Modern
Cronies

Modern Cronies

Southern Industrialism
from Gold Rush to
Convict Labor,
1829–1894

Kenneth H. Wheeler

K. H. Wheeler

THE UNIVERSITY OF
GEORGIA PRESS
ATHENS

*Inscribed, with warm
wishes, to Sharon
Christenson.*

Oct 19, 2021

© 2021 by the University of Georgia Press
Athens, Georgia 30602
www.ugapress.org
All rights reserved

Designed by Kaelin Chappell Broaddus
Set in 9.5/13.5 Miller Text by Kaelin Chappell Broaddus

Most University of Georgia Press titles are
available from popular e-book vendors.

Printed digitally

Library of Congress Cataloging-in-Publication Data

Names: Wheeler, Kenneth H., author.
Title: Modern cronies : southern industrialism from gold rush to
    convict labor, 1829–1894 / Kenneth H. Wheeler.
Description: Athens : The University of Georgia Press, [2021] |
    Includes bibliographical references and index.
Identifiers: LCCN 2020034685 | ISBN 9780820357508 (hardback)
    | ISBN 9780820357522 (paperback) | ISBN 9780820357515
    (ebook)
Subjects: LCSH: Industrialization—Southern States—History—
    19th century. | Industrialists—Southern States—History—
    19th century. | Gold mines and mining—Southern States—
    History—19th century. | Southern States—Economic
    conditions—19th century.
Classification: LCC HC107.A13 W44 2021 | DDC
    338.975009/034—dc23
LC record available at https://lccn.loc.gov/2020034685

CONTENTS

Modern Cronies

INTRODUCTION

—◦○◦—

AMERICANS RAPIDLY INDUSTRIALIZED THEIR NATION DURING THE late nineteenth century, building transcontinental railroads, factories, bridges, and skyscrapers. In Georgia, former governor Joseph E. Brown put together an integrated industrial enterprise; his coal mines, worked by convicts leased from the state, fueled iron furnaces he owned, and his coal and iron traveled on a railroad he leased and presided over. Georgia was becoming a different state than it had been, yet Brown had been learning how to run and oversee these industries since he was a boy and young man in northern Georgia, where a nascent industrial center formed as a result of the southern gold rush. At sites of veins of gold, miners erected stamping mills that pounded gold ore; a branch of the U.S. Mint turned gold into coins. Furnaces and forges yielded tons of iron, much of which was freighted on a new major railroad, the Western & Atlantic. At the terminus points of the railroad, the cities of Atlanta and Chattanooga emerged. Though the Civil War shut down, damaged, or destroyed much of this industrialization, people who industrialized antebellum northern Georgia were central to what came later, and the two eras were closely connected.

Numerous historians have explored southern industrialization, effectively countering the notion of an agrarian, antimodern South. Many scholars focus on one industry.[1] In this book, however, I document the interplay of different facets of industrialization, especially mining, railroading, and iron making, and trace a network of people who sought to develop and profit from industrial technologies. While reshaping the economic landscape, this group of people developed a comprehensive vision of an independent and economically diversified Southeast. On the eve of secession and the Civil War, they had seen great possibilities for themselves, which the war scattered. Afterward, members of this network settled in Atlanta, Chattanooga, and the new city of Birmingham, guiding the development of these southeastern cities. The reciprocal and reinforcing connections among this group of people and their endeavors are the focus of the book.

The precipitating event that set these industrial changes in motion was the southern gold rush, the largest in U.S. history to that time. Scholars have documented how the gold rush, beginning in 1829, brought about the expulsion of the Cherokees from the Cherokee Nation.[2] Generally, however, historians have treated the search for gold as disconnected from the subsequent development of the state and region, when in fact the gold rush attracted a group of people who saw in that rush a new vision that differed from a plantation-based and cotton-centric economy, one that led them down industrial paths with far-reaching implications.

The title of the book labels these people "modern cronies." By "modern," I mean simply that these southerners were fully invested in a diversified and dynamic economic future that would include farms, railroads, mines, mills, factories, and furnaces from which they expected to profit handsomely. Though they upheld racial slavery, they were also open to other labor systems. By "cronies," I mean a few things. First, the people I discuss were in league with each other—not all of them at one time, but together they formed a broad network of interlinking relationships. Second, the word "crony" evokes the phrase "crony capitalism," which I do intentionally. These actors saw government—the state—as a central player in their gambits, in ways far more important than, say, the granting of a corporate charter or the protection of property rights. Sometimes these cronies worked for the government or guided the government in its lawmaking and spending decisions, even as they moved to help themselves and their friends profit from those decisions. Other times they solicited the government for contracts, bailouts, or other support. Either way, they did not see government as irrelevant or set apart from their efforts. These cronies sometimes did things secretly, either because their political enemies would stifle their efforts if they could, or because the public would not approve if they knew of their actions, or because other people would imitate them, competing for the same opportunities.

The gold rush drew many of these cronies to the same places at about the same time. The gold rush lands stretched in a band running south-west across northern Georgia, along roughly the same route as the Etowah River. Much of this book revolves around two connected counties in northern Georgia—Cherokee and Cass (renamed Bartow in 1861), both in the Etowah Valley. Not coincidentally, these are two of the most mineral-rich counties in Georgia. The crony network that emerged was especially rooted in the desire to exploit the economic resources of these counties. This mineral belt, bisected by a major railroad line running roughly north-south, made this place unique and gave the members of the network a chance to take advantage of several opportunities around them. Notably, the gold rush attracted iron makers who began building the largest antebellum iron-making complex south of the Tredegar works in Richmond, Virginia. Several scholars have examined segments of the history of this important industrial site.[3] In this book I explain the development more completely.

Place mattered, as did people. The people described in this book were sometimes connected by family, sometimes by common interests, and sometimes by denominational association. Key figures were committed Baptists. While it is beyond the scope of this study to consider how Baptist theology shaped their values, I argue that a common denomination was an important means of establishing affinity and trust, emphasizing people as serious and responsible. In addition, several of these Baptists joined a temperance movement against alcohol consumption. As opposed to the more carefree environment at taverns, temperance groups connected energetic and ambitious people focused on future goals.

Though he does not appear until chapter 4, Joseph E. Brown is a central figure both because he is intrinsically important and because he connects to so many people. He is a linchpin and beneficiary of the network I describe. Brown was born in 1821 into a farming family in the South Carolina upcountry. The family moved when he was in his late teens to the gold fields of northern Georgia, where he became a schoolteacher and then a lawyer. He sought public office successfully, his career rocketed, and at age thirty-six, Brown won election as Georgia's governor and served four two-year terms. He led Georgia in seceding from the United States and served as the state's sole Confederate governor. His star then dimmed: by the summer of 1865 the Confederacy no longer existed, his home had been burned by U.S. soldiers, money he had invested in human slavery had evaporated, he went to jail for violating his probation, his political prospects looked dismal, and a good portion of his state was in disarray. Yet within a decade, Brown was again the most powerful person in Georgia.

One sign of his influence is that in 1880 Brown secretly finagled the resignation of a U.S. senator so he could have the seat, which he held for most of the rest of his life.

Some people called Brown the "miracle of Gaddistown," the inconspicuous place he had spent his late adolescence in northern Georgia. An investigation of the world he came from, though, reveals the underpinnings of the successes he enjoyed. Some people mined gold while others made money in railroad building, banking, iron making, and land speculation. Coerced labor, mostly that of enslaved people, was basic to these developments. As a teenager and young man, Brown saw these ingredients of wealth around him, and he applied the lessons to his advantage. When Brown became governor in 1857, he brought into his administration the people he knew and trusted from the Etowah Valley: temperance Baptists, grist millers, iron makers, gold seekers, and railroad developers. Brown's reordering of state governmental power brought these upcountry Baptists to prominence, displacing numerous planter-class figures who had predominantly overseen Georgia to that time.

These cronies were active in Georgia during the Civil War, but afterward they all faced serious questions about how to reestablish themselves in a greatly altered reality. Some found their way into an industrial future. That future was sometimes distant from the gold fields of northern Georgia, and the scale of industrialization had grown tremendously, but the skills and insights learned in the Etowah Valley were still valuable and applicable, demonstrating connections of antebellum industrialization to the late nineteenth century.

In this book, I also make a new argument about the origins of the convict lease system in Georgia. Scholarship on this system recognizes Joseph E. Brown's usage of convict labor, but not the pivotal role of Brown and his cronies in bringing it about in Georgia.[4] Brown, as head of the penitentiary committee of the state legislature in 1849 and 1850, argued that prisoners should work on state utilities. During Brown's governorship and after, his Etowah Valley cronies amplified and expanded this idea, suggesting that convicts be used in railroad or mining operations. State policy soon legalized a widespread convict lease system, which Brown dominated and profited from for decades.

To understand what happened, I utilize the personal papers of key figures in this network to explain their evolving relationships. Land records, usually at the county level, document part of what transpired. State records, including acts of incorporation and the actions of members of the network when in power, are also necessary for understanding their cronyism. Newspapers chronicle the relationships, interests, and involvement in a host of activities by members of the network. The combination of sources exposes relatively hidden relationships that powered decisions and actions, legislation and commitments.

In the first chapter, I introduce William Grisham and his founding of the town eventually known as Canton, which became the county seat of Cherokee County. In the midst of the Cherokee Nation and during the gold rush, Canton became an important base where major figures of this industry-minded network got to know each other, worshipped together, and hatched their specific ideas about how to develop their financial futures and participate in the development of the region as they built churches, courts, newspapers, schools, and roads.

In the second chapter I highlight the centrality of crony capitalism by describing how in the 1830s Georgians advocated for and built a state-owned railroad, the Western & Atlantic, across Cherokee Nation lands, creating at the railroad's ends the cities of Atlanta and Chattanooga. As a link for southern states from the Atlantic coast to the Ohio and Mississippi Valleys (via the Tennessee River), the Western & Atlantic was seen by promoters as a way to keep southern states in the economic mainstream of the nation while the interior of the continent was developed. Historians have narrated the building of the railroad; I explain the crony capitalism in the venture. Pivotal figures in Georgia's state government, in conjunction with their friends and relatives outside it, hatched plans to profit by purchasing key pieces of land along the planned railroad route. Their efforts affected the state government's dedication to building the railroad, the path of the railroad, and how it was constructed. Additionally, a new place was made possible by the expanding railroad: an Etowah Valley resort called Rowland Springs. Run by John S. Rowland, a member of the network, Rowland Springs became very popular in the late 1840s among Deep South elites who "watered" there in the summer months. Rowland Springs illustrates changes in the land after the Cherokees were removed, served as a retreat where Joseph E. Brown did much of his thinking about secession, and represents the conflicting emotions many southerners felt about connections with northern states.

In chapter 3, I show that the gold rush attracted other industrialists, particularly iron makers. The most important family was the German American Stroups, who migrated as soon as the Cherokees were removed and settled at a place just miles from where the Etowah River would be bisected by the Western & Atlantic. There they built the foundations of what became the Deep South's most extensive antebellum ironworks. In 1845 Moses Stroup partnered with Mark A. Cooper, a Georgia politician. Cooper, Stroup, and others believed in a diversified Georgia economy and founded the Southern Central Agricultural Society in 1846 to propagate their visions for the future of agriculture, transportation, and other industries.

Joseph E. Brown was profoundly affected by and connected to the events, figures, and developments outlined above. In chapter 4, I explain how Brown was influenced by the gold rush and migrated down the Etowah Valley to Canton, where he became an attorney, married into the Grisham family, and became a dedicated Baptist, ensconcing himself within the network of people who would fuel his political rise. As a representative in the state legislature, Brown advocated for the Western & Atlantic and promoted convict labor in support of it, a crucially important idea he and his cronies would amplify over the next few decades. Brown's successful marketing of a copper mine demonstrated his skill at utilizing his social network to capitalize on the potential for mineral wealth. In 1857, capping a meteoric rise in his political fortunes, the voters of Georgia propelled Brown into the governorship.

I argue in chapter 5 that the vision of an economically developed and diverse Georgia increasingly undergirded Governor Brown's political philosophy, and he advocated for state subsidies for industrial development. After Abraham Lincoln's election in 1860, Governor Brown ardently supported secession and the Confederate States of America. As the Civil War began, the Etowah Valley was a busy place. Mark Cooper sought war contracts to finance his iron business; soon, John S. Rowland ran the vitally important Western & Atlantic, and William Grisham worked for the railroad as Rowland's secretary.

In chapter 6, I describe how the destruction of the Cherokee Nation in northern Georgia was paralleled by the wreckage visited on the area in 1864 by federal soldiers, who destroyed much that Georgians had built in the Etowah Valley over the prior three decades. The ironworks were one target on General William T. Sherman's path to Atlanta, and Sherman's soldiers burned the county seats of both Cherokee and Bartow Counties. The end of the war brought emancipation to millions, and Joe Brown spent time in a Washington, D.C., prison after a federal commander believed he had violated his parole. Everyone pondered the future; the present was far from what they had imagined.

In the seventh chapter I show that while Brown's mentors were mostly deceased, Brown himself, only forty-four years old in 1865, had a future. Other capable people saw greater opportunity elsewhere and left or, in the case of Mark Cooper, stayed but were unsuccessful in creating new business ventures. Brown initially also faced difficulties and perils as he tried to figure out his path forward. His break came in 1870 when Brown successfully headed a partnership that leased the Western & Atlantic from the state for twenty years. As Brown purchased and developed coal mines in northwestern Georgia, he also acquired iron-making operations, leased convicts from the state to work the mines, and organized new corporate forms for his Dade Coal Company and its subsidiaries. Brown's influence and wealth were waxing, not waning. By 1876, Brown's integrated business empire was complete, and he continued to add to the power that empire gave him over the final decades of his life until his death in 1894.

In the epilogue, I argue that the influence of this network remained potent. Joe Brown's Baptist connection to the Boyce family resulted in a pivotal charitable donation by Brown to the Southern Baptist Theological Seminary, and Brown became chair of the board of trustees. The ongoing presence in Chattanooga of Tomlinson Fort Jr., who was the attorney for the Ker Boyce estate, is a reminder of the long-lasting family ties and connections to that city. Etowah Valley iron makers played a central role in the creation of Birmingham, Alabama, which became known as the "Pittsburgh of the South" because of its massive iron and steel mills. In Georgia, two-time governor Joseph Mackey Brown reminded all Georgians of how influential the Joe Brown network had been: even into the twentieth century some of the remaining members of that network propped up "Little Joe" Brown as a carrier of their interests.

CHAPTER 1

---⊸○⊶---

Ararat

ROM 1829 TO 1838, A MASSIVE UPHEAVAL IN THE ETOWAH VALLEY
of northern Georgia permanently altered the landscape and the
people who lived there. White settlers transformed what had been Cherokee Nation lands as they dug for gold, built new towns and roads, and ex-
pelled the Cherokee people. In this chapter, I especially focus on one in-
dividual, William Grisham, who helped create this white world. Grisham
was not unusual, but his importance as the founder of an important
county seat and as a future kinsman and partner of a significant person to
emerge from that place, Joseph E. Brown, makes Grisham's experience especially worth noting during these years when Cherokees and whites lived
side by side prior to the removal of the Cherokees in what would become
known as the Trail of Tears.

Born in 1803 in the upcountry of South Carolina, William Grisham
grew up around Pendleton. In the early 1820s, his prosperous and much
older brother Joseph established William as manager of one of the first two
stores on the square of a new settlement in northern Georgia called Decatur. When the state of Georgia made Decatur the county seat of DeKalb
County in December 1823, the twenty-year-old was made one of five town
commissioners with the authority to spend tax revenue and shape Decatur's development. The business Grisham ran from a log cabin was a dry
goods emporium that sold many useful items, such as pots, spoons, pocket-
knives, pencils, beads, buttons, pepper, cotton, gimlets, soup plates, paper,
shawls, and needles. Though Joseph Grisham would soon gain prominence
as a temperance advocate, William's store also sold "spiritous liquors," including wine, whiskey, and cordials.[1]

A descendant said that Grisham was initially known as "Wild Billy," and indeed the town had a group called "the wild boys of Decatur," who played rough practical jokes on various people. But Grisham was ambitious and sought respectability; the right marriage was a clear way to improve his social standing. Through the influence of his brother Joseph, he was introduced to a young woman, Susan Bradford, who lived on the Saluda River in South Carolina's Greenville District. Bradford was three years older than William and stood to inherit money and slaves since her father, a planter and state politician, had died recently. In January 1825, William wrote to his sister Melinda that he was anxious and hoped to "settle the uneasiness of my mind respecting this matrimony affair." He thought he might leave Decatur and return to Pendleton "unless miss Bradford will suit me and have me and live here." He felt some nostalgia for his boyhood home and wrote, "Sometimes it seems to me I'de like to live at fathers old place, the orchard and all things there at hand." He knew, however, that his future lay elsewhere: "But then I fear If I was to buy it I should not live satisfied there by myself as it were, on an old worn out piece of land." Grisham had to move on and create a future for himself in a new place. He found that "I am unable to do business without some help and I must either keep in partnership or marry, and I fear I cant marry to suit."[2]

Seeking to "marry to suit," Grisham wooed Bradford with earnest letters of love. In June he wrote to "Her Ladyship, Miss Susan Bradford" that his "whole happiness must be in waiting on you in the manner of a loving, dutiful and kind partner. . . . I have certainly great reasons for comfort, if not for joy—because [of] your very accomplished and truly extreme kindness to me at both interviews." Despite having met her perhaps only twice, Grisham was sad to be away from her: "I have been about but little since I came home, nor does company relish as well since my vows and devotion to thee." But later in his letter Grisham explained in detail that the Georgia state legislature had finished a two-week session "disposing & preparing to dispose of the late acquisition of Creek territory." Everything would be divided into lots of 202½ acres, and he mentioned that "tis said all the maids of 18 & over are to have a draw in this wheel of Fortune." Presumably if Susan were to relocate to Georgia, she might have a draw. And if she were to marry Grisham, she would be taking a different spin of the "wheel of Fortune." By September they determined to wed, and when Grisham returned to Decatur after another visit, he wrote, "Let us endeavor to sweeten the remaining hours of separation by offering ourselves as a living sacrifice

William Grisham, shown here in the 1850s,
helped to create the town of Canton, an
important location in the Etowah Valley.
Courtesy of William and Nell Galt Magruder.

to our Almighty Creator." Grisham said he was a changed man: "There
have come several girls and some persons say pretty too" to Decatur. "I ex-
pect the noticers of my previous conduct with the fair [sex] are in a wonder why I do not continue the round of gallantry." They soon found out.
Grisham and Bradford tied the knot late in 1825 and made their home in
Decatur. The following August, when the estate of Susan's father was dis-
tributed, her legacy went to the heirs of William Grisham, none of whom
had yet been born.[3]

The Grishams maintained the store, and William kept moving up in
social standing and respectability. "Wild Billy" was no more. In 1829, voters elected Grisham to be justice of the peace for Decatur. All manner of
local disputes would come before him, and his election was a sign of his
trusted reputation. The same year, Susan gave birth to their first child, a
daughter they named Melinda after William's sister. The household continued to expand in 1830, as Grisham began purchasing slaves. He spent

$300 to purchase Amy, "a certain negro Girl of Dark yellow complexion, about fourteen or fifteen years of age," who could presumably help with housework and care for Melinda, and another $350 for Tippoe, a boy of sixteen. Two years later Grisham purchased "a certain Mulatto child slave about five years old . . . named Rose" for $200 and spent $275 for "a certain mulatto Child Slave," nine or ten years of age, named Arminda.[4]

The view from Decatur helped young William Grisham see where his future might take him. Just a few dozen miles to the north lay the southern boundary of the Cherokee country, a nation of about sixteen thousand Cherokees, mostly in northwestern and north-central Georgia, though also including portions of Alabama, Tennessee, and North Carolina. The Cherokees were concentrated on small farms along the waterways, and many lived in the Etowah Valley, which stretched westward to the intersection of the Oostanaula and Etowah Rivers where they form the Coosa River in far western Georgia, the waters of which eventually empty into the Gulf of Mexico. People had lived in the Etowah Valley for millennia, and giant flat-topped mounds built by Mississippian peoples about five hundred years earlier stood in various places along the Etowah River, silent reminders of past inhabitants.[5]

Georgia whites had their eyes on the Cherokee Nation and fully expected to take control of the land. The federal government had promised, following the Yazoo scandal—political corruption involving a Georgia land swindle that occurred in the 1790s—to remove all Indians from Georgia in return for Georgia giving up its claims to the lands that became Alabama and Mississippi. The federal government, though, did not set a timetable or deadline for such removal. Meanwhile, the Cherokees in the 1820s, seeing whites eyeing their lands and already having ceded vast amounts of territory, embarked on a formidable effort to build up their defenses, in part by reducing the ways they were different from whites. With a leadership that included many biracial Cherokees and whites who had married into the nation, some Cherokees learned English, embraced Christianity, grew wheat instead of corn, and purchased slaves. The Cherokees developed their own written language, published a newspaper written in Cherokee and English, created a constitution patterned after the U.S. Constitution, and had attorneys who could access U.S. courts. Yet none of these changes helped them—in fact, at least one historian has argued that the changes made whites more determined to expel the Cherokees. Indians who could be depicted as "savage" were one thing; "civilized" Indians were, paradoxically, more threatening because they could write newspaper editorials, arouse sympathetic public opinion, and eloquently defend their nation in courts of law.[6]

The presidential election of 1828, which brought Andrew Jackson to the White House, may have foretold the doom of the Cherokees in Georgia, but during the following summer of 1829, when newspapers trumpeted the discovery of gold in northern Georgia, the Cherokees' situation worsened immediately. People had mined gold in North Carolina and, to a lesser extent, Virginia for decades, but when gold was discovered in northern Georgia it set off a rush, and thousands of people sought their fortunes within just the first few weeks. Everyone understood that the gold finds were extending into the Cherokee Nation, and thousands of whites immediately began inundating the Cherokee Nation as part of the "Great Intrusion." Most rushers panned for gold using a riffled iron skillet known as a "Georgia pan," and they looked for what was available on the surface. Only slightly more elaborate was a "rocking tom," a portable sorter that let people dump in soil or ore and then pour water through the tom to carry off the lighter soil and leave behind, caught by the riffles at the bottom, the heavier bits of gold.[7] Mobile and with low overhead costs, the miners appeared everywhere along the gold belt, which lay especially on the south side of the Etowah River, running in a mostly southwesterly direction across the Cherokee Nation.

The Cherokees appealed to the U.S. government to stop these invaders of their lands. The federal government, trying to keep order and concerned about the possibility of armed conflict, sent soldiers who patrolled the edges of the Cherokee Nation and arrested illegal miners, often burning any cabins or other buildings miners had constructed at mining sites. In 1830, at the Sixes gold mine along the Etowah River, soldiers drove off white miners and wrecked nineteen buildings. Whites were resourceful, though. When it became too difficult to mine gold during the day, miners would wait until nightfall, visit mining sites, pile ore into sacks, and carry them outside the Cherokee Nation. In the morning, they could then go through their plundered earth to find bits of gold. The small number of soldiers could not be everywhere at once. The result was continual unrest. Andrew Jackson ushered through Congress and signed into law in 1830 the Indian Removal Act, which provided for the relocation of existing southeastern tribes, including the Cherokees, west of the Mississippi River. Even so, ordinary whites resented the soldiers, and Georgia officials heard from their constituents. Later in 1830, Governor George Gilmer re-

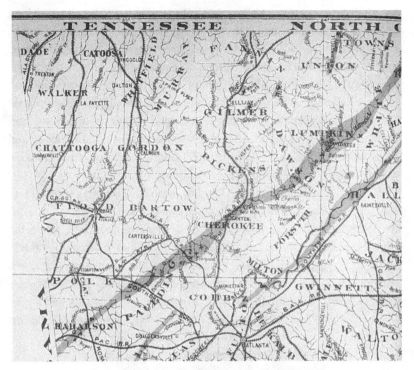

The gold belts attracted thousands of people to the
largest gold rush in U.S. history to that time.
Yeates, McCallie, and King, *A Preliminary Report on a
Part of the Gold Deposits of Georgia*.

quested that the federal soldiers withdraw, and he instituted a state force,
the Georgia Guard, in their place. Practically, the results were not much
different.[8]

Gilmer's position was politically precarious. He supported the acceptance of Cherokees' testimony in Georgia courts. He also viewed the gold
deposits as a public resource, to be used by the state rather than for private enrichment. Most white Georgians could not have disagreed more. In
the election of 1831 Wilson Lumpkin took advantage of these sentiments
to win the governorship over Gilmer. Soon the Cherokee lands would be
dispensed to white Georgians.[9]

Some whites, of course, had already been in the Cherokee Nation with
the permission of the Cherokees, including a Baptist missionary named
Duncan O'Bryant. O'Bryant preached and taught among the Cherokees
beginning in 1821, and in 1829 he opened a school along the Etowah near

the Cherokee town of Hickory Log. On land where William Grisham would soon found a town, O'Bryant had "two cabins, one crib and stable, one smokehouse and shed, nine peach trees, and three acres of 'cleared land of good quality.'" O'Bryant taught at his school and preached to a congregation of Cherokees. The description of the improvements to the land is a reminder that Cherokees and those whom the Cherokees permitted to live among them had cleared and cultivated thousands of acres of land and built thousands of houses and cabins, corncribs, potato houses, and other outbuildings, as well as gristmills, sawmills, and blacksmith shops, among other improvements.[10]

Despairing of remaining in Georgia, some of O'Bryant's congregants left: four families, including seven of his pupils, moved west in 1829. Others followed, and the school closed in early November 1831, when the Cherokees of Hickory Log, more than eighty families, packed up and left. O'Bryant, dedicated to his congregants and pupils, went west with them, leaving behind a less populated area that would soon be occupied again.[11] Under Governor Lumpkin, the state instituted a land lottery and a gold lottery to divide and distribute the Cherokee Nation lands in Georgia and put them into white hands, an event with massive implications.[12]

Until 1832, William Grisham could not be called much of a crony, notwithstanding his appointment as a town commissioner of Decatur and his election to local office as justice of the peace. But the Grishams relocated to Cherokee County at least by July 1832, when William Grisham became postmaster at a place called Cherokee Court House, virtually the site of O'Bryant's school until just months before. Being appointed postmaster was a political plum, and those who held the position ranked highly in society. Contemporary novelist Catherine Sedgwick described even a small village's postmaster as "the wheel of destiny for the community" and "the oracle to announce the voice of the divinities at Washington—the herald of all news, foreign and domestic, and the medium of all the good and evil tidings." The job paid, though the great majority earned less than $100 annually. The post office could run out of a small storefront, or even a counter in a law office or pharmacy, staffed with one's spouse or a clerk, so the job did not excessively tie a person down. Perhaps more important, especially for the politically ambitious, the position meant the postmaster would likely know personally anyone who sent or received letters or subscribed to a newspaper, and all those newspapers came directly to the postmaster, making him usually the best-informed person in the area.[13]

Grisham continued to embed himself into government. Cherokee Court House was on the south side of the Etowah River, on a bluff that made a fine town site. Originally, all of the Cherokee Nation lands were labeled Cherokee County, but in 1832 the state legislature divided the land into ten counties, which put Cherokee Court House at the center of a much smaller Cherokee County. Despite the name of the town, though, the location of the county seat was up in the air, and residents of another thriving place just eight miles to the southeast, Hickory Flat, lobbied to become the county seat. Three landowners at Cherokee Court House, however—Grisham, Joseph Donaldson, and John P. Brooke—cooperated to donate a large plot of land at the intersection of their three properties as a town center. In December 1833, the state of Georgia made that site a county seat called "Etowa," which was renamed Canton a year later. The state also made William Grisham one of five town commissioners. In a short period of time, Grisham became a postmaster, purchased land at a promising location, worked with others to make the location the county seat, and became a town commissioner once again. Getting in on the ground floor of the settlement created ongoing advantages and opportunities, which Grisham did not squander.[14]

The gold and land lotteries of 1832–1833 handed thousands of white Georgians land ownership in the Cherokee Nation. Some people kept their lots; others sold theirs. As the lotteries occurred, a Milledgeville newspaper, the *Federal Union*, issued a series of pamphlets, each called "Gold and Land Lottery Register." William Grisham purchased every pamphlet at five dollars each, and then assiduously took needle and thread and bound the entire collection together to create a catalog of the thousands of successful winners, where they lived, and the numbers of their land and gold lots, which could then be located on a map. These new owners could count on being contacted by people who wished to purchase their land. William Grisham, as a postmaster at the center of the gold rush, would have had frequent visitors who wished to consult his valuable information—the collection of pamphlets was well thumbed. The *Cherokee Phoenix* said the Cherokee Nation was inundated with whites, who "have been passing and repassing, single and in companies." They would hail people, "Ho, sir, where is the nearest line to this place, what District, number, corner, lot, station &c." As they descended, the *Phoenix* compared them to "the great flocks of pigeons, that hastens to the ground in search of their food. Every lot has been viewed, and as many paths beaten, by the passing and the

cross passing hunters." From the standpoint of Georgia, since the Cherokees were being removed, the state was simply handing out, in democratic
fashion, the lands that would soon be unoccupied. The law was that the
Cherokees could stay on lands they already had cleared, cultivated, and
improved until they were moved west. New settlers could not legally force
Cherokee residents off their land, even if the settlers had drawn it in the
land or gold lotteries.[15]

Constantly, whites and Indians jostled for control in isolated incidents
that were multiplied in hundreds and thousands of encounters. Unsurprisingly, whites had the upper hand. A federal emigrating agent esti-
mated in 1832 that of the five hundred white families living in the Cherokee Nation, "half might be honest in dealing with whites; but all took
advantage of Indians, who could not be a party to lawsuits." A Georgia law
passed in December 1834 provided that anyone who had drawn a lot in the
land or gold lotteries had the right, even if Cherokees were living on the
land, "to test the same for gold and operate thereon . . . providing said operations do not interfere with the actual cultivation or use of said lots by
Indians claiming the occupant rights." One can easily imagine the situations this law created. Certainly William Grisham, as he purchased land,
wanted full control over his possessions. Grisham spent the 1830s buying
land, and in 1834 he registered his stock mark with the county—"a swal-
low fork in each ear"—to distinguish his livestock. Years later, two boys
hunting birds on Grisham's land discovered Grisham's powerful sense of
ownership. Byron Waters and his older brother Emmett were out hunting
"in the wheat fields of Old Uncle Billy Gresham, west of Canton." Grisham
heard the gunshots and "came stalking across the field. He was a tall gaunt
man . . . with a very prominent Roman nose." Grisham yelled at the boys
for trampling his wheat, and when Emmett said he did not think they
were damaging the ankle-high wheat, Grisham "retorted angrily, 'You are
trampling down my wheat and killing my birds.'" Grisham demanded the
birds, which the boys handed over, whereupon Grisham "stamped them
into the ground, doing much more damage than we had done, and ordered us to leave by the shortest way we could go."[16] Even the birds that
flew across Grisham's land belonged to him. The deeds to the properties
Grisham purchased do not say whether Cherokees lived on the land or
whether they had cleared the land or had houses, barns, or orchards. The
deeds recorded property lines and left much unsaid.

Even powerful Cherokees lost their homes and land. Joseph Vann, who
commanded the labor of more than a hundred African American slaves

on his Diamond Hill plantation, lost an adjoining lot he owned, Spring Place, where Moravian missionaries invited by his family had conducted their school for years and years. On Christmas Eve 1832, the head of the Georgia Guard, Colonel William Bishop, showed up with title to the property, which had been dispensed in the 1832 lottery. Vann protested, but the Moravians were ousted, and Bishop assumed control over the property. In 1834, Bishop claimed that Vann had forfeited his home by violating a law that forbade Cherokees from hiring whites. Bishop, backed by twenty armed men, forced the Vann family to stay temporarily in one room of their home. The Vanns—Joseph, three adult women, and eleven children—shortly went to Tennessee. As historian Tiya Miles explains, the third generation to occupy the plantation had lost, in addition to their home, "805 acres of cultivated land, functional businesses, barns, stables, and dozens of log cabins and domestic outbuildings."[17]

Whites in the Cherokee Nation made their worldview clear. At the beginning of 1833, local attorney Howell Cobb began publishing the *Cherokee Intelligencer* from Cherokee Court House. The newspaper advocated strong support for President Andrew Jackson, took adamant positions in favor of the rights of states, and yet disagreed with South Carolina nullifiers. South Carolina had been locked in a conflict with the federal government over the right of states to nullify federal laws, and it had nullified the federal tariffs of 1828 and 1832. Even though South Carolina would eventually back down in the face of Jackson's violent threats and Congress's passage of the Force Act (1833), which authorized federal military action to enforce the tariff, the issue was fresh. The Grishams opposed nullification. Joseph wrote from South Carolina to William in Georgia, "I hope the Union party in your state will not permit their enemies to get the power as here & ruin their state & if you go with the nullifiers I have no doubt they will secede." Howell Cobb wrote in the announcement of his newspaper, "The State Rights' Doctrine as contended for by the best expounders of the constitution, are those we avow; we hold that each State has reserved to herself all and every right, not surrendered up and enumerated in the constitution of the United States. . . . While here, we remark, that we are uncompromising Union men, and feel and consider ourselves identified with all those that now rally under the standard of the twenty-four States." In the pages of the *Cherokee Intelligencer*, Cobb elaborated on this idea. He reprinted in his first issue an essay from the *Georgia Gazette* that answered the question "Can a State Secede?": "in our system, a *state cannot secede alone.* So on the assumption . . . that each of our states were ever perfectly sovereign, her right at this day to assume that attitude again, must necessarily depend on her physical power to maintain it." The plain meaning was that Georgians were sympathetic with South Carolina, but in the present circumstances, with both the state and federal governments bent on removing the Cherokees from Georgia, the white settlers in the Cherokee Nation had no intention to anger President Jackson or alter their trajectory. Rather, everything was going their way; the federal government was doing what Cherokee County whites wanted. The South Carolinians were on their own, which in no way impaired Cherokee County's dedication to states' rights. By 1838, Reuben F. and Nancy Daniel would open the State Rights Hotel in Canton.[18]

In 1833, William Grisham continued to build up the town he had founded. Voters elected him clerk of the Inferior Court of the county, and in July he participated in the Independence Day festivities. With many others, Grisham gathered at the courthouse to hear a reading of the Declaration of Independence, an oration, and Washington's Farewell Address. After dinner came numerous toasts "with great glee and highlarity." The celebrants toasted, among other things, *The Constitution of the United States*—A literal construction, its only safe guarantee . . . *The Union of the States and the Sovereignty of the States*—Without the latter the former cannot exist. . . . *The Etowa River*—The day is not far distant, we hope, when its surface will be as rich with floating commerce as its channel is with precious metals." And they praised themselves for what they had already built as Americans. Reuben F. Daniel toasted "the spirit of 76, it is seen and felt on the banks of Etowa." The newspaper that chronicled their day also carried the toast of Murray County revelers, who praised "the Indians—May they soon emigrate to a country congenial with their habits."[19]

Beyond these community rituals, whites founded community institutions. In August, the Grishams organized, with eight other individuals, a Baptist church in Canton. They chose to call their church Ararat, after the mountain or hill on which Noah's ark first rested following the great flood.[20] Indeed, like Noah's family on Mount Ararat in Genesis, they were both the survivors and the beneficiaries of the great destruction all about them.

By December the town had a school, chartered by the state of Georgia as the Etowah Academy. William Grisham was one of the five trustees, and in the summer of 1834 the Inferior Court granted them a city lot "in consideration of the advancement of Literature, Science and learning and the good wellfare and prospect of a good Academy" where they could build a schoolhouse. The school, it appears, stood remarkably close to where Duncan O'Bryant's Cherokee pupils had only a few years earlier learned their lessons.[21]

Throughout this period, gold powered the local economy. The *Cherokee Intelligencer* carried news about the gold lottery and advertisements for "Gold and Land Maps" of Cherokee County, which were for sale by Orange Green for only six dollars; for a "House of Entertainment" at the Sixes gold mine; and from people wanting to sell gold lots, including an offer to sell the Sixes gold mine itself. One mine not for sale was run by the "widow Franklin," her grown children, and dozens of slaves. The untimely death of her prominent husband, Bedney, in 1816 had left Mary Franklin with several children, but also substantial wealth. Within a few years, her oldest child and only daughter, Ann, married a future governor of the state, Charles J. McDonald. In the gold lottery of 1832, Mary Franklin drew a gold lot that turned out to be valuable. Soon she began the Franklin gold mine in the northeast corner of Cherokee County. By 1850, Franklin told the census taker she was worth more than $25,000, including more than thirty slaves. McDonald eventually owned a gold mine on land that adjoined his mother-in-law's property.[22]

Whites changed the landscape not only through their presence, but also through the ways they remade the land. The most obvious of these changes was through gold mining, though road building was also significant. For example, in 1835 the Inferior Court of Cherokee County appointed three men as commissioners "to lay out a new road from Canton to the Sixes Gold Mines to a new Ferry lately established on John Brewster's land and thence to intersect the road leading from Downing's Ferry towards Cassville and Alabama." And the following year the court ordered that a road that had been "reviewed and laid out" by three men "be worked out and kept in order as a public road."[23] Whites were reordering the landscape, deciding what places were most important and what routes people would use to travel through the Cherokee country. It was not just that the Cherokees were being pushed out—whites were altering the way the world looked in that place.

With this inundation, it is no surprise that violence sometimes resulted. In April 1832, a white man identified only as Mr. Tait accused a Cherokee named Tah-nah-ee of "killing a hog." Tait had been missing one of his hogs, and he and a companion searched until he found three Indians cleaning a slaughtered hog beside a pond. The other Indians escaped, but Tait and his helper "arrested" Tah-nah-ee, who spoke little or no English. Later, Tah-nah-ee indicated that he would lead Tait to the men who had been with him when Tait found the hog. Tait and a few other men bound the Cherokee man's hands, and he walked with them. Eventually, though, the whites concluded that he was not doing as he had said he would, so they started back. Tah-nah-ee tried to run away, and the men simply shot him and abandoned his dead body about five miles from the Sixes gold mines. The *Cherokee Phoenix* reported the incident and focused on the slain man's wife and young family, as well as the facts that he was unarmed, his hands were bound when he was shot, and his killers abandoned the body where it fell and left Tah-nah-ee for dead. General John Coffee of the Georgia Guard, writing to Governor Lumpkin, emphasized that Tait was "a respectable citizen"; Coffee was concerned that the killing might incite Indian retaliation. Months later, in December, just outside of Cherokee County to the northwest, two Indians killed four members of a white settler family at Pine Log and burned their home. In late April 1833, in a wild melee, about thirty whites fought thirty Indians near Scudder's gold mines, just outside Cherokee County to the northeast; no one lost his life, but "plenty had black eyes and broken bones." Whites were anxious because, as the *Cherokee Intelligencer* put it in May 1833, "We have not been able to discover any symptoms of a disposition amongst the natives to remove from this country: on the contrary . . . they do not intend moving to the Arkansas. We believe, too, that there has been a pretty general opinion prevailing amongst them of late, that they will yet recover their lands back from the Georgians." The editorial went on to emphasize the fait accompli the Indians were facing: "the whites have been pouring in . . . like bees into a hive, and will soon surround them on every side."[24]

Many Cherokees were understandably upset. In May 1834, a Cherokee man took a potshot at a white settler, Dr. James Burns. The bullet grazed Burns's head, but he was not seriously wounded. The reaction of other settlers, though, was panic. Militia general Eli McConnell wrote to Governor Wilson Lumpkin that the Cherokee natives in the area "are more desperate and hostile of late than is usual," and said the governor should send some soldiers, along with "arms and ammunition to the Court House" so that the whites could protect themselves, "as our citizens are in daily expectation of being massacred." Along with McConnell's letter came a report from a group of Cherokee County citizens, which probably included William Grisham, in which they explained, "Threats of the lives of our white citizens are daily and publicly made by the Indians," and "the citizens of Cherokee County are in constant danger of assassination, and other lawless violence." This group also resolved "that for every citizen of the County of Cherokee assassinated by a Cherokee Indian, and where the offender is not given up to the civil authorities within two weeks (or satisfactory evidence of their inability of arresting the offender) from the date of the offense, we will select three male Indians out of the County of Cherokee, and put them to death." They also wanted their resolution to be published, in Cherokee, in the *Cherokee Phoenix*.[25]

Governor Lumpkin, trying to avoid panic, instructed General McConnell that nothing had happened that could not be taken care of by civil authorities. If he dispatched soldiers to Cherokee County, then all the white settlements in the entire Cherokee country would want soldiers to protect them. After this incident, things settled down in Cherokee County, though Lumpkin, a bit irate at his citizens, had the last laugh. In their "haste," as the Cherokee County committee later explained, they had sent the governor the original copy of their resolutions, including that they were going to kill three Cherokees for every white slain, and they requested those papers be returned to them. Lumpkin sent them a reply in which he said he "should be pleased to oblige you if" he could, but those documents had become part of the official record of the governor's office and therefore could not be returned.[26]

The next month, Joseph Grisham wrote to William, "I had heard of the disturbances with the Indians, but did not believe there was any danger, the Indians are aware that if they commit any outrage the Georgians will exterminate them." It was a matter-of-fact assessment. Instead of vigilante justice, though, the criminal justice system in Cherokee County stepped in. Log-in-the-Water, or Teshatooska, was indicted on a charge of assault with intent to murder James Burns. Log-in-the-Water did not speak English, but his Cherokee interpreter, George Still, asked him if he had shot at Burns. Log-in-the-Water "replied that he did and gave as a reason for it that he was a little groggy." Log-in-the-Water was found guilty and sentenced to four years of labor in the Georgia state penitentiary.[27]

Whites also were brought to justice for their crimes against Indians. For example, Edward Edwards was an illiterate and penniless white man whom the court convicted of three counts of assault and battery for having beat up Poor Shoat, James Downing, and Elk, three Cherokees. Edwards testified that his horse had wandered to the house of Chewy, another

Cherokee, and Edwards had gone after his horse. The three Cherokees were drinking around a fire, and Edwards stopped to drink with them. Edwards, though, would not stop "frequently conversing about the Arkansas," which "enraged" the Indians, who "threatened to kill him and upon that occasion a general engagement took place immediately when [Edwards] protected himself as quick as possible." It was three against one, but perhaps the Cherokee men had been drinking for some time before Edwards got there, since he got the best of all three and was accused of trying to throw one of them in the fire. When the "respectable" Tait had shot and killed an unarmed Indian in cold blood in 1832, nothing had happened to him. But following the Burns shooting, when whites did not want to create any trouble, insults from a poor, illiterate white man could not be tolerated by the courts. Edwards was annoying, but if his account is believed, he acted in self-defense. Nonetheless, whites were unsympathetic. Seeing the handwriting on the wall, Edwards pleaded guilty and was sentenced to ten days in the county jail for each of the three charges.[28]

Eventually this strained and awkward comingling of peoples came to an end. The federal government got a small number of Cherokees to sign the Treaty of New Echota in 1835. Though the vast majority of Cherokees rejected the treaty and said the signatories did not speak for them, the U.S. Senate ratified the treaty (by one vote) in 1836 and set a deadline of May 23, 1838, when all of the Cherokees should have departed for the Arkansas Territory. Thousands of Cherokees were not willing to go voluntarily. The federal government arranged for the military to round up the Cherokees and send them on their way. General John E. Wool oversaw this effort in 1836 and 1837. Experienced and capable, Wool was primarily interested in avoiding problems that had arisen in Alabama and Florida, where antagonizing the Creeks and the Seminoles had led to dangerous and costly wars. Wool did everything in his power to pacify the Cherokees, which often meant taking their side in disputes with whites who wished to abuse Cherokees or dispossess them of their property. Yet everything Wool did was also designed to facilitate the Cherokees' removal to the West.[29]

Another military figure tasked with removing the Cherokees was Ezekiel Buffington. He raised a company of men in Hall County for service, and Buffington's company was based in New Echota for most of 1837, often protecting Cherokees from intrusive whites who seized livestock, homes, and land. In the late summer Buffington was ordered to establish a military post near Canton. Buffington chose land belonging to Moses Perkins, which was a few miles east of Canton, and arrived in mid-October. Over the next few months his soldiers constructed barracks, stables, corncribs, blockhouses, pickets, and a forge at a place they called Fort Buffington.[30]

Perkins was unhappy that Buffington had selected his land for the site of the removal fort. A member of the Ararat church, James Willson, complained that "brother Perkins unjustly accuses him with having caused the soldiers to come and dispossess him of his premises." Willson also claimed that Perkins had falsely accused Willson of being "a reporter of cases of white persons who trample on the Indians rights." Two months later the church minutes recorded simply that "the cause of dificulty between brethren Willson and Perkins . . . was settled," which leaves much unexplained. The implication of Willson's statement is that some whites were very upset when other whites reported their abuse of Indians. Perhaps Willson had connections to the military that made Perkins suspect that Willson had told soldiers about abuses—snitched on whites—or had even suggested for unknown reasons that they seize Perkins's land for their fort. The incident is a reminder that for whites' usurpation of Indian property and land to go uncontested, other whites had to turn a blind eye to what was happening all about them.[31]

In 1838, Buffington's soldiers readied the collection fort for its role as a gathering site for the Cherokees. Early in May, Colonel Wilson Lindsay, who had replaced Wool, wrote an order that specified how the Indians were to be dealt with, including the stipulation that Cherokees who fled the soldiers were not to be shot. The reality on the ground was often not so pleasant or professional. English immigrant George Featherstonhaugh saw a group of Georgia militiamen in 1837. Their dress was varied—"Some of the men had straw hats, some of them white felt hats, others had old black hats on with the rim torn off"—and they looked rough: "all of them were as unshaven and as dirty as they could well be. . . . Many of the men were stout young fellows, and they rode on, talking, and cursing and swearing, without any kind of discipline." When the soldiers went to work, however, they meant business. Fort Buffington had five hundred Cherokees camped there on the third day of the collection, and another six hundred Indians were collected at a station near the Sixes gold mines. Young Nathaniel Frank Reinhardt in northwest Cherokee County wrote in his diary that he "saw old Foekiller, a neighbor Indian, just after he had been arrested by the soldiers, who were carrying him to Fort Buffington. They treated him rather cruelly, which excited my sympathies very much in his favor. The old Indian desired to see father, who solicited better treatment in his behalf."[32]

Days after the New Echota deadline had passed, soldiers had embarked on their mission to round up the Cherokees; within a few weeks they forced thousands of Cherokees to the collection forts and stations erected throughout the Cherokee Nation. Nothing stopped the soldiers, who busted the locks on the jail in Canton and retrieved a Cherokee man imprisoned on a debt charge. When Inferior Court justices complained that the soldiers had just facilitated a jailbreak and ignored civilian courts, General Charles Floyd wrote back that he had no intention of colliding with civilian authorities, but he could not be held back by "every little cause of litigation" and his "instructions" were "to remove the Cherokees beyond the limits of the States, and *particularly of Georgia.*"[33]

We know almost nothing about what it was like for the Cherokees camped at Fort Buffington for the few weeks they were there. Some local whites were sympathetic, like the Reinhardt father who admonished the soldiers to be gentle with old Foekiller. One Canton family story is that "the women of Canton baked bread and delivered it to Fort Buffington when they heard that the Cherokee were starving." And yet these acts of kindness were done by people who were depending on the Indians being removed. Their white presence was predicated on the assumptions that the Cherokee Nation would no longer exist in Georgia, that the state of Georgia would be in control, and that Indian lands would pass into white hands. Only a few years earlier, the French traveler Alexis de Tocqueville had characterized a common attitude among whites: "This world here belongs to us, they tell themselves every day: the Indian race is destined for final destruction which one cannot prevent. . . . Besides I do not want to get mixed up in it. I will not do anything against them: I will limit myself to providing everything that will hasten their ruin. In time I will have their lands and will be innocent of their death."[34]

After preparations that had stretched for more than a year, the roundup in northern Georgia lasted only a few weeks, and fifteen or sixteen thousand Cherokees, the vast majority of those in the East, were on their way first to Ross's Landing or Gunter's Landing, two points on the Tennessee River, and thence to the Arkansas Territory (modern-day Oklahoma), where those who survived would be resettled. Thousands of Cherokees died on the Trail of Tears before reaching the West. They had been disrupted from their lands and normal sanitary habits, often lacked proper food and clothing, were exposed to the elements during a terribly hot summer followed by a harsh winter, and suffered from diseases that swept through their concentrated population. Callous treatment combined with bureaucratic inefficiency and the difficulty of moving so many people of all ages such a long distance compounded the tragedy and human suffering.[35]

It was a new order in Georgia. Cherokees, hundreds of their African American slaves, and some sympathetic whites were gone. The other whites and their own slaves who replaced them often lived in houses built by the Cherokees, farmed the fields Cherokee farmers had cleared (even harvested the crops that Cherokee farmers had planted in 1838), and stored their corn in the corncribs built by Cherokee hands. And meanwhile, the gold mining continued. White children attended the Etowah Academy, just as Duncan O'Bryant's Cherokee students had attended his Hickory Log school. William Grisham went about his life in the Cherokee country, absent the Cherokees, along with the gold diggers and the road builders and all the others who came to live there. The world might be full of destruction for others, but for Grisham a promising future lay ahead.

CHAPTER 2

A Railroad and
Rowland Springs

CRONY CAPITALISM WAS PIVOTAL IN THE CREATION OF A RAILROAD, the Western & Atlantic, that ran through the Cherokee country and, at its end points, created the nodes that became the cities of Atlanta and Chattanooga. The central figures in this story were financier and developer Farish Carter, surveyor and chief engineer Stephen Harriman Long, government banker Tomlinson Fort, and the governor of Georgia, Charles J. McDonald. As ordinary whites settled in the Cherokee country in the 1830s, the state of Georgia built a railroad to connect the Tennessee River (with access to the Ohio and Mississippi Valleys) with the rest of Georgia. Key state officials and other investors worked together secretly to exploit the economic opportunities created by the railroad. The Western & Atlantic Railroad also made possible a summer resort created by John S. Rowland: he would eventually superintend the railroad, but in the 1840s he developed Rowland Springs, which gathered wealthy whites, mostly from the coastal South. The following discussion of Rowland Springs reveals tensions inherent in the creation of the Western & Atlantic between southern whites' desire to connect to other parts of the country and whites' desire to stay in the South to avoid critiques of slavery, which grew ever more strident as time went on.

On January 1, 1838, a small gathering of people assembled near the Etowah River on "the bosom of the Allatoona heights" for a groundbreaking ceremony and commencement of the work of building a great railroad. The convener, General Abbott H. Brisbane, said a few words to those assembled—local citizens and two brigades of the Corps of Engineers—about the importance of this railroad, which he believed would be "revolutionary of the whole political, social and commercial character of society." The Western & Atlantic Railroad, said Brisbane, would link the "hardy yeomanry" of the West and the "ingenious" and "efficient" businessmen of the East to the "black labor" of the South. The Cherokees were also on his mind: "Where are the late proprietors . . . of the soil upon which we now stand? Their hearth-stones are still warm, and yet are we engaged in obliterating every trace of their possessions" in order to create among the different sections of the country "mutual trade, to beget social intercourse, and to foster political confidence." And Brisbane turned historian: he mentioned that "in 1825, Dr. Fort, of Milledgeville, introduced into the Legislature of the State, a bill" whose "purporting object is similar to the present enterprize." The bill had passed into law, but had not been executed. "At the present day, he was happy to say, no such thing could be."[1] The Western & Atlantic Railroad was happening.

Brisbane was politically astute when he called "Dr. Fort" the father of the Western & Atlantic because Tomlinson Fort was a crucial figure at the beginning of 1838, funding construction of the railroad as head of the state-controlled Central Bank of Georgia. Fort was a medical doctor, but more important, he was a politician of central importance. Born in 1787, Fort served in the Georgia state legislature from 1818 to 1825, during which time he advocated for internal improvements and also gained valuable expertise in banking affairs by serving on the legislature's banking committee from 1820 to 1823. Fort was a key figure in the creation of a short-lived state Board of Public Works that nevertheless, in its one year of existence, anticipated railroad transportation and laid out the goal of connecting Georgia's coast to the Tennessee River.[2]

Fort served from 1827 to 1829 in the U.S. Congress (where he became close friends with John C. Calhoun while living in the same boardinghouse), and by the time Fort returned to Georgia in 1829 he was serving as one of the directors of the branch of the Bank of Darien at Milledgeville, the capital of the state. So Fort was an expert in legislation, in internal improvements, and in banking. In 1830 Fort purchased the *Federal Union*, a Milledgeville newspaper in financial trouble, and turned it into a powerful political voice for his Union faction of the Democratic Party. In 1832, when Wilson Lumpkin became governor, Lumpkin named Fort as president of the Central Bank of Georgia. Soon, Georgia placed all assets of the state under the control of the Central Bank.[3]

During these years Tomlinson Fort was a wealthy man, with an annual income of about $10,000, including $1,500 annually from his salary as president of the Central Bank. As his wife recalled about these years,

"The prominent men of the State often congregated [in Milledgeville] and I knew them all. Dr. Fort's position made us entertain a good deal." The Forts, unsurprisingly, owned dozens of enslaved people, and Martha Fort remembered that though they "only owned enough for our house-servants, the ante-bellum usage demanded about a score." The Forts also had many children—thirteen by the time they were through, nine of whom lived to adulthood. Undoubtedly their slaves cared for the children as well as the many houseguests almost always on hand.[4]

Fort was not the only person in Georgia interested in internal improvements. In Eatonton, a promising town twenty miles north of Milledgeville, was another small group of budding industrialists, centered on the legal profession and the Baptist church. Mark A. Cooper, born in 1800, graduated from South Carolina College and moved in 1821 to Eatonton, where he practiced law. Cooper was baptized in Eatonton by his Baptist pastor, Jesse Mercer. Mercer also "frequently conversed" with a young Eatonton tavern owner, Zachariah H. Gordon, and played a part in propelling Gordon to become a Baptist minister in 1825. Zachariah Gordon moved away to work as a pastor, but almost certainly had later dealings with Mark Cooper, as I discuss below. In the meantime, Zachariah's brother Charles P., an attorney like Cooper, practiced law in Eatonton. In 1831, Charles Gordon and Cooper announced a September railroad convention in Eatonton. As a result of the convention, the legislative assembly later that year chartered the first railroad in Georgia, the Augusta and Eatonton Turnpike and Rail-Road Company, which was authorized to continue the railroad past Eatonton all the way to the Chattahoochee River.[5]

Across the nation, railroad technology was advancing by leaps and bounds. Train cars pulled by horses were soon replaced with steam engines; other improvements happened so fast that the passage of a year made one's knowledge and expectations obsolete. Canals had been the focus of many people interested in transportation in the late 1810s and 1820s, and the success of the Erie Canal across New York state inspired numerous imitators. In most of the South, though, soil, topography, and climate all worked against a successful canal-building plan. Many southerners recognized railroads as a huge boon that could avoid many of the deficiencies of southern canals, and railroad enthusiasm grew.[6]

In Charleston, South Carolina, leaders were worried about the economic life of the city during the 1820s and feared that other cities, especially Savannah, were thriving instead. This led first to the Charleston and Hamburg Railroad, completed in 1833, which at 136 miles was the longest railroad in the world at that time. Hamburg lay on the South Carolina side of the Savannah River, close to Augusta, and Charlestonians hoped to divert the trade then flowing from Augusta to Savannah onto the railroad and thence to Charleston. Enthused by their success in building the railroad to Hamburg, South Carolinians attempted an incredibly ambitious railroad, the Louisville, Cincinnati, and Charleston Railroad, which would extend 700 miles across the Appalachian Mountains and connect South Carolina to the Ohio and Mississippi Valleys. It was a great concern in the coastal Southeast that much of the commerce of the vast interior of the country was headed to New York, Baltimore, and Philadelphia because of the Erie Canal and the National Road or, alternatively, down the Mississippi River to New Orleans. Perhaps the Louisville, Cincinnati, and Charleston could arrest stagnation and make Charleston thrive economically.[7]

A much shorter and more affordable alternative existed, however. In 1835, John C. Calhoun wrote to Farish Carter, a wealthy and entrepreneurial Georgian based in Milledgeville. Calhoun was pleased that now Georgia was considering a similar plan for a southeastern railroad that would connect to the Tennessee River (a water highway to the Ohio River). Calhoun recommended that Carter and some other "strong Capitalists" form a company so that when the survey for the proposed railroad was complete, "the company might secure all the collateral advantages, such as purchasing all the favourable sites" along the route. Calhoun said he had communicated with "Mr. Boyce," who thought Calhoun's ideas were sound. "Mr. Boyce" was Ker Boyce, the head of the Bank of Charleston and an extremely wealthy investor. It is no accident that Calhoun wrote to Farish Carter, who was quite similar to Boyce; Carter was one of the wealthiest men in antebellum Georgia. Born in upcountry South Carolina in 1780, following the death of his father, a major in the American Revolution, Carter made money and gained considerable experience as a contractor to the military during the War of 1812. After that he had his hand in cotton and sugar cane plantations—and enslaved laborers—across the South. He invested in stores, warehouses, mills, shipping, railroads, and gold mines. If anyone had the resources to invest in such a project, it was Farish Carter.[8]

A conference in Macon in November 1836 helped to galvanize support for a railroad to connect Georgia to the Tennessee and Ohio Valleys. Farish Carter was still in contact with John C. Calhoun on this subject and wrote him within days of the conference's close. Both Carter and Calhoun owned gold mines in northern Georgia—Calhoun had a highly productive mine, the Obarr mine, just three miles south of Dahlonega in Lumpkin County—and Carter said he agreed with Calhoun that gold mining was quite expensive. Workers found it lucrative, but much of the owner's profit was swept away by the costs. Carter thought gold mining still showed profit potential, but admitted, "I do not wish to increase my interest in the gold region as I cannot give it my personal attention." He continued, "You have to watch it constantly to keep off the Swindlers and even then you have a large part of the gold abstracted by those rogues." He added that the railroad convention in Macon had ended on a promising note, and it seemed that the state legislature would respond.[9]

Indeed, on December 21, 1836, Georgia's state legislature chartered a state railroad, which would become the Western & Atlantic. The railroad was to run from the south side of the Chattahoochee River northward to the Tennessee state line. The goal was to connect to the Tennessee River. Water and railroad, then, would connect the interior of the United States to the southeastern coast if the railroads from Augusta and Savannah extending into Georgia would link to the state railroad, which their owners would no doubt wish to do.[10]

Georgia needed to find the right path for the railroad, and in May 1837, with the consent of the War Department, Georgia governor William Schley appointed Colonel Stephen Harriman Long as the chief engineer. Long was an auspicious choice. Born in New Hampshire in 1784, Long graduated from Dartmouth College and wound up an engineer in the army. In 1819, as secretary of war, John C. Calhoun sent Long on a trans-Mississippi expedition that deepened the knowledge that Meriwether Lewis and William Clark's expedition had yielded. That successful foray, followed by another on the Minnesota River, made Long quite prominent. Long surveyed the path of the Baltimore and Ohio Railroad; in 1830 he wrote the first American treatise on how to build railroads; and he did initial surveys in 1832 that made South Carolinians enthusiastic about their trans-Appalachian railroad possibilities.[11]

Beginning in July 1837, Long and his assistants did their work; by November they supplied to the state of Georgia and to the War Department their survey of a proposed route. On December 23 the Georgia legislature passed an act that accepted Long's proposal. And three days later, Long made a private agreement principally with Farish Carter authorizing Long to spend tens of thousands of dollars to purchase key plots of land along the planned route. So Carter went into business with Long, who knew every bit of the route for the railroad. It was a marriage of investment capital with detailed knowledge and expertise.[12]

At the ground-breaking for the railroad on January 1, 1838, Long was absent. Brisbane handled the speaking duties, and no wonder—Long was busy spending money. In letters to Farish Carter he described how he had purchased May's Ferry across the Etowah River, bought "Seales Ferry," bought "Woodall's place at the junction of . . . the Alabama and Tennessee Roads," and had a verbal agreement to purchase another three parcels. Next he went south to the Chattahoochee River, where he had negotiated an opportunity to purchase 940 acres that included Montgomery's Ferry and two mill sites, one already developed into a gristmill and sawmill, for $5,000. Long and Carter were not advertising their actions, which might have aroused competition or opposition and raised asking prices. "Our concerns at the Etowah still remain a profound secret," wrote Long. "As yet there is not a suspicion afloat in reference to these matters." Before the end of January, Long wrote from May's Ferry on the Etowah River that he had purchased eight land lots, and if he and Carter played their cards right, they could own a two-mile stretch of riverfront. Long also informed Carter that he had received a letter "from our mutual friend Mr. Calhoun," who still encouraged "our scheme of Improvements." By February 8, Long reported twenty-seven lots purchased and recommended several more that he hoped they could acquire. If they could purchase them, "we shall have the entire [Etowah] river and its valley in our possession from May's Ferry upward, . . . embracing a distance of more than two and a half miles, and one of the most noble water-powers within the limits of Georgia." Long was anticipating building a bridge, a supply depot, a hotel, and a bank branch. In a short period of time, Long spent more than $32,000. Secrets are hard to keep forever, though, and in December Georgia's general assembly barred engineers working on the Western & Atlantic Railroad from purchasing land within three miles of the railroad. But it was too late—Long's work was complete.[13]

At the end of April 1838 Long reported that for his bank branch at the ferry he hoped to work with the Western Bank of Georgia, headquartered in Rome. But the economy was becoming a shambles, and the economic effects of the Panic of 1837 were already damaging some Georgia banks. Long wrote to Carter, "I refer you to our mutual friend Dr. Fort for information of any kind touching the affairs of the Bank at Rome. I believe all

Farish Carter and other cronies
secretly bought land along the
planned route of the Western &
Atlantic.

Cunyus, *History of Bartow County, Georgia*.
Courtesy of the Southern Historical Press.

Tomlinson Fort, shown
here about 1820, leveraged
his position as head of the
state-owned Central Bank
to his benefit.

Fort, *Memoirs of the Fort
and Fannin Families*.

Governor Charles McDonald, shown here probably
in the 1850s, brother-in-law of Farish Carter,
promoted the Western & Atlantic Railroad.
Avery, History of the State of Georgia.

is safe there." As Long pointed out, Carter and Fort were friends at least
as early as 1829, when Carter and Fort served together as directors of the
Milledgeville branch of the Bank of Darien. In 1831 the Georgia state legislature granted Carter, Fort, and two other men mill-race rights for a cotton and woolen mill they planned to build in Milledgeville. So Farish Carter and Tomlinson Fort became business partners.[14]

Fort could see just as easily as others that money-making opportunities awaited in the Cherokee country as a result of the Western & Atlantic Railroad. And Fort had an ally in the form of Zachariah B. Hargrove,
who married a relative of Fort and who could help Fort take advantage of
the situation. Hargrove, born in 1800, was in the Cherokee country early.
He was an attorney who in 1833 became one of the first town commissioners of Cassville, the county seat of Cass County, and he was one of the
founders of Rome, Georgia, in 1834. Fort and Hargrove began working
together.[15]

Because the Tennessee River does not flow through Georgia, Georgia could build a railroad to its state border not far from the Tennessee River, but would have to rely on cooperation from Tennessee in order to make the railroad connect, and it was an open question where the railroad in Tennessee might intersect with the river. That spot, of course, would become valuable real estate. One obvious place where the railroad might intersect the river was Ross's Landing. The landing was named for John Ross, a Cherokee leader with both white and Cherokee ancestry, who ran a ferry there. In 1838, Ross's Landing became the central collection point for thousands of the Cherokees forced off their lands who were about to travel west of the Mississippi River.

Even before Cherokee Removal, Samuel Williams, who lived near Ross's Landing, saw great potential for profits in land speculation and began negotiating an arrangement with Zachariah Hargrove. On February 5, 1838, Samuel Williams and his brother George created an investment company in partnership with Tomlinson Fort and Zachariah Hargrove, known as the Hargrove Company. Within months, Samuel Williams and another local, James A. Whiteside, teamed with Farish Carter and three Milledgeville men—Richard K. Hines, John Thomas, and George Lane— to form the Hines Company. Lane was the son-in-law of South Carolinian Ker Boyce and soon sold out his interest to him.[16]

These efforts intersected. Hargrove visited Farish Carter's large plantation along the Coosawattee River in northern Georgia during the summer of 1838. (Five years earlier, Carter had purchased fifteen thousand acres close to the plantation that had belonged to the Vann family.) Stephen H. Long wrote to Carter that he should not let Hargrove "get too fat." Long's teasing continued: "Rather keep him on short allowance, for I begin to fear that the attractions at Coosawattee will out-weigh his partialities for Cherokee." Matters turned serious, though, when Hargrove fell ill, and Long's next letter to Carter informed him that Fort had just arrived in Marietta and was hastily traveling to tend to Hargrove. The episode passed, apparently, and soon Tomlinson Fort, Zachariah Hargrove, Farish Carter, and Samuel Williams negotiated a substantial land purchase near Ross's Landing. Within a few years, they had spent more than $40,000 at this Tennessee site alone. Long wrote to Carter, "I think it best for us to keep the great Tennessee object in view," but he urged that they also pursue other ventures too small to attract the attention of many but that would nonetheless be profitable. At the time, though, it seemed their speculation on the "grand object" would pay off. "I have a letter from the

Messrs Williams," Hargrove wrote to Fort in December 1838, "in which they say that our investment will pay from *one to three hundred per cent* and much more should the Road terminate at their Landing. This is now to be regarded as settled." He continued, "I have no doubt of our making a considerable Sum of money." One sign that the investments paid off is that Samuel Williams, Farish Carter, and Ker Boyce all had streets named after them in early Chattanooga, the town that emerged at Ross's Landing. As Stephen Long wrote to Carter, "You own nearly one half of the Town site."[17]

Chattanooga, though, did not have a Hargrove Street. Life can be uncertain, plans sometimes have to yield to the unexpected, and Hargrove, who had not been in good health, died in January 1839, a particularly inconvenient time. His business partners needed financial flexibility; Hargrove's death suddenly froze a portion of the assets. Also, Hargrove had invested heavily in the Western Bank of Georgia: he owned 498 shares, more than any other investor. The bank, like many others caught in the Panic of 1837, had been forced to suspend specie payments and looked unsound. Tomlinson Fort's father-in-law was financially invested in Fort and Hargrove's deals, and he was not happy now that thousands of his dollars were tied up with the Hargrove estate. Fort tried to get cash out of the estate, but the process took years.[18]

Meanwhile, in the middle of 1839 the economy worsened (it would stay terrible in Georgia in 1840–1841), and the Western Bank of Georgia failed altogether. Fort had been fired from his position as president of the Central Bank, and with his money tied up in undeveloped real estate and in the Western Bank in the midst of financial meltdown, Fort's situation became so dire that friends recommended he declare bankruptcy. Instead, Fort took a $20,000 loan, a substantial amount, from a friend. The identity of the friend is unknown, though Farish Carter is the most obvious potential source.[19] Fort was hurting financially, and Carter and Long were financially extended and vulnerable in the economic depression. But they had two major things going for them.

The first advantage is that Stephen Harriman Long did not only oversee the survey but stayed on to direct the building of the Western & Atlantic Railroad. Second, late in 1839 Georgians elected Charles McDonald as their new governor. McDonald, who had married gold mine owner Mary Franklin's daughter, was an attorney, a state militia general, and a charismatic politician who was closely tied to banking; he worked with both Farish Carter and Tomlinson Fort as the attorney for the Bank of

Darien while both Carter and Fort were directors.[20] Most important, Farish Carter had married a sister of Charles McDonald in 1811, and the two
men knew each other and had had financial dealings since that time. In
1835 McDonald had joined with Carter and another partner to form a
gold mining company, the Chestatee Mining Company. Just before he was
elected governor in 1839, McDonald wrote to Carter asking for a loan of
$1,000.[21] In other words, Farish Carter had his brother-in-law and busi-
ness partner in the governor's mansion. Further, McDonald's first wife,
Ann, had died, and in 1839 the widower McDonald married Eliza Ruf-
fin Roane, who was a close friend and former schoolmate of Martha Low
Fort, the wife of Tomlinson Fort. Tomlinson Fort and Governor McDonald
also were friends. In January 1840, one of the first things McDonald did as
governor was return Fort to the board of directors of the Central Bank. In
sum, a tight-knit web of personal, familial, and business ties among these
top politicians and perhaps the richest man in Georgia had significant implications for the Western & Atlantic and the development of the state.[22]

The Central Bank of Georgia had been suffering in the economic de-
pression. It was loaded with debt and had precious little revenue. And yet,
during McDonald's first term of two years, with Fort at the helm of the
Central Bank, work on the Western & Atlantic continued apace and did
not stop until December 1841. By that time, the War Department had reclaimed Stephen Harriman Long, and the person McDonald got to re-
place Long was former governor Wilson Lumpkin. Lumpkin came aboard
only to find that in five years of railroad construction, not one rail had
been laid. Long had put all the efforts and more than $2 million into grad-
ing the land along the entire 140 miles, including many remote places with
very inhospitable terrain. Lumpkin was astonished; it was so inefficient.
Why had Long not built part of the railroad, gotten that section operating, and then extended it, using what had already been built to transport
materials and workers where they were needed?[23] What Lumpkin did not
know, or was unwilling to discuss publicly, was the extent of Long's real estate investments along the railroad route. Stephen Harriman Long's highest priority had been to get the railroad route locked into place all the way
to the northern border of the state, which would secure the importance
and value of his and his partners' land purchases, and to push Tennessee
to connect to the railroad via Ross's Landing. Since Long built no bridges,
there would have been steady paying traffic at the ferry sites he and his
partners owned.

Needless to say, Long and Fort, with apparently the cooperation of Governor McDonald, were mixing their public responsibilities with their personal desires to gain wealth, and those personal desires affected the decisions they made in their public offices. Farish Carter, Ker Boyce, and other investors were counting on their connections to public officials to help them make their investments pan out. It was a clear case of crony capitalism.[24]

Even though the work stopped at the end of 1841 for a few years, the Central Bank had already poured in more than $2 million, which meant the investment was so great that the state could hardly abandon the project. When better economic times arrived, the railroad was completed: first to Marietta and Cartersville (named after Farish Carter) by 1845, and all the way to the Tennessee River by 1850. As Chattanooga grew, Carter, Fort, Boyce, and their associates owned key pieces of land throughout the city. Tomlinson Fort was able to pay back his $20,000 loan. In 1846 the Forts named their newborn daughter after Eliza McDonald, Charles Mc-Donald's wife. It seemed the least they could do.[25]

This new railroad shaped the lives of many people who lived in northern Georgia, including John S. Rowland. Rowland, born in 1795, became a tax collector in the Pendleton District, served in the War of 1812, and in 1816 married Frances W. Lewis. In 1839, Rowland purchased a plantation along the Etowah River and soon acquired more than two thousand acres of land a few miles away. Rowland in time would become a superintendent of the Western & Atlantic, and William Grisham would work as his secretary.[26]

In the meantime, Rowland could see the possibilities that existed because of the Western & Atlantic. On the additional two thousand acres he had purchased were mineral springs, and Rowland began developing a summer resort called Rowland Springs. Resorts, where the coastal planter class could repair to avoid the heat, humidity, and mosquitoes of the subtropical summers, had been a staple of elite southern society since the 1790s. As the Cherokee country became accessible via the Western & Atlantic and connecting lines, Rowland Springs and several other resort locations emerged as places for the planter class to mingle, discuss the issues of the day, relax, and sometimes lobby politically or seek votes. Rowland Springs was not distinctive; resorts varied somewhat in their emphasis, but pretty much they were of a type, and they did not differ in any meaningful ways. That was part of their attraction.[27]

The Western & Atlantic opened to Cartersville in October 1845; the following June, a woman named Sarah Alexander came to the "Altona hills" and vacationed at Rowland's resort, which she described in a letter to her daughter as a relaxing "Arcadia." From her "large log cabin," one of half a dozen, she could watch ducks swimming on a stream fed by "two beautiful springs of sulphur and chalybeate water." A bathing house, a springhouse, and a "large framed house" being built constituted the only improvements, but she noted that "the sound of hammers is going all the day." The letter writer felt refreshed by her stay and noted that "they have a piano, and plenty of books and periodicals and papers." She and her husband, though, were almost the only guests.[28]

John S. Rowland and his enslaved laborers continued to improve Rowland Springs. In 1847, more people stayed there from mid-June through October. A promotional letter in Macon's *Georgia Telegraph* praised the easy accessibility via the Western & Atlantic, the wonderful springs, and the hosting abilities of Rowland. The hammers Sarah Alexander heard had "just completed one of the most commodious and best appointed Hotels in the county." Rowland's slaves also had built "acqueducts from a neighboring mountain, one mile and twenty rods distant, which will elevate the water fifty-five feet in front of the Hotel; where [Rowland] is preparing to erect one or more beautiful fountains." The anonymous writer revealed that "quite a number of gentlemen from Charleston, Savannah and Augusta, have already engaged rooms for themselves and families, and there is not the least doubt but that they will be better patronized the coming season, than any watering place in the Southern country."[29]

Upon arrival at the springs, visitors were greeted by the proprietor. One guest described Rowland as "so obliging, courteous and anxious to please, that the petulance of the weary traveller, the crabbedness of old age, and the peevishness of ill-health, are disarmed and subdued." A writer described Rowland as "an extremely courteous and obliging gentleman." Those who wished to be left alone could vacation unmolested, while others "can flirt, or 'trip it on the light fantastic toe,' to their heart's content." Another informant thought that Rowland's physiognomy indicated his personality: his "cheerful countenance and portly form give him assurance of good cheer and pleasant company."[30]

A letter to the editor of the *Charleston Courier* in July 1849 detailed the comforts available. The main building sat at the top of a hill, and there were "several two story frame buildings" where guests could live. Visitors could amble along graveled pathways past "ornamental shrubbery" and view the completed fountain, which shot "six jets" of water fifteen feet into the air. During the day, guests could walk through the garden or the orchards, practice their skills at the "ten pin alley," or select their preferences from a bar "abundantly supplied with choice Liquors, Wines, Segars, &c., of every description." By 1851, Rowland Springs included a pistol gallery, and the directors kept "a supply of carriage, buggy and saddle horses at the Springs, for the accommodation of pleasure parties, &c." Guests enjoyed the spring waters, and "commodious baths hot and cold, [were] kept in constant readiness." Breakfast was served in the morning, followed by lunch at 11:00, dinner at 2:00, and supper at 7:00. In the evening, following supper, music encouraged dancing. In at least one year the proprietors engaged a brass band from Savannah for the season.[31]

People often went to more than one resort in the summer; sometimes, they made a tour of several of them. If bored in one place or if the company wore thin, visitors could take off for another resort, see different scenery, and meet different people. A number of resorts flourished in Georgia, including one not far from Rowland Springs. Zachariah H. Gordon, the Baptist minister from Eatonton and brother of Charles P., in the late 1840s lived in Walker County in northern Georgia, where he opened Medicinal Springs, later Gordon Springs. The springs were twelve miles from the Western & Atlantic station at Dalton at the base of Taylor's Ridge. In 1847, the first year Medicinal Springs was open, the Gordons had just enough room to accommodate a small number of visitors, perhaps a dozen to twenty at a time. Yet so many people showed up that some had to sleep on the floor. The attraction was at least ten springs, of varying temperatures, which would fall off or spring from the mountain quite close to each other, variously infused with "Iron, Sulphur, Magnesia, Epson salts, &c. &c." Puff pieces in newspapers called on one and all to visit, especially people with maladies, including liver problems. Over the next few years the Gordons made improvements, though in 1849 a visitor complained that the place was "over-run with company." By 1852 the Gordon family claimed to be able to host 250 people at a time.[32]

Rowland Springs was likewise busy. Joseph Le Conte and his new bride honeymooned there, and in 1847 both the Democratic and Whig candidates for governor met there and "cracked with each other several hearty jokes." The throngs numbered about two hundred people, especially from Georgia and South Carolina. A correspondent said that Rowland Springs was "overflowing with visitors." And the writer recognized the Western & Atlantic as "of incalculable importance to this beautiful region," an acknowledgment that these resorts depended on the railroad to bring their guests.[33]

At times the papers waxed eloquent about the people who had so recently lived there, romanticizing the Cherokees. One 1847 visitor to Rowland Springs wrote that people could walk about the springs where "of late, the red prince of the forest was wont to slake his thirst and repose himself when the chase was ended." The writer had heard that Cherokees would meet there "in great numbers, pitch their temporary wigwams, and secure for the infirm and decrepid of their untutored race, the healing properties of these fountains of health, prepared for them as for us, by a beneficent God." Another letter writer said, "One looks in vain for some traces or memorials of the aborigines. They have hardly left a monument to mark their occupation of the soil. An occasional hard beaten trail, or cleared space, now fast being reclaimed by nature, where once was an Indian hearth stone, is all that remains, and soon hardly a monument will stand to denote their long possession."[34] This romantic language, an intentional misremembering of Cherokee cultural ways and how they ceased to be the inhabitants of the place, was frequent, a way of allaying guilty feelings about the tragic and cruel circumstances of their expulsion.

Rowland Springs would not have existed without the Western & Atlantic. In 1849, advertisements claimed Rowland Springs was only thirty hours of travel away from Charleston. One would leave Charleston by train at 10:00 a.m., arrive in Augusta at 6:00 p.m., eat supper, and leave at 8:00 that evening for Atlanta on the overnight train. Passengers would eat breakfast in Atlanta during their four-hour layover before taking the railroad to Cartersville, where they would hire a hack, which were allegedly always waiting at the station, for the ride of six miles to the springs. Including the price of supper and breakfast, one could travel the full distance for $11.75, and once arrived, pay to stay per day for $1.25, per week for $7, or for a month for $24.[35]

Newspapers published pieces that wondered why people would travel to northern states at all to vacation. In 1846, "G" wrote in a Savannah newspaper that he could foresee the day when Georgians would simply remain in the state, whether in search of "health, rest, novelty, or amusement," since the Cherokee area was so pleasant. Having left Marietta on the train, the writer and other passengers enjoyed the landscape, "the primeval forests," and the cutaway hillsides by the tracks that revealed lead and gold mines. A letter published in the *Charleston Mercury* and reprinted in Savannah's *Georgian* also emphasized how pleasant it might be to stay in the region rather than travel to the North and urged people to visit Rowland Springs. Rowland Springs was again extolled as a better alternative to a northern tour in 1848, when a Macon newspaper editor claimed "it were a thousand times better" for people to stay in Georgia and spend their money "at one of the many delightful places with which upper-Georgia abounds, than to dwaddle away the Season amid the dissolute follies of up-start fashionables at some Northern watering-place, where all the knowledge gained had better be unlearned." Some white southern-ers were clearly anxious about leaving the region lest they encounter anti-slavery opinions. Better to spend one's money and time close to home. The Macon newspaper editor wrote that for those who could go, they should, and railroads made these resorts highly accessible. Of Rowland Springs, the editor said, "it is unnecessary to say any thing, they are already so well known among us." That theme, the well-known and much-visited Row-land Springs, sounded again and again. In 1849, one of the South's leading authors, William Gilmore Simms, who was living in Charleston, published a novel entitled *Father Abbot; or, The Home Tourist*. In one bit of dialogue in the book, when a member of a fictive South Carolina monastery men-tions having been to Georgia, the abbot immediately asks, "What, Row-land Springs?" only to be told, "No indeed! I remembered too well your fa-vorite maxim, never to go where all the world goes."[36]

Not everyone, though, was going to Rowland Springs; some people es-caped from it. In early August 1849, four enslaved men belonging to John S. Rowland fled the place, leading Rowland to post a substantial reward for the capture of Tim, a "first rate blacksmith"; Guff, a carpenter; Her-cules, a tinner; and Levi, a literate and "first rate carpenter." They were valuable men. The carpenters certainly would have built and repaired buildings at Rowland Springs, and quite possibly all had participated in building the long aqueduct that fed the fountains. Unable to believe these men would have left of their own volition, Rowland wrote, "I have rea-son to believe these negroes have been decoyed off by some thief or ab-olition emissary," and he offered $300 for their seducer's conviction and another $200 for the four men, or $50 for each of them.[37] Not long af-ter, a correspondent from Rowland Springs, "E. F. G.," began his letter, which appeared in the major Macon newspaper, with the usual descrip-tions of the weather, the visitors, and the activities. But the writer then noted the escape of "four likely negro men" who "had without cause or provocation suddenly disappeared" on a Saturday night. "They were all mechanics, and were worth over six thousand dollars to" John S. Rowland.

Suddenly the letter writer veered into a complaint that "nothing is more common in Georgia, than to hear the Statesmen of South Carolina spoken of contemptuously" for resisting "the progressive encroachments of the federal government upon their rights in the matter of slavery. 'The chivalry,' 'hot-heads,' 'disunionists,' are the reproachful epithets frequently applied to them," yet "every Southern man and every Southern state" should support Calhoun and South Carolina. The writer continued, "When fugitive slaves have been demanded from the free States—when persons have gone into them in pursuit of property," these law-abiding southerners had been met with "mob-law," and "death has resulted." The "despicable fanatics" with "mad designs" were having greater and greater political influence, resulting in ending slavery in Washington, D.C., attacking interstate slave trades, and preventing the expansion of slavery into U.S. territories. Some people said not to be "excited now—that when the time comes the whole South will be united." But the writer was already worked up and wanted to know how many times the Constitution had to be violated before they would act.[38] Unable to address the reality of enslaved people running for their freedom, the writer invoked the grievances of a white South with northerners who would sympathize with or even act in favor of such runaways, and he scolded Georgians for distancing themselves from Calhoun's ideas and the state of South Carolina. The white South must be united.

Two weeks after they fled, the escaped men were captured in Barbourville, Kentucky, more than 250 miles from Rowland Springs, beyond the Cumberland Gap. Rowland went to get them and reported, "When taken they were worn down with fatigue and hunger, and much discouraged." Kentucky was crawling with men looking for runaways, and Rowland thought it "almost impossible for a Negro to get through." He speculated that "if Negroes of such intelligence as these cannot get on, I think others may give it up."[39]

Rowland hoped this was true, but he was aware of the unsettling situation in which a railroad connecting the coastal South with not only the upcountry of Georgia but also the vast interior of the continent also connected that South to free states with different politics and priorities. Whites at Rowland Springs could not imagine enslaved people wishing for freedom, so they made up thieves and abolitionist emissaries as culprits allegedly misleading steady servants who wished to do no more than to stay in their traces. One can see in the newspaper letters and editorials both an interest in transportation that would connect the coastal South to places like Rowland Springs, and a hesitance to embrace connection with the rest of the country. Abbott Brisbane's full-throated endorsement of bringing the sections together, of creating mutual trade, social intercourse, and political confidence over the hearthstones of the vanquished Cherokees did not ring with the same enthusiasm a decade later. The railroad had created new geographies and new places of relaxation, and it had connected those places to wider worlds, different worlds, both tantalizing and threatening.

The same minerals that infused the waters of Rowland Springs and made them attractive to people seeking pleasure and health were indicative of other possibilities, which did not go unnoticed. Discussions of Rowland Springs sometimes remarked, as a Georgia newspaper did in 1848, that "a few miles distant, on the Etowah River, are the Iron works and the great Flouring Mills of Cooper & Stroup—objects, to persons who have never seen similar ones, of much curiosity."[40] The iron-making facilities along the Etowah River and its tributaries in the 1840s and 1850s constituted an expansive industrial enterprise, which is the subject of the next chapter.

CHAPTER 3

Iron

AT THE INTERSECTION OF THE GOLD RUSH AND THE WESTERN & Atlantic Railroad emerged a crucial industrial site: the most extensive ironworks in the antebellum Deep South. A Carolina family, the Stroups, brought iron manufacture to Georgia and prospered amid the relative wealth of the gold fields. Moses Stroup used his South Carolina connections in 1837 to travel north on the East Coast to learn the most up-to-date iron-manufacturing methods. He eventually rejoined his father, Jacob, in the Etowah Valley and put his knowledge to use. Iron manufacture looked highly promising there, as the Western & Atlantic Railroad opened the possibility of markets far afield. Other talented people, especially the railroad promoter from Eatonton, Mark A. Cooper, were attracted to this fundamental dimension of southern industrialization. Cooper's founding in 1846 of an agricultural society dedicated to economic diversification and scientific improvement reveals an added aspect of this industrial outlook, which included a strong desire for self-sufficiency and a diversified economy. Moses Stroup's development of the iron industry in Alabama represented a continuation and extension of his existing iron network, and it had implications for the future.

Jacob Stroup and his son Moses were the premier iron makers in the Deep South from the late 1820s to the 1860s. They were from a large community of German American iron makers centered in Lincoln County, North Carolina, the descendants of iron-making Germans who migrated to Pennsylvania and Maryland during the late 1600s and early 1700s. Among these people were Mathias Stroup, an ironworker, and Johann Peter Stroup, who settled in Coalbrookdale, Pennsylvania, which had one of the earliest furnaces in the American colonies. These immigrants made iron for people such as William Penn and Lord Baltimore at a time when most iron production in America was pig iron—bars of iron manufactured near the coast for shipping to England—in keeping with mercantilist philosophies. Adam Stroup, born in 1746 in Baltimore County, Maryland, was related to these Stroups, and in the mid-1770s he and his family, along with numerous other German American ironworking families, migrated southward to western North Carolina. There, far from the coast, most iron served local needs for nails, horseshoes, hinges, pots, kettles, skillets, tools, and guns. This meant that furnaces were usually connected to forges for the finishing work, even if this violated mercantilist trade laws. During the American Revolution, these backcountry German Americans were staunch Patriots; they were led by Jacob Forney, a hero of the revolution in the South.[1]

Jacob Stroup was born in 1771 in York County, Pennsylvania, and moved as a young boy with his family to Lincoln County, North Carolina, the center of iron production, where he soon took up the family craft. By 1815 he showed up along the Broad River in nearby South Carolina, where he and Edward Fewell partnered in an iron-making operation. The furnaces that Jacob Stroup built were very similar to one another. When complete, they resembled flat-topped pyramids. Built of stone that was stacked without using mortar, these furnaces were routinely twenty to thirty feet wide at their base and extended in height more than twenty feet. Built next to a hillside or cliff, the furnaces were fed via a small bridge that led to the top of the furnace, where mined iron ore, charcoal, and limestone (used as a flux) were poured in. A charcoal fire burned constantly when the furnace was in use, for as long as forty weeks at a time, at a temperature of about 2500 degrees Fahrenheit. Inside, the iron ore melted, and impurities burned away. When a plug was removed twice daily, the tapped molten iron would come rolling out of the furnace into troughs to form bars (pig iron) that could be reworked in a forge into wrought-iron products, or the molten iron would be ladled into precast molds to make the skillets, gears, and other items iron customers sought. Making iron was an art, and skilled men worked the furnaces as keepers, forge men, fillers, and gutter men.[2]

Furnaces had ripple effects. Area farmers would cut the timber used to make charcoal, and the average furnace ate as much as 255 acres of timber each year, with pronounced ecological effects over time. Some people mined ore or limestone, while some worked as teamsters to bring the charcoal, the ore, and the limestone to the furnace or to take away the iron

The remains of an iron furnace built by Mark A. Cooper in 1859.
Courtesy of Joe Head, Etowah Valley Historical Society.

products and distribute them in different markets. In the early nineteenth-century rural South, where a tavern could be a community center, these iron plantations were huge economic engines. They were so important that in many cash-starved areas, bar iron substituted for currency. Iron makers used their product to pay wages and school tuition, pay off notes and lawsuits, purchase land and horses, and settle store accounts.[3]

In South Carolina, Fewell built an iron furnace, while Stroup built a forge, and together they owned hundreds of acres that supplied their iron ore and timber for charcoal. This arrangement was dashed in 1822 when Fewell died and flooding wiped out their operation. Stroup married Fewell's widow, supported her children, and went on to build another works, the King's Creek Ironworks, which he sold in 1825 and then moved on to develop yet another operation on the Broad River.[4]

In the summer of 1829, when the gold rush began, early strikes were reported in Habersham County, a short distance from Stroup's Broad River site; by December, Jacob Stroup had purchased property in Habersham, even though he had not yet sold his unfinished South Carolina furnace. In Habersham County, he and his son Moses built an iron forge and furnace on the same watercourse, the Soquee, as Shelton's gold mine. Habersham County had the waterpower, iron ore, and timber that Stroup needed to run an ironworks. Also, because Habersham County was not in the Cherokee country of Georgia, one could obtain secure land titles to property there. Thousands of miners were intruding on Cherokee lands, and the Stroups supplied these first prospectors, who worked over the surface deposits, with "Georgia pans," skillets made of sheet iron.[5]

In Habersham County over the next few years, Jacob Stroup continued to purchase land lots that would provide his furnace and forge with the iron ore, limestone, and timber for charcoal that he needed to fuel his enterprise. He was assisted in this by helpers who followed him for decades, including his attorney and son-in-law James Strain, his bookkeeper and assistant Noah Goode, and a couple of his sons, Alexander and Andrew. (The name of Andrew Jackson Stroup, born in 1824, indicates Jacob's political loyalties.) By 1837 Stroup had amassed 4,250 acres of land and harnessed the river to provide waterpower for a gristmill and sawmills. Jacob Stroup's pattern during his life, however, was to sell his operations after they had matured and move to a new, undeveloped site to begin again. During the first part of 1837 Stroup sold for $16,000 his entire works to a group of Augusta-based investors interested in building a railroad in the area. Stroup paid off his debts and pocketed the rest of his money; his timing was lucky. The Panic of 1837 ripped through the economy, and the purchasers of the Habersham Ironworks failed to summon the resources necessary to sustain the business, which went bankrupt.[6]

Meanwhile, Moses Stroup traveled in a different direction. By the mid-1830s, he was employed by the well-connected politician and iron maker Wilson Nesbitt. Nesbitt joined with other investors in the South Carolina Manufacturing Company, which in 1834 acquired, built, and rebuilt iron furnaces and mills. Almost certainly Stroup worked on these projects.[7]

Nesbitt also trusted Stroup as a key figure in his next enterprise. In December 1836, Nesbitt and several other wealthy and prominent South Carolinians founded the Nesbitt Iron Manufacturing Company, which operated along the Broad River south of Spartanburg. The stockholders included South Carolina's governor and the head of the Bank of South Carolina. Moses Stroup was also a stockholder. Nesbitt served as president, and in August 1837 he announced to the other stockholders that "before the formation of the company Mr. M. Stroup was in my employ at the rate of $800 pr. annum. He remains in the service of the company." The company did not intend to replicate the ironworks that had existed in South Carolina to that time—short stack furnaces using cold blast techniques with charcoal as the exclusive fuel. They set their sights higher.[8]

In September and October 1837, the company sent Nesbitt and Stroup on a trip up the East Coast to purchase machinery, hire workers, and school themselves on the most modern methods of American iron making to help them build a top-notch facility. Both Nesbitt and Stroup reported on their trip upon their return. Nesbitt explained that he and Stroup first went to Washington, D.C., where Congress was in session. Nesbitt, a former congressman, garnered letters of introduction from a number of representatives and senators, and then Nesbitt and Stroup traveled to Ellicott's rolling mill, which operated fifteen miles outside Baltimore. For Moses Stroup, the trip was a return to the places his grandfather had lived and worked in the mid-1700s. They presented their letters of introduction to Nathaniel Ellicott, who "politely" received them and "appeared with pleasure" to tell them all about his operation, which mostly supplied iron to naval yards.[9]

From Ellicott's works, the South Carolina travelers went to York County, Pennsylvania, where Adam Stroup had been working when his son Jacob was born in 1771, and they visited Grubb's furnace. One Grubb family member had recently returned from a trip to Europe, where he studied the hot blast technique. Stroup and Nesbitt, in turn, studied Grubb's furnace, which was "built after the plan of the Furnaces in England." Without the hot air blast, the furnace produced seventeen to twenty tons of iron weekly, but with the hot air blast, the furnace output increased to an average of thirty-one tons weekly. Nesbitt looked at Grubb's books and took notes, and they arranged to have Grubb send them the patterns for the necessary pipes. From there, the pair traveled to another furnace, Henry Slaymaker's, which also used the hot air blast.[10]

From there Stroup and Nesbitt went to Philadelphia, where they visited two rolling mills up the Schuylkill River. Neither mill was in operation, and both were patterned similarly to Ellicott's, so they pressed on to the West Point Foundry in New York, a "very extensive Establishment," including a rolling mill that routinely produced 60 tons of iron weekly and could handle as much as 125 tons each week. Stroup and Nesbitt studied the rolling mill closely, then proceeded to the workshop of the West Point operation. There, Stroup purchased a range of items that shows the extent to which the enterprise rested on his abilities. He ordered machinery, including piston rods, a lathe with cutting shears, a vise, and a drill, and he also purchased bells, tin plate, iron plate, glass panes, putty, leveling instruments, surveyor's equipment, drawing instruments, blasting needles, glass gauges, and mercury.[11]

Stroup also acquired expertise. He contracted with an iron molder, Samuel Lawson, and another man, John Conlon, to come to South Carolina to work for six months. Lawson helped Stroup pick out and order the machinery they needed from the West Point Foundry in New York. It appears that Lawson's molding skills were to be used to make the piping for a hot blast furnace.[12]

At this point, the pair split. Nesbitt, eager to be frugal, sent Stroup to Boston alone and returned to South Carolina. Stroup, highly impressed by the South Boston Iron Company, spent thousands of dollars for "the most Dificult part of the machinery" before he too departed for the South. Between Boston and New York, Stroup spent more than $4,000 on behalf of the Nesbitt Company.[13]

During this time, new technological advancements in England were making their way to the United States. Stroup was familiar with the technologies that his father and other ancestors had utilized, and he now incorporated the latest discoveries, although in their infancy, into his knowledge. As Stroup recounted to the company in a November letter, he had "visited the North" and "asertained all the information which was to be had in that quarter on the subject of Iron Making" by visiting "the Best" iron manufactories "in the country." Three processes struck Moses Stroup as particularly relevant. Furnaces had air blasted into them, but Stroup discovered that some furnaces were heating the air before releasing it on the charge of fuel and ore. "The hot air Blast applied to the Furnace . . . apears to be the greatest modern improvement in the Manufactor of Iron," Stroup reported. He also examined the reheating of pig iron, which turned the iron into a doughy mass that could be reworked in rolling mills. "The Pudling of Iron . . . I inquired into very particular." Stroup was impressed because puddling "apears to Be a great saveing in making of Bar Iron," but he was worried because puddled iron did not bring so high a price, though its supporters said this was not because of inferior quality, but only because of prejudice against puddled iron. Finally, Stroup mentioned "the Roling mill which I was Disapointed in as I could not see any plan that I could adopt and of course had [to] make a plan of my own."[14]

Stroup's account and the records that document his trip reveal someone intently interested in adding to his knowledge, and Stroup was now acquainted with the most advanced methods of iron making in the United States. Though most British furnaces had converted to coal production of iron, partly because of the unavailability of timber, in the United States in 1837 almost all furnaces still operated with charcoal as the heat source.

As late as 1844, John C. Calhoun's son-in-law, the mining expert Thomas G. Clemson, noted that "no furnaces are in successful operation in [Pennsylvania], that are supplied from any other combustible than charcoal, save one or two with anthracite. The experiments that have been made with mineral coal have signally failed." By 1847, a decade after Stroup's trip, only 25 percent of the iron produced in the United States was produced by coal-fired furnaces; charcoal-fired furnaces were still the norm.[15] In 1837, with Moses Stroup, the Nesbitt Company had a promising and experienced furnace builder who knew how to build an advanced ironworks in the Lower South.

When the hot blast patterns had not arrived by late January 1838, prominent stockholder Benjamin T. Elmore "immediately ordered the patterns to be made under Stroup's direction, which would take 3 or 4 weeks, with a fair chance of failing, tho Stroup was confidant of succeeding." But Stroup's confidence was misplaced; a year later, the furnaces were producing tons of iron daily, and Elmore reported that "Stroup was about to try the hot blast again." Ultimately, the hot blast never was successful at the Nesbitt ironworks. Beyond the strain on the pipes, the possibility of breakdown was high, so ultimately the company chose to proceed with the more standard cold blast procedure in its two furnaces, but added to its facility various finishing capabilities.[16]

In March 1838, the Nesbitt Company contracted with Moses Stroup to build a substantial physical plant. First Stroup would build a "foundry with reverberatory furnaces" that would enable him to create the machinery for the rest of the facility. This foundry would be built in an enclosed "frame building of wood seventy feet long by forty wide." Stroup would then also build a "Black-Smith shop with four fire places and a triphammer, two turning lathes and a drilling machine" in another building 120 feet by 34 feet, along with a store. The next portion would be major: "one Forge and Rolling Mill—the forge to contain eight fires; the Rolling Mill to work eight sets of Rollers in five frames," which would make flat bars, square bars, round rods, and boiler plate. The forge and rolling mill would be housed in a building that measured 170 feet by 80 feet. All of the operations would be powered by water from the Broad River run through stone-lined races to the wheels, fires, and bellows of the plant. The provisions of this contract were to be completed by April 1, 1839, a year later.[17]

Stroup's responsibilities were enormous and wide-ranging. Besides overseeing all aspects of the construction, Stroup was in charge of gristmills and sawmills, he had to improve the navigability of the Broad River, and he even appraised for the company the value of the slaves who were working on the project. The company had a superintendent who hired people, handled payroll, and conducted the business generally, but the enterprise rested heavily on Stroup's shoulders.[18]

Unfortunately for the owners of the Nesbitt Iron Manufacturing Company, they had chosen a major economic investment at precisely the time when the national economy crashed in the Panic of 1837. Even before the company made its contract with Stroup, it was clear that banks, not just in the United States, were in serious trouble financially. The company had the advantage of including as a major shareholder the head of the Bank of South Carolina, Franklin H. Elmore, but there was only so much Elmore could do, and he was constantly trying to acquire capital from bank investors in the scramble that the panic caused. As a sign of the scale of the new enterprise, consider that Jacob Stroup usually had sold his ironworks for somewhere between $16,000 and $20,000. And yet by 1841 the Nesbitt Company owed more than $90,000 to the Bank of South Carolina. Bankruptcy of the Nesbitt Company threatened to topple the bank into failure.[19]

One place the Nesbitt Company looked for relief was the federal government. In May 1838, the company submitted a memorial to the House of Representatives, "Praying the Establishment of a National Foundry," and explained the company and its prospects. Its location, amid "inexhaustible" beds of high-quality iron ore, allowed the company to access the Broad River, which flowed through Columbia and on to Charleston. The Nesbitt Company owned eight thousand acres of forests, three thousand acres of iron ore fields, and five hundred acres of limestone. In addition to the two iron furnaces already in production, it was expanding so it could produce three thousand tons of iron product each year. The petitioners anticipated that the Louisville, Cincinnati, and Charleston Railroad, "now in progress from Charleston to the West, will either pass by the works, or so near as to induce a connexion with it by a branch, which will be completed without delay."[20]

The admission that the company's location was remote from any existing railroad highlighted a critical weakness, as did the petitioners' acknowledgment that the area contained no coal deposits. Congress referred the memorial to the Select Committee on a National Foundry. The Nesbitt Company received some orders for cannons and shot during the 1840s but had a hard time winning enough government contracts to make the business flourish. The anticipated railroad near the works was never built.

Eventually the company went completely bankrupt and was sold in 1850 to Swedish and German investors, who formed the Swedish Iron Manufacturing Company of South Carolina. Moses Stroup had finished his contract, but the economic and geographical conditions worked against fulfillment of the early promise of the Nesbitt Iron Manufacturing Company. The momentum was already moving in a new direction, and Moses's father, Jacob, was taking the lead. Moses would soon move to where the action was.[21]

Having sold his Habersham Ironworks in 1837, Jacob Stroup moved westward, farther into the heart of the gold fields. Since 1832 it had been possible to have secure land title in the Cherokee Nation, and Stroup found an area that was central to the gold rush and rich with the materials needed to make iron. Years before he sold his Habersham operation, on August 22, 1833, Jacob Stroup had purchased a forty-acre land lot in Cass County. He moved there in 1837, built a forge, purchased more land, and in 1839 began construction of an iron furnace there. Stroup was evidently not the only person who recognized the possibilities of the site. In February 1838, Stephen H. Long wrote from Etowah to Farish Carter that "Genl. Taylor passed through this place a few days since, and spoke in terms of high approbation of our prospect for establishing iron-works." It was Jacob Stroup, though, who developed iron manufacturing in the area. He also did more than just supply the gold miners around him. His son recalled that Jacob "lost heavily in a gold mine" investment.[22]

Stroup built his furnace on Stamp Creek, a tributary of the Etowah River and a prime location for making iron. High-quality iron ore was abundant, as was limestone, and Stamp Creek, a powerful and largely spring-fed stream that hardly ever flooded or went dry, provided constant waterpower. The surrounding hills were covered with "poplar, beech, oak, walnut, chestnut, ash, and hickory," which would provide the charcoal necessary for the furnace.[23] Besides the gold mining in the area, the other enterprise of greatest significance was the Western & Atlantic Railroad, running just four miles west of Stroup's furnace. The problem that had bedeviled the Nesbitt Company in South Carolina—lack of access to railway networks—would not afflict the Etowah area.[24]

From the beginning of Jacob Stroup's Stamp Creek operation in 1839 until 1845, the Stroup family had the iron business virtually to themselves. Moses Stroup left the employ of the Nesbitt Company and migrated from South Carolina to the Etowah area to join his father. In March 1845, Jacob's first furnace was producing iron, and Jacob and Moses were building

Moses Stroup played a
central role in the iron
industry of the Deep South.
Armes, *Story of Coal and
Iron in Alabama.*

Mark A. Cooper

MARK A. COOPER.

Mark A. Cooper was a politician who promoted
railroads and banks before he partnered with
Moses Stroup to make iron.
Courtesy of the Prints and Photographs
Division, Library of Congress.

a second furnace. They made pig iron, cast iron, "pots, ovens, and other
kitchen utensils." Including the families of their workers, 150 people were
employed or supported by their operation.[25]

The business was modeled after what Jacob Stroup had been doing all
his life. Moses, after his experiences with the Nesbitt Company, envisioned
greater possibilities, but financing was the key. In 1845 Moses Stroup
forged a new business partnership with Mark A. Cooper, the wealthy
Georgia politician, banker, and railroad enthusiast from Eatonton who
had promoted the first railroad convention in the state. A few years earlier, while Cooper was campaigning for political office, he had stayed one
night with Moses Stroup and later said he was "inspired" and "fascinated
with the grand scenery and water power." In May 1845, Stroup and Cooper announced the creation of their business alliance and urged "Farmers, Placers, Merchants, Machinists, and Founders" to "examine our products and prices." The invocation of "placers," people who panned for gold,
shows the ongoing connection to the gold rush, but clearly their business
was wide ranging.[26]

Cooper was born in 1800 to a prominent family. He graduated from South Carolina College in 1819, whereupon he became an attorney and practiced law in Eatonton. The planter life did not especially interest him, and he put his energies briefly into a cotton mill, only to turn more extensively to banking in Columbus, Georgia. In the 1830s he served in the state legislature, where he promoted railroad construction and a states' rights philosophy, and beginning in 1838 he served three terms in the U.S. House of Representatives, initially as a member of the States' Rights Party of Georgia and later as a states' rights Democrat. He resigned his seat in 1843 to run unsuccessfully as a Democrat for governor. Though he soured on electoral politics after 1843, Cooper had plenty of remaining ambition. Because he was a classmate of Nesbitt Company investor Franklin H. Elmore at South Carolina College and the two served at the same time in Congress, it is easy to imagine that Cooper knew something about the iron industry from Elmore's experience. Beginning in 1845, for several years Cooper put his money and energies into expanding the industrial plant the Stroups had begun.[27]

Early in 1846 the media-savvy Cooper published a letter entitled "Southern Independence" in a number of southern newspapers and explained that in the Etowah Valley the two iron furnaces were producing as much as twenty-five tons of iron weekly. The furnaces were supplying gears and cast-iron machinery for factories and mills. Further harnessing the abundant waterpower, Cooper and Stroup ran a corn grist and a flour mill, and they were building a much more expansive merchant mill—four and a half stories, built of stone—that would serve markets far beyond the local subsistence farmers since it could turn out between twenty thousand and thirty-eight thousand barrels of flour each year. Newspapers reported, unsurprisingly, that "all the wrought and cast iron used in the mill was manufactured at the adjoining iron works of the same proprietors, where the machinery was also fitted up." Beyond the flour mill, the clearest sign of what was to come is that Cooper and Stroup had begun building an iron rolling mill, as Stroup had done for the Nesbitt Company. With the growing needs of the Western & Atlantic Railroad, there was a market for the iron rails rolled in the mill.[28]

The iron business could be boom and bust, but Cooper found his flour mill could contribute steadily to the bottom line. In 1848, the chief engineer of the Western & Atlantic reported to Georgia's governor that "the Etowah mills and others erected, or in process of erection for the manufacture of flour, are stimulating the production of wheat to an unprece-

The village surrounding the rolling mill housed ironworkers and their families.
Courtesy of the Atlanta History Center.

Cooper's flouring mill promoted wheat cultivation in the Etowah Valley.
Courtesy of the Atlanta History Center.

dented extent. . . . Wheat and flour are to be important articles of transportation on this Road." Advertisements for Etowah Mills flour appeared
in newspapers in the interior cities of Macon and Augusta, as well as the
coastal cities of Charleston and Savannah. Years later, as Cooper recalled
that era in his memoir, he wrote that his barrels of flour "drove the northern flour back to the seaboard and with the help of the other mills built afterward Georgia flour took the market in Georgia; and wheat in Cherokee
County, Georgia was grown as a staple." Here were the ancillary effects of
a growing railroad network and Etowah River waterpower used to power
a large mill: area farmers found themselves drawn into a growing market
economy, and their wheat production expanded tremendously during the
1850s.[29]

During the first half of 1846 Cooper and Stroup brought in another
partner, Leroy M. Wiley, who added excellent financial backing. Wiley,
born in Georgia in 1794, had a good head for business. Starting out in
Milledgeville, by the 1830s he was involved in significant national business
concerns, especially wholesaling, in Charleston and New York, had business dealings and corresponded regularly with Farish Carter, and retained
a major interest in economic opportunities in Georgia. As a director of the
Bank of Milledgeville, along with Farish Carter, Tomlinson Fort, and Ker
Boyce, and with connections to the Bank of Macon, Wiley was aware of
the economic possibilities along the route of the Western & Atlantic Railroad. He turned down an offer from Carter to invest in Ross's Landing,
but when Cooper visited Wiley's New York wholesaling firm on business,
Wiley asked Cooper if he could acquire a stake in the Cooper and Stroup
enterprise. Wiley invested $15,000 and became a full partner.[30]

Also in 1846, Cooper took another significant step in his vision of a fully
developed southern economy when he created the Southern Central Agricultural Society, which sponsored an annual fair in Georgia. In 1851, Cooper explained the origins of the society in a letter in which he recalled a
conversation with a Stone Mountain hotel owner, who wondered how to
increase the visibility and business of his hotel. Cooper suggested an agricultural fair to be held at Stone Mountain and issued calls in newspapers
for interested people to gather there in the summer of 1846 because "now
the Rail Road had opened the rich valleys of Cherokee to Middle Georgia,
the products of this farming region might meet the plantation products
at the Stone Mountain." The fair would "advance the general welfare" and
"call public attention to the vast and varied resources of Georgia, and especially those of her mountain territory."[31]

In August 1846, a few dozen people gathered at Stone Mountain to organize the fair. Cooper took the leading role. Moses Stroup was also a founding member. The founders agreed that the Southern Central Agricultural Society should exhibit and sell "all such products of Agriculture and Horticulture," including "animal and vegetable products of the Plantation, Farms, Gardens, and Orchards and Dairy," along with "Agricultural implements and articles of Domestic Manufacture useful to the Planter or Farmer." Herein lay the expansiveness of Cooper's vision for the society, which at this first meeting endorsed a resolution to call for a convention that would draw people from several southern states to Atlanta "to consider the advantages of the Rail Road system, and the means of extending it so as to connect the Mississippi valley with the Southern Atlantic States and cities." To further emphasize what Cooper had in mind, the account of the meeting reported that those gathered "examined a specimen of stove fitted up for a dining or breakfast room by Messrs. Cooper, Stroup and Wiley, at their Works in Cass County." The society and its annual fair would be far more than a display of fruits, vegetables, and grains; additionally, the society was a vehicle of advertisement specifically for Cooper, Stroup, and Wiley and a lobbying organization in favor of more railroads.[32]

At the first fair in August 1847, three thousand attendees gathered. A correspondent writing for the Savannah *Georgian* complained of sleeping crammed in a room with twenty-eight people, many of whom snored, and he awakened the next morning to find that "pedestrians, carts, carriages and wagons are arriving every moment." Fruits of the field were in abundance, and participants also attended a meeting concerning "the Magnetic Telegraph."[33]

Following the success of the first agricultural fair, in the announcement of the second fair in 1848, Cooper, Stroup, and Wiley offered "a silver medal for the best bushel of wheat" and encouraged everyone to try for it. It was a smart move, perfectly in keeping with an agricultural fair and also designed to bring attention to the flour mill that was a mainstay of their Etowah business enterprise. Among the 250 entries in the competition, Cooper won second place for his corn, beating Moses Stroup, who came in third in that category. Cooper also displayed potatoes, white onions grown from seed, a nutmeg melon, garden vegetables, a heifer, and "a variety of specimens of the manufacturing of Iron—railroad iron, rolled iron, hollow ware, [and] castings of different kinds." Cooper, Stroup, and Wiley also won an honor for their entry of "Mott's Patent Furnace, with boiler complete." Taken as a whole, the agricultural fair exemplified Cooper's dream of a well-developed, multidimensional southern economy, one with a full complement of railroads, a vigorous manufacturing class, and agriculturalists receptive to scientific advances. Moses Stroup not only tied himself to Cooper as a business partner, but was also a fellow founder of the fair and an exhibitor, someone who shared Cooper's vision for the South.[34]

The rolled iron at the fair in 1848 indicates the fruition of the rolling mill Stroup had been building since 1846. This mill was not as large as the one Stroup had built a decade earlier for the Nesbitt Company, but it was advantageously located and one of only thirteen antebellum rolling mills in the South, which were mostly in Kentucky and Virginia. Technologically, the rolling mill was important because it introduced coal as a heat source into the iron-making process without transferring impurities to the iron ore. Iron created in charcoal furnaces could be reheated using coal in the puddling process, which wound up with the iron ore being squeezed into thin sheets in the rolling mill. One could produce with this method much more iron in bar form, which could be used for railroad rails among many other uses. With both furnaces and the rolling mill in action, the Etowah Iron Works normally produced between six and eight tons daily.[35]

Via a combination of the Western & Atlantic Railroad and wagons where the railroad was not yet complete, the Etowah mills got their coal from Dade County in northwestern Georgia, almost a hundred miles distant. When the Western & Atlantic opened the full distance to Chattanooga in 1851, the Etowah Iron Works was the primary customer for the coal transported through Chattanooga. Cooper purchased Dade County coal mines. So the gold rush and the railroad stimulated the iron industry, which then created a need for coal production and transportation via the railroad.[36]

Beyond Cooper, Stroup, and Wiley, other people got into the iron-making business in the area. John W. Lewis built a furnace and then sold it in 1848 to his brother-in-law Samuel Maxey Earle, previously a shareholder in the Nesbitt Company. As initial investors in 1836, when the company formed, Samuel M. Earle and Bayliss J. Earle had delivered thirty-five slaves to Wilson Nesbitt "in payment of their portions of the stock" in the company. These slaves then became a portion of the labor force that worked at Moses Stroup's direction, building the iron-making facility. The arrangement did not last, however. Sometime over the next year or two the Earles were in dispute with the rest of the company about how much their slaves were worth; the Earles believed they had overpaid for their stock. What presumably complicated the valuation of their investment was that many of the enslaved people had specialized skills. As Franklin H. El-more explained to potential investors in the company in December 1838, the company possessed "between 130 & 140 valuable slaves—many of them mechanics & nearly all the males, trained to the various employments of the business." The same month, though, the company reached agreement with the Earles to accept the return of their shares in the company and re-turn to the Earles the slaves that had been their investment.[37]

At this point the Earles presumably looked for another place for their slaves to work profitably. Samuel's brother-in-law John W. Lewis, after he moved to Canton, promptly began purchasing iron ore properties and be-came authorized by the Georgia legislature in 1841 to build a dam across the Etowah River, which would supply waterpower to any enterprise he might build. Lewis ultimately built a mill or factory site in 1845 on Stamp Creek, which fed into the Etowah River, and in 1847 he completed an iron furnace, also on Stamp Creek. The same year, Samuel M. Earle relocated to the area, and his slaves mined gold before Earle purchased Lewis's fur-nace and returned his unfree workforce to the iron ore and limestone min-ing with which they were more familiar: making charcoal, feeding the fur-nace, building roads, and working as teamsters, hauling away iron product in ox carts and wagons.[38] Significantly, these enslaved workers were mi-grating between industries; their skilled labor could be used in different extractive mining efforts to produce both iron and gold.

This dynamic iron-producing place, along a major railroad in a re-gion still dotted by gold mines, produced a diverse workforce. Anne Kelly Knowles has argued that southern dependence on enslaved laborers made southern iron making conservative and unable to embrace technological change, but she notes that the Etowah area was less resistant to a cosmo-politan workforce. "Skilled workers from England, Wales, Scotland, Ger-many, Massachusetts, Pennsylvania, and a number of Southern states" appeared in the 1850 U.S. Census of the area, and at least one of these workers was creating innovative technology. In 1851 two notices in *Scien-tific American* reported patent applications from Mark M. Ison. He was working at Etowah on both spike and nail machinery and, at a time when people were still figuring out how to secure railroad rails to the ties, on a machine that would make "chairs" to hold the rails.[39]

A visitor to the Cooper works in September 1849 observed that "the workmen here were almost exclusively whites," and he noted a certain esprit de corps among them. "The firemen at the pudling furnaces," he wrote, "were uniformed, and their dress was sufficiently simple to please the veriest utilitarian. It consisted of striped pants, fastened round the waist, and a small close-fitting cap, ornamented with a tassel. Shirts and waistcoats they hold in detestation." Here were no degraded laborers, but men wearing distinctive pants and tasseled headgear, quite different from most iron-making operations in a slave society.[40]

These workers had options about whom their employer would be, since Cooper's furnaces and rolling mill were the centerpiece of a growing iron-making center. Up and down the Etowah River and along its tributaries, other people were also building iron furnaces, so that by the late 1850s a total of six charcoal furnaces and another forge, in addition to Cooper's rolling mill, were all complete and producing tons of iron product. During the 1850s Etowah iron found markets in Georgia, Alabama, Tennessee, and even Ohio and Pennsylvania.[41]

This was now a major industrial area. In 1861, the Etowah rolling mill was the only industrial complex south of the Tredegar Iron Works in Richmond that could produce railroad car axles. Cooper's furnaces and mills alone were producing thousands of tons of iron to be turned into railroad rails, and for the consumer market they were producing "Boilers, Pots, Ovens, Spiders, Skillets, Fire Dogs," and sundry other cast-iron pieces. Cooper augmented his furnace and rolling mill with a nail factory and a spike machine. In 1858 Cooper employed or supported between 400 and 600 people; there were 1,200 people living around Etowah, which had a post office, a store, a boardinghouse, a brewery, a house of prostitution, and a Baptist church built by Cooper that doubled as a schoolhouse.[42] From the perspective of the late 1850s, with the furnaces, mills, and other industry in the area, including potash works and saltpeter and gold mines, along a major trunk railroad line with access to both the coast and the great interior of the nation, the future looked rich with possibilities.

By this time, though, Moses Stroup had moved on. In late 1848 or 1849, after the rolling mill he was building with Cooper and Wiley was complete, Stroup sold his portion of the enterprise to Cooper and went farther down the Etowah River to the Coosa River, into which the Etowah flowed, into Cherokee County, Alabama. He scouted Cherokee County in 1848, acquired land rich with iron ore, and in 1849 started to build his Round Mountain furnace, which began operating in 1852. Stroup was not alone in this venture. He renewed an old partnership by joining again with his old employer, Wilson Nesbitt. During the 1840s, Nesbitt had tried to nurse along the Nesbitt Iron Manufacturing Company, which eventually went completely bankrupt and was sold in 1850. Now Nesbitt turned his sights toward his old furnace builder, who presumably needed some financing, and in 1850 the Alabama General Assembly chartered the Alabama Mining and Manufacturing Company, headed by Nesbitt and Stroup. The 1850 U.S. Census shows that Henry and Barbara Veitch had also moved to Cherokee County, Alabama, along with their six sons and Henry's mother.[43]

Henry Veitch and his descendants would form a crucial part of the technological network of the Stroups stretching into the late nineteenth and early twentieth centuries. Henry F. Veitch was born in New York in 1808 or 1809 into an impoverished iron-making family that migrated to Lincoln County, North Carolina. The Stroups and Veitches reportedly worked together in Lincoln County beginning in 1832. Henry Veitch married Barbara Costner, also from an iron-making family, in 1834. In 1837–1838 he worked for the Nesbitt Iron Manufacturing Company in close association with Moses Stroup. Census records indicate that Henry and Barbara Veitch moved to Georgia by 1841, and in 1843 they buried a daughter in the furnace cemetery along the Etowah River, which adjoined the four cemetery plots that eventually held Jacob Stroup, who died in 1846; Jacob's wife, Sarah Fewell Stroup; and two of their boys, Thomas B. Stroup and Edmond Monroe Fewell (son of Sarah's first husband). Henry Veitch worked for Jacob Stroup in 1845 at Stroup's Allatoona Iron Works, and Henry and Barbara's sons spent their boyhood in this iron-making area in the 1840s. So Nesbitt and Stroup continued to work with people they had been associated with for decades.[44]

Technologically, the Round Mountain furnace was much more akin to what Jacob Stroup had normally done, rather than what Moses had been involved with for the previous fifteen years. Jacob had a talent for constructing a small furnace and forge, which he then sold for a profit. Moses seems more to have escaped indebtedness in the case of the Nesbitt Company and the Etowah Iron Works rather than made money, and perhaps he was thinking that his father had the better business model.

In 1855, Moses Stroup sold the Round Mountain furnace and went to Tannehill in Roupes Valley in central Alabama. Here again, Stroup worked with people he knew, including adding as a partner John Alexander, whom Stroup had known for probably two decades. Alexander got his start in the iron business in South Carolina in 1836, and a John Alexander showed up on the pay records of the Nesbitt Iron Manufacturing Company in 1837 when Moses Stroup was working there. At Tannehill, Stroup built another iron furnace.[45]

While Stroup was still using charcoal for these furnaces, he knew that coal production of iron was coming, and people sought his ideas on the topic. In 1859, for example, the *American Railway Times* quoted "the intelligent iron master" Stroup on the possibilities of coal for iron production in Alabama. After Stroup's experiences in South Carolina and Georgia, he could not have failed to recognize that a modern iron production facility, with coal and iron ore at hand and immediate railroad access, was the direction the industry was headed.[46]

Overall, the lives of Jacob and Moses Stroup illuminate the growing symbiotic interconnections among the gold rush, railroads, the iron industry, and fledgling coal mining. It was not just that Jacob Stroup invested in a gold mine, but that the gold rush provided an unusual and lucrative market for his iron goods. Moses Stroup, after his experience with the Nesbitt Company in remote South Carolina, recognized that railroad transportation in the Etowah Valley provided the missing ingredient that had doomed the Nesbitt Company. The Western & Atlantic Railroad benefited from carrying the iron forged in furnaces and the flour ground in Cooper's mill as area farmers turned increasingly to selling wheat in the market economy. Enslaved workers who mined iron ore and limestone in South Carolina were transported to Allatoona by their owner, Samuel Maxey Earle, where he had them digging for gold before he purchased his brother-in-law John W. Lewis's iron furnace and returned his workforce to their accustomed endeavors. As the iron industry grew along the Etowah River to include a rolling mill, the railroad brought the necessary coal from a distance. It is no wonder that Cooper promoted the agricultural fair at Stone Mountain and saw the economic interdependence and economic diversity as independence, turning a raw-material-producing area into a self-sufficient region.

CHAPTER 4

◦◦

The Education of
Joseph E. Brown

THE BROWN FAMILY FLOATED INTO EXTREME DANGER. THEY must have known the risk they were taking, but they set off in a flatboat in April 1788 and headed down the Tennessee River. James Brown, the father, had fought bravely for the Patriots in North Carolina during the American Revolution. For his service, he was awarded lands in Tennessee on the Cumberland and Duck Rivers near Nashville, and he was taking his family—his wife, four sons, and three daughters—there to settle. The only land route was through Kentucky, a great distance away, so he chose instead to traverse the Tennessee River. His son Joseph Brown recalled, "As one or two boats had been built in East Tennessee in 1786 or 7, and come down the Tennessee and up the Ohio and Cumberland river to Nashville, getting there safely, my father concluded to go the same route." Several other travelers, including slaves belonging to the Browns, rounded out the company.[1]

Their path led them straight into lands controlled by the Cherokees, Chickamaugas, and Creeks. Indians spotted the Browns' flatboat as they "passed the Chickamauga towns, and they sent runners" downstream; soon, four Creek canoes approached the Browns on the river, "meeting us with flags, and had their guns and tomahawks covered with blankets in the bottom of their canoes." The Browns were alarmed, and James Brown shouted that there "was too many of them coming at one time!" One mixed-race man named John Vann reassured Brown in English that "it was a peaceable time between them and us . . . and they only wanted to see where we were going, and to trade with us, if we had any thing to trade on." Thus, Joseph Brown wrote, "they succeeded in getting on board of us." Soon other canoes, which had been hidden in a cane bottom, appeared, and the flatboat landed "at the mouth of the branch" of Nicka-jack Creek "that ran into the river near the middle of the town" by the same name. The whites and the Indians talked for a short time, but when one man grabbed fifteen-year-old Joseph Brown, his father "took hold" of the Indian "and informed him that I was one of his little boys, and he must not touch me." The man let Joseph go, but as soon as James turned his back, the Indian took a sword he carried and "struck" James "with the sword, cutting his head nearly off." Having seen his father slain before his eyes, Joseph was taken prisoner, as were his mother, his three sisters, his youngest brother, and the slaves, while Joseph's two older brothers, five other men, and a woman on the flatboat were in a short time all shot and killed. Joseph "heard the guns firing for the slaughter of my poor broth-ers and the other young men; but I was so foolish, as to suppose that they were only trying the guns they had taken out of the boat."[2]

Joseph's life hung in the balance. Some Indians thought he was too small to kill, while others said he would grow into a man and, having seen what he had, would avenge his family if he lived. In the end, conflict and mistrust among the various captors led to Joseph's survival. He was ad-opted into a family that cut his hair—"shaved the entire sides of my head, leaving only a small scalp-lock on the top of it to tie a bunch of feathers to"—dressed him in about four feet of coarse cloth, and put him to work in the fields, incorporating him into their family and saving his life. Long-term survival was highly uncertain, but Joseph lived and was eventually, along with some other family members, exchanged for Indian prisoners whom whites had taken. He had remained in captivity almost a full year; his younger brother was not released for five years.[3]

Joseph Brown remained in Tennessee and tangled with Indians over the next several years. In 1794 he helped guide six hundred men to sur-prise the Indians at Nickajack town, where his family members had been killed. The main body attacked one end of the town while Brown and about twenty men secreted at the other end surprised fleeing people. They soon found themselves in "a severe fight of it in the cane-brake." About seventy Indians perished. Joseph Brown had realized the fears of some of his captors, that not killing him would eventually lead to destruction for the Indians. Brown spoke with some people he had known while he lived among them as their prisoner and told them in Cherokee they would not be massacred. Brown later fought with Andrew Jackson against the Creeks in the War of 1812, and he even recovered, with Jackson's help, "the negroes and their increase—15 in all," who had been taken from his father. This Joseph Brown was the cousin of another Joseph Brown, who fathered Mackey Brown, the father of Joseph E. Brown, and it seems certain this family story was told often and committed to memory.[4] It was a tale of conflict on the frontier, of white people seeking opportunity despite very high risks and danger.

Mackey Brown, like his father's cousin, also fought with Andrew Jackson in the War of 1812 and was at the Battle of New Orleans. After the war, he married Sally Rice, who gave birth in 1821 to Joseph Emerson Brown, their first child to survive. The family lived in the southern Appalachian Mountains just inside the South Carolina border close to both Georgia and North Carolina, along Long Creek in the Pickens District. As a boy of fifteen or sixteen, in the mid-1830s Joe Brown moved with his parents and younger siblings to the headwaters of the Etowah River in the midst of Georgia's booming gold fields, just four miles from Dahlonega. Thousands of miners hunted for gold, many of them full time, but almost any farmer could search some of the time, panning for placer deposits (reachable on the surface) in creeks. Larger mining corporations, some of them international, cut shafts and tunnels into hillsides, mountains, and almost anywhere they thought they could pull out the value in veins of gold ore. It was often a guessing game of speculation, and land prices rose and collapsed as people bought and sold property, mineral rights, and mining rights, and as they struck it rich or became discouraged. Unsurprisingly, many lawyers were at work handling these transactions. The gold-mining town of Auraria, with one thousand residents in 1833, had a dozen law firms. There, the Brown family farmed, built a gristmill on the headwaters of the Etowah River, and made money off the gold miners. Family friend Ira Foster said, "Joe cultivated a little scrap of hillside land with a pair of bull calves, and every Saturday hauled to town some potatoes, cabbages, lightwood, or other truck, and took back something for the family."[5]

The environmental effects of gold mining were visible everywhere. One writer told his readers that "approaching Dahlonega I noticed that the water-courses had all been mutilated with the spade and pickaxe, and that their waters were of a deep yellow; and having explored the country since then, I find that such is the condition of all streams within a circuit of many miles." Streams and even rivers no longer ran in their old beds and were "thereby deprived of their original beauty. And of all the hills in the vicinity of Dahlonega which I have visited, I have not yet seen one which is not actually riddled with shafts and tunnels." Joe Brown spent his late teens amid this scene, observing as miners endlessly dug mines, stamped ore, swirled slurry in a Georgia pan, and paid for supplies with gold dust. Potential wealth was everywhere. "Several auriferous veins traverse" Dahlonega, the visitor reported, "and it is common after a rain to see the inhabitants busily engaged in *hunting* for gold in the streets."[6]

The nearest mint was in Philadelphia, a long and inconvenient distance, so John C. Calhoun and others lobbied for a mint in northern Georgia that could process mined gold. In 1835 the federal government approved a federal branch mint in Dahlonega and authorized twenty-five tons of machinery. By 1838, the mint was operational; the gold came in, and so did sightseers. Brown almost certainly saw the building going up and then watched the mint stamp out gold coins.[7]

Brown, though, did not see an immediate future in gold mining. The Brown family believed in education, and Joe Brown attended country schools in South Carolina and northern Georgia; one biographer claimed to have met Joe Brown's first teacher, who "informed me that Joe Brown, and Mack[e]y, his father, went to school to him at the same time." Most white boys in that world received at most a few years of education, enough to make them functionally literate, and then they farmed for the rest of their lives. But Joe Brown in 1840, at the age of nineteen, left home and returned to his native state, where he entered the Calhoun Academy in Anderson District. He had no money to pay his tuition and sold "a yoke of steers" to pay for his board; he stayed eight months, returned home, taught school for three months, paid off his tuition debt, and then continued at the school. His teacher Wesley Leverett and Brown were quite attached to each other, and when Leverett changed schools Brown followed him. Over time, Brown acquired a meaningful education that would serve him well.[8]

Brown then moved to Canton, Georgia. A Georgian who knew the Brown family, Ira Foster, said that he found Joe Brown walking to Canton "to get something to do." At that time, about 1839, Brown was just a humble country boy from an "exceedingly poor" family, to hear Foster tell it: "I was riding to Canton in a buggy, and I overtook a young man walking in a very muddy lane. He had a striped bag hung over his shoulder and looked very tired. I asked him if he would not take a seat, and he looked down at himself and said he was too muddy, and that he would dirty up the buggy. I insisted and he broke off a splinter from a rail and scraped his shoes and got in." Years later he arrived looking far less bedraggled. In 1843, twenty-two-year-old Joe Brown moved to Canton with a recommendation from Leverett attesting to his fitness as a teacher. "I have supervised the Education of Joseph Brown," wrote Leverett, "and I take great pleasure in giving him the sanction of my name, as a gentleman of great moral worth and reputable attainments, of much energy and decision of character, all combining to constitute him a judicious and efficient Instructor of youth." In January 1844, Brown began teaching at the Etowah Academy, the school William Grisham helped found. Brown was an immediate success; his students blossomed from six to sixty. He also immersed himself in the Baptist community by joining the church as soon as he arrived. Mackey Brown and Joseph Grisham were friends, so it seems probable that Joe Brown was already acquainted with or known to William Grisham, who perhaps recruited Brown to teach at the school. The other relationship Brown soon made was with his pastor, John W. Lewis.[9]

Lewis, born in Spartanburg in 1801, became one of the most important figures in Brown's life. The wealthy South Carolinian trained primarily as a doctor, but was also a minister, politician, businessman, land speculator, and developer. In letters Joseph Grisham sent to his brother William in the late 1830s Joseph mentioned Lewis constantly, and it was clear that Lewis was thinking about moving to Georgia. Lewis preached in Canton at the Baptist church in August 1837 and kept making visits there. Joseph Grisham especially appreciated Lewis as an ally in the fight against alcohol. Joseph called "whisky . . . a curse on our Land!—I am more & more determined to have nothing to do with spirits—I do not believe a Baptist ought to be alowed to make or sell spirits." Lewis had another connection to the Etowah Valley: John S. Rowland had married Lewis's sister Frances. After Cherokee Removal, Lewis relocated to Cherokee County and built a house just east of Canton; in 1840, he became the minister at the Baptist church in Canton founded by William and Susan Grisham, and Lewis also embarked on a host of other enterprises. As Joseph E. Brown said of Lewis decades later, he "was one of the wealthiest men of his day in upper Georgia. He was distinguished for his high order of talent, large grasp of mind in business matters and unfailing energy which generally gave him success in everything he undertook." When Lewis met Brown, he took him under his wing.[10]

John W. Lewis saw great promise in Brown. Late in 1844, Brown left his teaching position at the Etowah Academy, boarded with the Lewis family, and tutored Lewis's children to pay for his keep. Brown read law in the evenings. After a year, Lewis loaned Brown money to obtain some legal education at Yale College. Brown had in August 1845 been admitted to the bar by the Cherokee County Superior Court to act as an "attor-

John W. Lewis, shown here late in life,
pastored and mentored Joseph E. Brown.
Courtesy of Trey and Jeannine Rollins.

ney, solicitor and counsellor," yet he traveled to Connecticut in September
or October and stayed until March. Evincing a keen intellectual curiosity,
Brown went beyond his legal education and heard lectures from, among
others, Benjamin Silliman on chemistry and geology, Nathaniel William
Taylor on mental philosophy, and Jonathan Knight on anatomy. During
the Christmas holiday, Brown spent time in Washington, D.C., where he
met with Senator John C. Calhoun. How Brown arranged the meeting is
unknown, but his family was from the same upcountry area as Calhoun,
Calhoun's gold mines were not far from where the Brown family lived in
Union County, and John W. Lewis had served in the South Carolina state
legislature, so Brown might have been introduced. At their meeting, Calhoun told Brown to settle in Atlanta. Calhoun "pointed out to him the
different railroads since built and with a crook in his first finger (a ges-
ture of his) and looking him in the eye said, 'I tell you, Mr. Brown, Atla-
nata is the gateway or will be the great inland city of Ga. if not of the whole
South.'" Brown would wind up in Atlanta, but first he finished at Yale and

returned to Canton, where he threw himself into a budding legal practice; he earned $1,200 in the first year and continued to increase his income thereafter.[11]

Meanwhile, William Grisham lost his bid for reelection as clerk of the Superior Court. His brother Joseph expressed his condolences and wrote that he was even "more sorry" because Joseph had learned that a possible business venture between William and John W. Lewis was on hold. "But you need not fear," consoled Joseph, "you can make a living any way." William Grisham was farming; by 1840 he had a tanyard, he may have been connected to some mills, and he still had some extra income from his work as postmaster, but he was seeking additional revenue. William intended to open up another store, presumably similar to the one he had run in Decatur. Joseph replied to William's "intention to commence merchandizing" and said, "It will afford me pleasure to aid you in any way in my power." The store never materialized, but in 1844 William landed an appointment as a clerk at the mint in Dahlonega.[12] Dahlonega was less than fifty miles from Canton, so though Grisham lived apart from his family, they were able to get together at times, and they exchanged many letters.

Also in 1844, perhaps not coincidentally, the eldest Grisham daughter, Melinda, just fifteen years old, wed twenty-seven-year-old Joel L. Galt, and Galt immediately began overseeing Grisham's farms, finances, and other interests in Cherokee County. Joel Galt's father, Jabez, was in business with John W. Lewis, a nephew of Jabez's wife. Joel's middle name was Lewis. So Joel was an insider, and he frequently wrote letters to his new father-in-law about what he was doing and what was happening. Overall, they describe the locale that Joseph E. Brown was becoming accustomed to, where gold was still basic to the economy. Many times, Joel Galt and other people Grisham knew forwarded mined gold to Grisham, who had it turned into coins, which Grisham then safely returned to the owners.[13]

Joseph Brown, though, rather than being preoccupied by precious metals, had a more immediate concern. In 1847 he married Elizabeth Grisham, a daughter of Joseph and Mary Steele Grisham and a niece of William Grisham. Elizabeth was born in the Pickens District of South Carolina in 1826. Her parents believed in a sound education for both boys and girls, and she and her younger brother went to a boarding school in Greenville when she was fourteen years old. A few days before Christmas 1846, she was at home when Brown stopped and asked to stay the night as he and a friend passed through on the way to visit relatives. Brown acted as though his stop was random, but it was surely not. Brown, a young

Joseph E. Brown, shown here at age
twenty-nine, incorporated the lessons
of the Etowah Valley into his plans
for the future.
Avery, *History of the State of Georgia*.

Elizabeth Grisham and Joseph
E. Brown's 1847 marriage linked
their two families. She is shown
here several years later.
Courtesy of the Hargrett Rare Book and
Manuscript Library, University of Georgia.

and promising lawyer in Canton, needed a good helpmate. With John W. Lewis as the most influential person in Brown's life at the time, and with William Grisham in the church, it was only natural that someone would have mentioned the wealthy Joseph Grisham's daughter to Brown.[14]

Elizabeth Grisham claimed later in life that a cousin had asked her in 1846 for her description of the man she hoped to marry. She told him the man "must be saving, not stingy, industrious, a member of a temperance society, not given to dissipations of any description; must not chew tobacco (will allow him to smoke a cigar occasionally, though very seldom), religiously inclined, would prefer his being a member of the Baptist church, intelligent, sociable, benevolent, must pay the preacher and take a newspaper." Elizabeth did not stint on her descriptions of his ideal physical figure and his clothing, summer and winter, and she concluded that he ought to be "about twenty-three years of age; worth from four to ten thousand dollars, though if he had all those good qualities, I should rate him at half a million. Must be a merchant, farmer or lawyer." When Joe Brown appeared, Elizabeth Grisham did not hesitate. She told her friend Matilda right then, "Yes, he is the one I have been looking for, that is the one I am going to marry." Elizabeth then welcomed Brown to their home.[15]

Joseph Grisham came to the door and heard, "How are you, Col. Grisham, my name is Brown." Joseph replied, "Are you the son of my old friend, Mackey Brown, why I have seen you at your father's when he lived on Long Creek." Brown sat and talked that evening with Joseph Grisham, telling Grisham about the telegraph Brown had seen in Washington, D.C., and how it worked. Brown departed the next day, but returned the same way, making sure to stop at the Grishams' once again. The next month he began to write to Elizabeth, and after he visited her for a week in both April and June, they married in July 1847. After the wedding, the Browns made their way over a few days the 130 miles to Canton, where they would live in the home of William and Susan Grisham until their own home down the street was ready to occupy. Elizabeth brought with her three cakes that had not been eaten at her wedding reception, and as she wrote later, "I gave one to Mrs. John W. Lewis and one to Aunt Susan Grisham." Those were nice gestures from the new resident, though Canton was probably not a strange or new place for Elizabeth. Years earlier her father had written to William about plans for Elizabeth to visit Canton. So the newly married Browns were ensconced among prosperous Baptists in a community that offered friendship, support, and opportunity.[16]

The temperance commitments of these people mattered. Elizabeth preferred her eventual husband to be Baptist, but she required him to be a temperance man. Joseph Grisham, her father, was becoming a well-known temperance advocate who strongly approved of John W. Lewis. As historian W. J. Rorabaugh has argued, the antebellum temperance movement was "forward-looking, progressive, and modern." The Sons of Temperance, the leading organization, "appealed to the most powerful and influential men in the community." As opposed to taverns, where one would interact with dissipated men going nowhere in life, temperance organizations provided a network that could "facilitate interaction among bright young men looking for entrepreneurial and professional opportunities." Membership indicated that a person was ambitious and serious about the future. Joe Brown joined the Sons of Temperance in the 1840s, and his mentoring by Lewis and his acceptance as the son-in-law of Joseph Grisham show he was clearly cut from the kind of cloth they approved of.[17]

In the 1840s, when Joe Brown was working closely with John W. Lewis, Lewis was pursuing opportunities in the iron industry. He had married Maria Earle, who came from an iron-making family. Elias Earle had moved to South Carolina from Virginia in 1787 and invested heavily in land in the Pendleton District. After 1811 he built an ironworks that produced guns for the federal government. The Earle family remained involved with iron, and two Earles, including Maria's brother, were heavily invested as stockholders in the Nesbitt Iron Company.[18]

It appears that Lewis talked with William Grisham about getting into the fledgling iron industry being built by Jacob Stroup on Stamp Creek and the Etowah River. William, as usual, wrote to his older brother Joseph for advice, and Joseph replied, "My dear brother I know but little of Iron works but think I know enough to keep clear of it now in this country." It was expensive, required numerous employees, and demanded neverending attention, he argued. William stayed out of the iron industry, but Lewis jumped in. After John, Maria, and their children moved to Canton, Lewis purchased a large amount of land along the Etowah downstream from Canton in Cass County. Soon Lewis sold land to other iron makers and began building an iron furnace. In 1847 Lewis's furnace was complete; the next year Lewis sold the furnace to his wife's brother, Samuel Maxey Earle. The attorney on the deal was Joe Brown. The same day, Lewis gave Brown a lot in Canton, evidently payment for Brown's work, though the legal papers said Lewis was giving Brown the lot "in consideration of the friendship good will and esteem which he has and bears for the said Brown."[19]

After the sale of the furnace to his brother-in-law, Lewis kept his hand in the iron business. On Stamp Creek, just five hundred yards downstream from a mill or factory site Lewis had built in 1845, Lewis joined with B. G. Poole to build an iron forge in 1849. In time they replaced the forge with an iron furnace. Lewis was becoming a major figure in the growth of an iron-making area in antebellum Georgia. Lewis also became a founding member of the Southern Central Agricultural Society, indicating his ties not only to other Etowah iron makers, but also to their economic vision. Joe Brown undoubtedly was well acquainted with these ventures, being so closely tied to Lewis. In addition, Brown did legal work in both Cass and Cherokee Counties, so he often traveled from one to the other, crossing the path of the Western & Atlantic. Beginning in 1851, Brown also collected money owed to the iron business run by Mark A. Cooper and Leroy M. Wiley, which he delivered to them as he passed by their ironworks.[20]

Iron is heavy, of course, and though it was only miles from the furnaces to the Western & Atlantic Railroad, the iron makers logically thought about how to ease their transportation burden. In 1847, a group of men known for their connections to the iron industry obtained a charter from the state legislature to incorporate the Etowah Railroad Company. The incorporators, who included Mark Anthony Cooper, Moses Stroup, Leroy M. Wiley, John W. Lewis, and Jabez Galt, were authorized to build a railroad "from the State Road, thence up the bank or along the valley of said river, by the Etowah River opposite Canton, thence up and along said river to or near Dahlonega." The group of incorporators shows that Cooper, Stroup, and Wiley were working in concert with Lewis and Galt, Lewis's relation. The immediate goal was a railroad spur that would facilitate getting their iron product easily onto the trunk line, but they also envisioned a lengthier railroad that would follow the Etowah River through the gold fields all the way to Dahlonega.[21]

Meanwhile, the builders of the Western & Atlantic Railroad were quite close to the completion of their project. At the end of October 1849, workers finished tunneling through a hill in northern Georgia that would finally make the Western & Atlantic complete from Atlanta to Chattanooga. They held a celebration and, among the toasts and other festivities, listened to a speech from Mark Anthony Cooper, who had brought a cannon "sent up from the Iron Works in Cass County," which fired "seven salutes." In his speech, Cooper praised this "first connection of the Atlantic and the Mississippi," and said, "this quiet opening of its grand tunnel is emblematic of its peaceful end." But then Cooper said something strange: "The roar of Georgia's native cannon over our mountain top indicates that in time of peace we are prepared for war." War with whom? one might ask. Cooper was announcing the same anxieties and ambivalence about connection with the rest of the country that others before him had professed. He wanted the railroad, he wanted to have access to what the railroad could bring, and he wanted to sell his products in faraway markets. Yet he came to a celebration of those connections to other places and fired a warning shot.[22]

Also late in 1849, another chapter in the education of Joseph E. Brown began when Brown won election as a state senator representing both Cobb and Cherokee Counties and immediately took a leading role in the legislative session from November 1849 through February 1850. During the legislative session, Brown was immersed in the issues of the day. Slavery—and the question of its extension into the territories of the United States—was the key national issue under discussion. The end of the war with Mexico in 1848 had brought with it much of northern Mexico, and the discovery of gold at Sutter's mill that same year had led to an exodus of people, some of whom undoubtedly Brown knew, for the gold fields of California. California's application for admission into the Union as a free state worried many white Georgians, who were concerned that the political balance between free states and slave states in the U.S. Senate would be lost, making slaveholding states vulnerable to attacks on the institution of slavery. Georgia's state legislators expressed discontent with the Wilmot Proviso (1846), a failed federal effort to prevent the extension of slavery into any territory acquired from Mexico; complained about the three-fifths compromise in the Constitution, which they felt unjustly hampered southern congressional representation by counting the enslaved population at only 60 percent of their actual numbers; and were angered by efforts to outlaw slavery in the District of Columbia and by a lack of enforcement of the fugitive slave clause in the Constitution.[23]

Issues that would preoccupy Brown for several years were part of this legislative session. Governor George W. Towns in a message to the legislature mentioned that the state had been using convicts as laborers inside the penitentiary for the previous two years. This was especially relevant to Brown, who was appointed to the Joint Standing Committee on Penitentiaries, of which he became chair. His committee reported that convict labor had proved quite financially beneficial, so much so that the penitentiary was not requesting any funds for operation from the state and had actually retired thousands of dollars of debt. Brown's committee proposed to move some convicts "to Atlanta or some point on the Western and Atlantic Rail Road" to perform work on the railroad, and Brown introduced a bill "for the removal of a portion of the convicts in the Penitentiary to Atlanta."[24] Significantly, in his first experience with elective office, Brown immediately dealt with the issue of convict labor and proved himself a proponent of using convicts outside the penitentiary to work on the state's railroad.

Brown clearly cared about railroads, especially the Western & Atlantic. As the track was being completed, people saw it as a valuable asset. The legislature repealed a law authorizing the governor to sell the Western & Atlantic if anyone would offer $1 million. Joe Brown's leadership came in a dispute over the train schedule of the Western & Atlantic. Until 1849, the Western & Atlantic had a daytime schedule of departures and arrivals. But this placed a burden on connecting roads, which had to operate at night to reduce layover times and run the entire railroad system efficiently. Backers of the Macon and Western Railroad, which linked to the Western & Atlantic, wanted changes that would not oblige the Macon and Western to have night runs in order to coordinate with the Western & Atlantic. Brown would have none of it. He proposed legislation that would guarantee day-time runs for the Western & Atlantic, arguing that the hilly northern Georgia countryside necessitated, for safety's sake, a daytime schedule. Brown wanted to "insist" on a day schedule "in all their future contracts with the Post Office Department." The Senate passed Brown's bill.[25]

One other thing Governor Towns said in his message to the legislature at the beginning of its session was that the revenue he expected from the Western & Atlantic Railroad "will furnish a fund by which a system of common schools can be extended throughout the State." Brown, who had worked so hard for the education he obtained, proposed a committee to look into the state of education in Georgia, and the Senate passed "a bill to incorporate the Southern Education Society."[26]

Brown showed that he understood diplomacy when the Georgia branch of the Sons of Temperance requested incorporation by the state. It was a political hot potato because temperance was controversial in Georgia. Opponents worried that the Sons of Temperance, if they could not sway enough people to join their cause voluntarily, would seek legislative action to enforce their will. Brown got the bill sent to a select committee on which he served, and when the committee reported, Brown, on behalf of the committee, argued that the Sons of Temperance should not be incorporated by the state. He said the committee believed that the Sons of Temperance were doing good work, but the committee, most of whom were members of the temperance group, did not wish "to inflame the public mind," and since the Sons of Temperance had said they wished for no legislation on temperance, the committee opposed the incorporation. No doubt feeling relieved, all thirty-two members of the legislature who were present voted unanimously to uphold the recommendation.[27]

One other legislative topic was a proposed Georgia convention to respond to everything relating to slavery and the territories. In the end, the state called a convention. In Cherokee County, John W. Lewis, Eli McConnell, Samuel Tate, and John P. Brooke published an open letter to the people of the county asking for election to the convention to respond to the crisis over slavery. They evidently anticipated concerns that the convention would advocate secession and said their primary objective would be to promote "our own prosperity and security, by erecting" cotton mills, "by making Iron and things made of Iron," and by setting up woolen mills and leather tanning and manufacture—"in a word, by making *at home*, as near as we can, what we need." They wanted self-sufficiency, not immediate secession.[28]

After his stint in the legislature, Brown returned to Canton, practiced law, and stayed active in the Canton Baptist church. John W. Lewis gave up his preaching there at the end of 1850, but William Grisham had returned from Dahlonega, and soon the congregation was augmented by Joseph and Mary Grisham, who in 1849 decided to sell their property in South Carolina and move closer to their daughter Elizabeth Brown's family in Cherokee County. Joseph Grisham placed for sale "20,000 acres" of land, along with "Good Flour, Corn, Rice, and Saw Mills" and "Cotton and Threshing Machines." Though he wished to sell these properties, he was amenable to a leasing arrangement "to honest, industrious, temperance men, (none others need apply) and Baptists of the right sort will be preferred." Grisham was particular about the character of people he did business with, and he saw temperance dedication and Baptist church membership as markers of respectability and trustworthiness. Having moved to Cherokee County in 1851 Grisham conducted business with his son-in-law. Brown set up special pages in his account book that show he borrowed thousands of dollars from Grisham, especially in 1852 and 1853, usually at 10 percent interest. Grisham trusted Brown, who was a "Baptist of the right sort." In the church, Brown was an active member and a leading contributor to a fund to buy books for a church library. In fact, the only other congregants to match Brown's five dollar pledge were William and Joseph Grisham. Nobody else pledged more than two dollars. The amounts not only indicate Brown's continuing interest in education, but also reflect his (and the Grishams') prominence in the church. Brown was on the committee to obtain the books, and soon they had a library of more than fifty volumes of varied Christian literature, including a concordance and numerous volumes of theology, and they also purchased three volumes of George Bancroft's *History of the United States*. Soon, the church put Brown, William Grisham, and Reuben F. Daniel in charge of having a bookcase constructed and installed, and they set up the borrowing rules.[29]

Brown believed in education; sometimes he imparted lessons. In 1856 Elizabeth Brown wrote in her diary, "Mr. Brown whipped Emma for nothing to show me he was master."[30] Brown had not been reared in a slaveholding family, but his stern and sometimes imperious character adapted to the violence inherent in the institution of slavery, in this instance as a means of demonstrating to his wife who was in charge.

Brown's interest in education was shared by many of the significant people in his life. The best evidence of this is the creation in Cassville of two schools: Cassville Female College, which originated in 1853 under

Methodist auspices, and Cherokee Baptist College, a school for boys, begun the next year. The trustees of the Cherokee Baptist College included
Farish Carter, Mark Anthony Cooper, John W. Lewis, Ira R. Foster, and by
1858 John S. Rowland. Foster was in charge of donations from Cherokee
County supporters, including William Grisham. The youngest daughter
of William and Susan Grisham, Elizabeth, attended the Cassville Female
College. The people of Cassville, having been bypassed by the Western &
Atlantic Railroad, were building up their town as a premier educational
center in northwestern Georgia.[31]

Even though the western gold rush had siphoned off many gold diggers, various mines continued in operation throughout the Etowah Valley;
the most prominent was the Franklin mine. Mary Franklin was in charge
of scores of enslaved laborers, who operated a complex plantation operation. Franklin's daily diary for 1853, her "journal of time and how em-
ployd," gives an indication of the work that went on, including "Repairing
Negro Houses," "Tunnel repairing," and "working at the Mill Race," while
"women in the Hous" was a frequent entry. Men killed hogs, and women
"attend[ed] to Lard." Many days, Franklin noted "miners at their work."
There was plowing, "haling wood," and cutting "coal wood," which was to
be turned into charcoal. Men worked in the "Shop and Saw Mill," while
"Women [were] Plowing." Some of Franklin's adult sons helped, but Mary
Franklin was closely involved with the daily work.[32]

In the 1850s, a new mining possibility excited people. To the north, in
the far southeastern corner of Tennessee, copper had been discovered at a
place called Ducktown, leading to the development of numerous copper
mines both there and in nearby Fannin County, Georgia. Farther south, in
Cherokee County, Joseph E. Brown purchased an inexpensive land lot in
1854 with a good stand of timber on it, and he then sold twenty-five acres
of it, along with one-fourth interest in any minerals in those twenty-five
acres, to William Grisham. Two months later, in October, Brown granted
permission for W. F. and Skidmore Harris to investigate the property on a
"mining interest lease." The Harris brothers thought there might be copper
deposits on the property. In a sign that people were getting excited about
the mining possibilities in the area, in late October Grisham's son-in-law
Joel Galt wrote to Grisham in a letter marked *Confidentially* at the top, "I
want you if you can to get a leas on Mrs. Watsons lot, for if Brown & Harris
strikes coper the streak must run across the corner of her lot." In December,
Brown gave the Harris brothers the option of purchasing one-eighth of the
mineral rights for $2,000. The Harris brothers began digging.[33]

Enslaved black workers regularly
performed mining duties.
Harper's, August 1857.

Attention to the Canton copper mine grew with the publication in the November 1855 issue of *Mining Magazine* of Julien Marc Deby's assessment of its prospects. Deby was a twenty-year-old Belgian mining engineer who had inspected the Canton mine. How Deby came to be hired to examine the mine is unknown, but it appears that Joe Brown was thinking about drawing investors nationally. In a brief report, Deby explained what shafts and tunnels had already been dug and assessed that the "ores extracted from the Canton mine, very poor at the onset, have gradually increased in value as the vein was worked deeper." Mostly the ore was copper pyrites, but it included some lead and various other minerals. "I believe," Deby concluded, "this mine will prove to be among the most valuable in Georgia," and he speculated that as the mine went deeper "the ore extracted will pay well for shipment, and compare well with the best product of the Ducktown mines." In fact, claimed Deby, "the ore, even now, at Canton is as rich in per centage of copper as that from Ducktown, and is more compact and portable," and the "proportion of silver in the Canton ores is considerable."

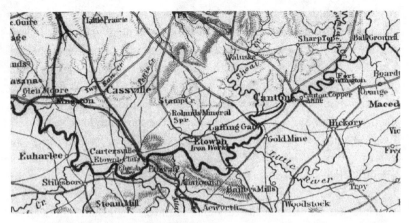

The antebellum Etowah Valley. *Right to left*, the Etowah River, including
Fort Buffington, where the Cherokees were collected before relocation; Joe
Brown's copper mine; Canton; a gold mine; the Etowah ironworks; Rowland
Springs; the route of the Western & Atlantic; Cartersville; and Cassville.
Courtesy of the Library of Congress.

Since there were other salutary conditions, including the proximity to the
Western & Atlantic Railroad, Deby predicted "a prosperous future and a
rich harvest for its owners." At a time before the professionalization of science, people like Deby functioned partially as scientists and partially as
boosters and enthusiasts drumming up investors' interest.[34]

The following year, an even more extensive investigation was published
by Charles Upham Shepard, an established mineralogist who had taught
at both Yale and the Medical College of Charleston in South Carolina. It is
unknown how Shepard came to inspect the Canton copper mine, but it is
likely that Joseph E. Brown and Shepard were acquaintances, or that they
were connected through Professor Benjamin Silliman, whose lectures
Brown had attended at Yale. Shepard, born in New England, had worked
as an assistant to Silliman and even married an adopted daughter of Silliman. Shepard kept a home in New Haven and lectured on natural history
at Yale for years, including the time Brown was there. Shepard also taught
in Charleston each winter and was well known in the South.[35]

Shepard's published *Report on the Copper and Silver-Lead Mine at
Canton, Cherokee County, Georgia* buttressed Deby's enthusiasm about
the mine's potential. Shepard said interest in the mine first had developed
a year and a half prior when a local man, Skidmore Harris, noticed that
rocks at the surface resembled those at the Ducktown mines. Harris and

his brother sank a shaft down 96 feet, where "they struck the stratum of mica-slate." From there, they went east and west, digging tunnels, following the vein, and they created another set of tunnels at 116 feet. Shepard also discovered a tiny cross-vein that had been ignored, but that "contains an ore of copper exceedingly rich and valuable. . . . In fine, it is precisely the same compound as that which is formed by the Chemist, by melting copper and Sulphur together." Shepard said the compound had never been found in a natural state, and he named the new mineral harrisite after "the enterprising discoverers of the Canton mine." He thought the mine also might contain manganese; there were only a few such mines in the entire United States. At 145 feet deep, Shepard discovered another new mineral, which he named hitchcockite "in honor of the distinguished American geologist, Dr. [Edward] Hitchcock." Shepard named a third mineral he discovered cherokine "after the Indian tribe who lately occupied this region." Overall, Shepard said, the mine's ores were comparable to the best copper mine in the nation. In a note, Shepard added, "This mine has within a few years yielded nearly $250,000 of copper, and now has half a million dollars worth of ore in full view." In addition, the Canton mine had galena, a valuable lead ore made more desirable because of its silver content. Many other minerals and ores were also present in various amounts, and when Shepard considered the mine as a whole, he concluded it would defy "all previous experience in respect to Mines, if so many valuable ores should co-exist within so circumscribed a locality, and not be in connection with a profitable Mine." Like Deby, Shepard thought that the deeper the mine went, the more likely it was to pay off. Shepard wrote that $18,000 had already been invested, and the mine seemed on the verge of producing great profits.[36]

This report, issued at the end of March 1856, was a glowing recommendation for the mine, and a second edition in mid-June contained excerpts from letters Shepard had received from the Harrises, which confirmed everything Shepard had predicted. The Harrises sent along specimens of their ore, and Shepard reiterated that "no mine-viewer can look upon these productions of the Canton mine, without being impressed with the idea, that the depository from which they come, is destined to yield a still richer supply." This was enough for the Canton Mining Company, chartered in December 1855—which had been doing the work to that point while only leasing the land—to outright purchase the land from Brown and Grisham. Brown walked away on July 10, 1856, with $20,000, and William Grisham with $7,000. Brown had turned an ordinary piece of land into great wealth, and his fellow churchman, his wife's uncle, also benefited greatly. Brown's time at Yale had provided far more than legal knowledge; it probably introduced him to Shepard or Silliman. That connection almost certainly led to the report that spoke so certainly of the profit potential of Brown's land and earned Brown far more than even a well-paid attorney could have made in years.[37]

By then, Brown had reentered public employment. In 1855 he expanded his political reach when he ran successfully for circuit judge of eleven northwestern Georgia counties. Riding the circuit, usually twice each year, was an excellent way to get to know many people, and Brown, both ambitious and competent, probably attracted positive notice in many places. Nobody, however, could have anticipated what happened next. In 1857, the Democrats nominated Brown as their candidate for governor. Lewis, who had relocated to Cass County, was a delegate to the Democratic convention and supported his friend and mentee. Brown, though, was not even at the convention and learned of his nomination at home from his friend Samuel Weil. A political myth would emerge that Brown was in his field gathering wheat when he was told. The truth was only slightly different. Years later, Brown pointed out the field to companions and told how one afternoon he checked to see how the work was coming along. "I had four men cutting wheat with common cradles, and the binders were very much behind, and I pulled off my coat and pitched in about half after two o'clock, p.m., on the 15th of June, 1857. The weather was very warm, but I ordered my binders to keep up with me, and I tell you it made me sweat, but I pushed my binders all the evening." With the daylight fading, Brown "went home, and was shaving myself and preparing to wash myself for supper" when up rode Weil, who asked Brown to guess who was the nominee for governor. Brown guessed wrong. "'No,' said Colonel Weil, 'it is Joseph E. Brown, of Cherokee.'" Weil had been in Marietta when a telegram arrived announcing the nomination, and he had hurried to tell Brown. "I subsequently ascertained that the nomination had been made about three o'clock that day," said Brown, "and at the very time I was tying wheat in this field." The image of farmer Brown working in his wheat field was a convenient one, presenting him as an industrious, self-made, common man. The workers Brown was driving, though, were presumably enslaved men he owned. The account never says so directly, but Brown had been acquiring slaves, and he says he "ordered" the field hands to keep up with him. At the same time, Brown exemplified the diversified economy he supported, working in a field not of cotton, but of wheat, which he sent to be ground at one of the gristmills that dotted the Etowah River.[38]

Understandably, the thirty-six-year-old Brown was a little uncertain of how to respond to his unexpected political good fortune, so he went to the house of a friend, former governor Charles J. McDonald. McDonald, following his two terms as governor, had settled in Marietta. He retained his Cherokee County gold mine investments, including the mine on a lot adjoining Mary Franklin's gold mine. McDonald also invested in a textile mill along Sweetwater Creek, southwest of Marietta. He became a founding member of the Southern Central Agricultural Society. When Brown began to forge a close friendship with McDonald is unclear, though the Browns had him for meals at least five times in 1854 and 1855, and the Browns visited the McDonalds in Marietta and spent the night there. At the McDonalds' home, after the two men discussed an appropriate response, Brown composed his letter of reply to the convention that had nominated him. Two years later, the Browns named their new son Charles McDonald Brown, a sign of the importance of their relationship.[39]

From the time Joe Brown moved to Canton to teach school in 1844 until his nomination in 1857, much had happened. Brown understood gold mining, and in Canton he became, in part through marriage, closely tied to wealthy, influential temperance Baptists who further acquainted him with iron manufacture. He saw firsthand the operation of the Western & Atlantic, advocated for education and railroads as a state legislator, and seized an opportunity when people became interested in the possibility of copper mining on his land. He purchased slaves and also considered how to utilize convict labor to achieve his goals. Many people he knew were involved in aspects of the swift alterations taking place in northern Georgia, but Joseph E. Brown was exposed to and positioned to take advantage of the full array, from mining and manufacture, to education, to railroading, to convict labor in a search for power and influence in a multifaceted economy. To voters, though, Brown was the up-from-humble-origins wheat binder from the northern Georgia mountains, a pious, temperance-minded Baptist ready to apply his hard-earned education and insights in the service of the state. Perhaps there were risks ahead, as there had been for his relatives on the Tennessee, even deadly ones that could not be entirely foreseen or prevented, but the voters of Georgia believed that Brown was the right person to lead them into that unknown future.

CHAPTER 5

The Republic of Georgia

OSEPH E. BROWN'S ACCESSION TO THE GOVERNORSHIP REPRE-
sented a marked political change in Georgia. Brown's background
as an upcountry temperance Baptist departed from the Georgia norm of
electing upper-crust politicians—who were often planters but never Baptists from mountainous northern Georgia.[1] People recognized that change
but may have missed another element: Brown's mining involvement and
his close ties to other miners, millers, iron manufacturers, and railroad
builders whom he installed in key positions in state government. As governor, Brown performed public service in keeping with his implicit ide-
ology of industrialization, which meant a special regard for his own interests and those of his friends. Crucially, Brown's first years as governor
intersected with the key years of sectional tension that led to the outbreak
of the U.S. Civil War. In the crisis Brown became a secessionist, perhaps
the pivotal figure in Georgia's break from the United States, which offered
enormous possibilities and perils for everyone in Brown's network and, of
course, far beyond.

One of Brown's first decisions was to install John W. Lewis, his men-
tor and former pastor, the man who had lent Brown the money to enroll at
Yale, as superintendent of the Western & Atlantic Railroad. The decision
was both personal and politically shrewd. Brown trusted Lewis, a man of
considerable talents who immediately improved the railroad while cutting expenses simultaneously, generating revenue for the state. Brown and
Lewis fired numerous employees who had obtained their jobs through patronage, and they replaced them with their own choices. The *Cassville
Standard* complained that Brown and Lewis had transformed this public utility into the "Cherokee Baptist Railroad." Frank Brown, one of the

governor's sons, pasted into his scrapbook a humorous anecdote from the *Augusta Dispatch* that told the apocryphal story of Brown and Lewis proceeding "up the line of the road to deliver the 'walking papers'" to those being dismissed. At one depot, though, they encountered a wily station agent. When they arrived, an underling said the agent would return momentarily. "In a few minutes he came up the steps singing with the most approved nasal intonation: 'I'll take my cross and follow thee.'" Having sung the "right tune just in time," as the headline declared, Brown and Lewis allegedly changed their minds about dismissing him, "renewed his commission and went on their way."[2] Clearly the Baptist commitments in the state's highest offices registered with Georgians. Whatever the truth of the contention that Brown and Lewis especially handed out patronage to Baptists, this altered power structure in Georgia would have lasting effects.

Like Lewis, Ira Foster was another Cherokee Baptist favored by Brown. Born in 1811 in the Spartanburg District of South Carolina, Foster taught school, studied medicine and law, and in the 1830s moved to Dahlonega, where the people elected him county coroner. He served as an Inferior Court justice and Georgia state senator, fought the Seminoles in Florida, and became a brigadier general in the state militia. Foster worked as an attorney and lived in Cumming, the seat of Forsyth County, where he advocated temperance. In 1843, Foster leased a gold lot and by the end of the 1840s bought a mill site on the Etowah River in southwestern Cherokee County. Foster intended to sell his property in Forsyth County and move to Cherokee County, where he figured he could triple his income. By 1851, Foster had executed his plan; his business sent sacks of flour at least as far as Charleston, South Carolina.[3]

In 1854 Foster became a trustee of the Cherokee Baptist College. The next year he acted as treasurer for the Middle Cherokee Baptist Association. Foster was ensconced in Brown's cohort, a temperance Baptist running a gristmill and not neglecting gold mining. His property abutted Mark Cooper's land, and Foster provided John W. Lewis and B. G. Poole with wheat bran and flour, which they needed to feed their employees.[4]

Following Brown's nomination for governor in 1857, Foster asked Brown for an appointment and soon thereafter delivered a speech extolling Brown at the ratification meeting in Cherokee County. Upon Brown's election, the new governor appointed Foster as a route agent on the Western & Atlantic. Their relationship deepened as Foster sent Brown political gossip. Brown thanked Foster for keeping him "posted at all times in the movements of my enemies," and the following year he worked to gain Foster a federal appointment working with the mail, describing Foster as "a man of untiring energy uprightness and integrity, a very shrewed man."[5]

Brown also brought into state government Henry Hawley Waters, yet another temperance advocate, lawyer, and gold seeker who also ran both a sawmill and a gristmill six miles downriver from Canton. In 1858 Governor Brown made him his executive secretary and a colonel. From then until 1865, letter after letter that issued from the governor's office in Milledgeville had Colonel H. H. Waters's name on it. Waters's youngest son, Byron, later described a symbol of the abilities and emphases of the new administration. The Waters family lived about a mile south of the capitol building; during their first winter the Oconee River flooded and backed up a creek that passed between the Waters home and the town, causing the family to travel far out of their way to get to work and school. After the flooding subsided, Henry Waters constructed a suspension foot bridge higher than the floodwaters had reached, which locals "considered a unique attraction, as it was the only example of such construction in that section of the country."[6]

Eli McConnell, another miller and gold miner Brown brought to Milledgeville, built the first merchant flouring mill in Cherokee County and in 1849 purchased another mill, later known as Cherokee Mills, near the Brown farm. McConnell was a frequent dinner guest of the Browns in the mid-1850s. Brown made McConnell the "principal keeper" of the state penitentiary. McConnell immediately echoed Brown's earlier thoughts as a state legislator about how the convicts in his care could be used away from the penitentiary. In McConnell's first report to Governor Brown in October 1858, McConnell pointed out the "dilapidated" penitentiary buildings and the inadequacy of the facilities, including workshops, the hospital, cells, and the outer wall. Only "the vigilance of the Guard" had kept any convicts from escaping during McConnell's tenure. In the workshops, the prisoners made cars for the Western & Atlantic Railroad, but McConnell thought that those incarcerated had mostly been "gathered up from the haunts of dissipation, being loafers and vagabonds who have never been accustomed to labor, and consequently are not mechanics or tradesmen of any kind." McConnell mentioned that "the subject of removal of the Penitentiary has frequently been brought to the notice of the Legislature," and he wondered if it would "not be better to select some suitable location on the Western & Atlantic Railroad, where [the convicts] could be employed in making Iron, such as Pig Iron, Nails, and all the different kinds of Iron used by the country."[7] McConnell did not say that the most viable place where the convicts could be so employed would be Mark A. Cooper's iron-works. McConnell elaborated on the benefits, but his essential point—that convicts should be used in industrial pursuits connected to the Western & Atlantic—was very similar to what Brown had argued as a young legisla-tor less than a decade earlier. McConnell, though, thought convicts might be useful working in private enterprise, not just on public works.

During the late 1850s, the nation was locked in tension over slav-ery and abolitionism. While Brown and his cronies began their work in Milledgeville, some leaders remaining in the Etowah Valley extended their desire for economic diversification and self-sufficiency into a call for educational independence from corrupting northern influences. On July 14, 1858, politician and diplomat William Henry Stiles gave a commence-ment address at the Cherokee Baptist College in Cassville. Stiles was lo-cal, living on a plantation called Etowah Cliffs, and he began immedi-ately with a justification of Cherokee Removal, contrasting the area two decades earlier, when it was "the dwelling place of the savage," with "the rich valleys that now teem with industry." The changes had happened so quickly that a person could, while riding in a railroad car, still spy "those narrow trails, the highway of the 'red-man,'" which were not yet entirely gone. Further misrepresenting what the area had been like while the Cherokees lived there, Stiles claimed that the most important change was the replacement of "the rude wigwam of the savage" with the Cherokee Baptist College. There had been a time when southern youth could safely travel to the North and receive an education there, but in these days of "deadly hostility," Stiles believed it necessary to discuss "the *Educational Independence of the South*."[8]

Stiles hated that the South had become "dependent upon" and "tribu-tary to" another portion of the country, and he thought the lack of agree-ment among southerners about what to do in response was because many southerners had received their education outside the region. Stiles thought it was foolish that southerners spent their money on books and schooling in the North, and he believed that southerners needed to educate their own children. He thought the South must secure independence in busi-ness and monetary affairs, which could not happen before it became in-dependent in education. Stiles contrasted the educations offered by the Athenians and Spartans to their youths and meditated on what a failure it would have been for the children of one group to have been educated by the other. Likewise, schools in the South and North "differ as widely . . . as ever did those of Athens and Sparta. The institutions of the one are based upon *slavery*, the institutions of the other are based upon what they are pleased to call *freedom*. One section is unalterably identified with *slave* institutions, *slave* property and *slave* labor, the other equally identified with *free* society, *free* labor and even *free* love." Stiles railed against fanatical professors at Harvard and Yale and against "abolition textbooks." He thought the "whole moral atmosphere" of New England was more poisonous than "the contracted hold of a slave-ship." Unsuspecting young southerners went north only to be ambushed by "fallacious arguments drawn from the 'Declaration of Independence' and the 'Golden rule,'" which often destroyed their usefulness on their return home.[9]

The crisis now existing, argued Stiles, was much greater than what propelled the Patriots to declare their independence from Great Britain. He expounded on the idea that slavery had existed in all civilized nations throughout history, and not just that, but those nations had achieved their greatest heights of civilization at the very same time that they held slaves. Stiles then launched into a whirlwind examination of the world since that time. Every example proved his point: slavery was not only age-old but went hand in hand with "the highest civilization and greatest prosperity," which was lost when slavery was abolished. Only through a southern education built around the necessity of the preservation of slavery could whites maintain their wealthy southern society. Stiles concluded by warning the instructors to teach the boys about "the obligations to right and honor, they should unhesitatingly maintain, even at the cost of a dissolution of this confederacy." In matters of education, "our motto *shall* be, *Independence now, Independence forever!*"[10]

A week later, another Cass County resident spoke to those gathered for the commencement at Cassville Female College. The Reverend Charles W. Howard was a prominent minister and writer who had moved to Cass County by 1842, and his address also spoke of slavery. He reminded the graduating young women that "our life . . . is materially influenced by the existence among us of a peculiar form of labor." The plantation mistress must be as good to her slaves as to her husband and her children. These women would "preside over that system of slavery, which is one, not of oppression, but of protection to the laborer." Howard also spoke of the reverence with which all Americans should regard George Washington, and he said that honoring Washington would "rebuke" people who cursed the American hero as a slaveholder.[11] Both speakers, Stiles and Howard, told aspects of the same story: a slaveholding region in the American tradition defending itself against slander and attacks. Their support for education in northern Georgia was tied to maintaining the existing social system.

Months later, Mark Cooper fired off a cannon; it was time to celebrate the completion of a railroad spur that ran to his iron furnaces and mills from the Western & Atlantic. His railroad was not lengthy—a barely four-mile track—but he had done it himself, and when one thinks about the tons of iron product coming from his furnaces and rolling mill daily, and the number of carts, horse teams, and teamsters required to transport heavy iron to the railroad, those four miles were highly significant. It is no wonder Cooper did not intend to stop shooting off his cannon. He said he planned to fire the cannon every morning until a formal celebration was held. Around the state, newspaper editors congratulated Cooper. The *Augusta Constitutionalist* pointed out that at "the last session of the Legislature, he applied for aid to build a Rail Road from his Iron Works at Etowah to the State Road," since he sent so much business on the Western & Atlantic, but once refused, he "built it himself, without aid from any quarter." The editor of the *Cartersville Express* lamented the shortsightedness of local people and the state legislature for not recognizing how important Cooper's railroad was and for not helping him build it.[12] Cooper had used the charter granted in 1847. Maybe in time the spur would be expanded farther into the gold belt of Georgia, as the original charter had authorized.

The chief engineer on the railroad spur was Eugene LeHardy. Born in 1818 in Belgium, LeHardy was educated at the University of Brussels and became a civil engineer. After the revolutions of 1848, in which he sided with the Republicans, he and others, mostly family members, left for the United States and settled on the Etowah River in Rome, Georgia, where they comprised a small Belgian agricultural colony of about twenty-five people. LeHardy became active in the community; he was acquainted with John S. Rowland and Rowland Springs and evidently became close to one of Jacob Stroup's sons: in 1854, Jacob Decatur Stroup and his wife, Dorcas, named their new son Eugene LeHardy Stroup. LeHardy advertised himself as a "Civil and Topographical Engineer, Surveyor, and Architect," and in 1858 John W. Lewis made him the chief engineer of the Western & Atlantic.[13]

Brown and Lewis both wanted Cooper's extension to be only the beginning of a longer railroad line. The state legislature in late 1858 authorized the Etowah and Canton Railroad Company to have old railroad rails replaced on the Western & Atlantic. Eugene LeHardy responded to a letter

Eugene LeHardy, shown here probably in the late
1860s, worked on the Western & Atlantic and on
Cooper's spur to his ironworks before he left for
Europe to purchase arms for the Confederacy.
Battey, *History of Rome and Floyd County*.

from Governor Brown in January 1859, just months after the completion
of Cooper's four miles, and LeHardy's reply indicates his close relationship
with both Brown and Lewis. LeHardy apologized for not writing earlier,
but he had anticipated running into Brown along the path of the railroad,
which Brown loved to travel on. LeHardy had spoken with Lewis about
the best path for railroad tracks to Canton, and LeHardy believed the railroad could be extended within one year to within six or eight miles of Canton. "As soon as the Directors of the Road will give me instructions to that
effect I will push the Road with vigor & energy," LeHardy promised.[14]

The vigor and energy in Georgia's state government, though, soon
shifted to protection of the state. In October 1859, abolitionist John
Brown's deadly raid on the Harpers Ferry armory in Virginia deeply dis-
turbed the slaveholding South, where whites feared that Brown's plan to
incite a slave rebellion indicated a strong possibility of a race war. In Geor-

gia, Joseph E. Brown won reelection that year, and early in 1860 Brown arranged for Mark Cooper to travel through the northern United States and purchase $75,000 worth of arms and munitions for the state. Cooper was in Boston by April, and he spent the next several weeks in Massachusetts, Connecticut, New York, Washington, D.C., and Maryland arranging for the purchase of rifles, bayonets, sabers, ammunition, cannons, tents, and various accoutrements, such as bayonet scabbards and cartridge boxes. Where these items had "US" stamped on them, Cooper arranged for the national designation "to be substituted by the Coat of Arms of Georgia." Arms manufacturers, such as Eli Whitney and the Ames Manufacturing Company of Massachusetts, were accustomed to supplying state militias and freely sold what they produced.[15]

Cooper was not the only person Brown sent north. Brown persuaded the Georgia legislature to appropriate funds for the construction of an armory; in May 1860, he appointed Ira Foster and two other men to a committee on the founding of an armory in Georgia.[16] Foster and his committee visited the principal armories in the United States and when they returned wrote a report about what it would take to build an armory and foundry in Georgia that could produce five thousand rifled muskets annually. They noted that private armories were almost wholly lacking in the southern states. And while many nations procured cannons from private establishments, almost all countries had public armories capable of producing small arms. The commissioners recommended that Georgia build an armory. Excess capacity could be sold to "sister states," and the result would not only equip and protect Georgia but also "exhibit to the civilized world the spirit of manhood and independence at the South, which dares resist oppression and misrule and uphold freedom and justice though the price paid be the baptismal blood of her sons."[17] Foster and his fellow commissioners believed that the proposed armory would help Georgia maintain its independence if the state left the Union. John Brown's raid and the upcoming national elections, with a growing Republican Party that was hostile to the expansion of slavery, inspired thoughts of self-protection and self-sufficiency in Georgia. Brown's state government prepared for war.

Brown probably read this report at Rowland Springs. The previous few summers Brown's family had escaped the heat of middle Georgia by returning to Canton, but the Browns were friends of the Rowland family, and during the summer of 1860 John S. Rowland provided the Browns with a house at Rowland Springs. The resort was no longer open to the public, so it was a respite, and Brown was among friends. Given that John W. Lewis's home was a half mile away, that Lewis's sister was married to Rowland, that Cooper's ironworks were just four miles away, and that Ira Foster's mill was just beyond, it seems likely that Brown conversed frequently with Lewis, Rowland, Cooper, and Foster—and perhaps with Eugene LeHardy and Henry Hawley Waters—about national politics and the upcoming elections and read newspapers as fast as they arrived. Doubtless, Brown was also thinking through what to say in his letter to the incoming legislature in November.[18]

On November 7, one day after Abraham Lincoln's election to the presidency, Brown delivered a special message to the gathered legislators. Brown did not neglect the headlines. His special message argued that the constitutional rights belonging to Georgians and people of other states where slavery was legal had been violated. These states were justified in whatever they believed necessary to protect their rights. Brown discussed northerners' complicity in American slavery and the rise of abolitionists. He claimed that many abolitionists supported freeing those held as slaves, letting them "intermarry with our children, amalgamate with us, and be placed, in all respects, upon a basis of perfect equality with our free white population." Now that "the Black Republican party" of Lincoln and his supporters had won the presidency and vice presidency of the nation, Brown said that white people in the South must protect themselves against actions that he feared would result in "a war of extermination between the black and white races."[19]

As for what would happen if the slaveholding states left the Union, Brown maintained that calm would prevail. Enslaved black people would never revolt, he claimed, because "nine-tenths of them are truly and devotedly attached to their masters and mistresses, and would shed in their defence, the last drop of their blood. They feel and recognize their inferiority as a race . . . and few of them have any ambition beyond their present comfort and enjoyment." Brown said that even poor southern whites supported slavery because they did not wish to compete with black people in the labor market or "associate with them, and their children as equals." Should "the madness and folly" of northerners create a cleavage between the two sections of the country, the southern states—powerful, prosperous—would be just fine. Brown asked the legislature for $1 million to be placed into a military fund, and he concluded with a declaration that Georgia would not compromise its rights in any way.[20]

The same day, Brown delivered a more traditional and general address to both houses of the general assembly, which laid out his educational and industrial agendas. Brown echoed William Stiles when he urged the legislature to support the University of Georgia adequately so that "the sons of the South" could get a fine education "without subjecting them to abolition taint or New England fanaticism." Brown reported on how difficult it was to purchase and have delivered the firearms and accoutrements with the $75,000 the legislature had authorized the previous year, and he presented the legislators with the report written by Ira Foster and the two other commissioners. Brown recommended that the legislature appropriate funds for the building of an armory or authorize Brown himself to arrange for a private company to build a foundry in Georgia that could make the implements of war. Then, Brown brought up Mark A. Cooper. Brown said Cooper could quickly build a foundry and supply the needs of the state. Brown said that nobody had done more to develop the state's mineral wealth than Cooper, that Cooper's enterprises had paid more than $100,000 into the state coffers just to ship his freight on the Western & Atlantic, and that his business had sustained the lives of more than a thousand people, counting the families of his workers. But in doing so Cooper had gone into debt and was now at a point where he might have to suspend his operations. Brown carried a request from Cooper and endorsed it; Brown recommended a $250,000 loan from the state to Cooper. If Cooper could not repay the loan, the state could foreclose on his valuable properties, including twelve thousand acres of land. Brown emphasized that he was not trying to revive a failing business. Rather, "the State has a large interest at stake," given how much revenue came to Georgia because of the amount of business Cooper did with the Western & Atlantic. Brown asked the legislators "whether justice and sound policy do not dictate that the necessary relief be granted."[21] The cronyism inherent in Brown's life was on display. Brown asked Cooper to do things to help out Brown and the state of Georgia, and then Brown asked the legislature to assist Cooper. Some of Brown's words probably came directly from Cooper's mouth, heard by Brown over the summer while he was living at Rowland Springs.

More generally, Brown reiterated a request he had made the year before for the legislature to appoint a geologist and chemist for Georgia. Brown invoked the idea that there was enough iron ore in northern Georgia to satisfy demand across the South. He reminded the legislature that "the coal fields of Georgia and Tennessee are in close proximity, and a railroad communication is already established between the two." In addition to the ingredients for iron, "gold, silver, copper, lead, manganese, and other valuable minerals and metals, have also been found in different sections of our State."[22] These were the priorities of a man who anticipated an industrial future for Georgia and who wanted to assist mining industries, from which he had already profited greatly.

The legislature balked at a specific bailout of Cooper but granted $1 million for the defense of Georgia and also arranged an election for January 2, 1861, of delegates who would meet in a state convention. It was not clear in Brown's November address that he favored secession, but over the next few weeks many prominent Georgians called for the state to leave the Union. Brown also heard from Joseph Barbier, a Tennessean who had just returned from a mission to Belgium with Eugene LeHardy to facilitate more direct trade between the southern states and European countries. Barbier concluded that their mission "was a Complete Success—and will sustain the following couplet: The star spangled banner / long may she wave / over the land of the free / and the home of the Slave."[23]

By early December, Brown was a clear secessionist. And he once again, in a letter of December 7, held out the specter of black and white equality. Poor whites, said Brown, would fare worst if slavery were ended, since they would be put on an equal level with "the negroes" when whites "are a superior race." Brown listed all the ways blacks and whites would be equals—in schools, on juries, and in the military. Interracial sex would be the final indignity: whites and blacks would "enter each others' houses in social intercourse as equals; and very soon their children must marry together as equals." Lest anyone think they were safe because they lived in the northern mountains of Georgia, far from where most black people lived, Brown predicted that the end of slavery would bring black people by the thousands to northern Georgia. "We should have them plundering and stealing, robbing and killing, in all the lovely vallies of the mountains." That was too much for Brown, who waxed rhapsodic about his years spent in the northern Georgia mountains and about the poor, yet "brave, honest, patriotic, and pure hearted" white people who lived there. To prevent black people from coming to their "lovely vallies," Brown had no doubt the whites would fight valiantly. As historians have pointed out, upcountry Georgians were the most resistant to secession, and Brown's cheerleading was a crucial factor in the state's vote for secession. As his December 7 message makes clear, Brown based his racist arguments to white northern Georgians about leaving the United States on negrophobia.[24]

Once South Carolina seceded from the Union in December, Brown

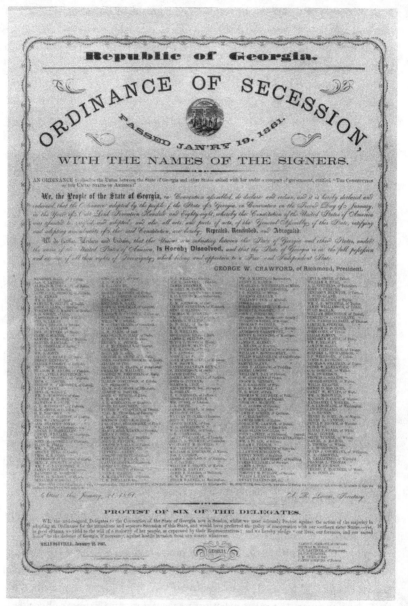

During the weeks between Georgia's secession from the United States and the formation of the Confederate States of America, Joseph E. Brown was the head of a country, the Republic of Georgia.

Courtesy of the Hargrett Rare Book and Manuscript Library, University of Georgia.

acted quickly. Brown prevailed on Eugene LeHardy, the railroad builder who had accompanied Joseph Barbier to Belgium months earlier, to return to Europe and purchase war materials for Georgia. On January 2, 1861, the same day as the election for the Georgia state convention, which resulted in a slight victory for delegates who supported secession, LeHardy departed for Europe. On January 19 the Georgia convention voted narrowly for secession, 166–130, and Georgia was out of the Union. At that time, though, the Confederate States of America did not exist. Georgia became, for a few weeks, the Republic of Georgia, not part of any other country, headed by its own governor, Joseph E. Brown. But Brown had not waited for the declaration of secession; he seized the empty federal Fort Pulaski on the coast and also took possession of both a federal arsenal in Augusta and the mint in Dahlonega, which he knew so well.[25]

It is important to see how the world must have looked to Brown in late January. Several southern states had seceded from the Union, and it seemed quite possible that the rest of the United States would simply let them go. Outgoing president James Buchanan was doing nothing to tie his successor's hands, but that also meant he was sitting idly while states seized federal installations without any federal reaction. Joseph E. Brown had every reason to think a southern Confederacy could be established, and Georgia would be unquestionably a most important state, a linchpin of the Confederacy. Brown, as he surveyed his state, saw prosperity, and he knew Georgia was incubating an extractive and industrial economy in addition to its vast cotton plantations, with critical railroads, human talent, and massive potential. Brown intended to guide Georgia into that future. Representatives of the seceded states met in Montgomery, Alabama, on February 4, 1861, and announced the creation of a Confederate nation, one that would secure the advantages of slavery. It was a new American nation, which stripped out the abolitionists and their vehicle to political power, the Republican Party.[26]

Back home in Georgia, plenty of people were ready to get into the fight. Less than two weeks after the Confederacy formed, Governor Brown received a letter from Skid Harris, who wrote from the Canton copper mine. Harris wanted Brown to know that the soldiers he led all had uniforms and lacked nothing but weapons. Harris seemed anxious that the conflict would be resolved before they could be mobilized. If there were no fighting or even deployment, the money spent on uniforms would be wasted.[27]

The departures of campaigning soldiers were marked by encouraging speeches. William Grisham wrote one for the Cherokee Brown Riflemen, who were addressed by Grisham's granddaughter, fifteen-year-old Susan Galt, as they set out. Galt reminded the soldiers, "We are now free citizens of a free and independent republic," having broken every connection "to that Union which Abolition fanaticism had made detestable." Galt presented the soldiers with a banner made by women in the Canton area. She knew that they would fight valiantly against invaders, and "should the protection of our independence and the institutions of our fathers require the effusion of your blood, or, the sacrifice of your devoted lives; should fates decree that the battlefield should be your grave, your imperishable fame shall ever live in the hearts of your countrymen."[28] And the men marched away; many did not return alive.

To Mark Anthony Cooper, the election of Lincoln and the secession crisis looked like a gigantic business opportunity. A week after the election and Brown's message to the legislature, Cooper wrote to Brown requesting that his ironworks be the site of the $250,000 armory. The armory would supply all the arms Georgia required and make Georgia a strong state. The next month, Cooper was negotiating to supply arms to Alabama, Mississippi, and South Carolina. In February, one week after the creation of the Confederate States of America, Mark Cooper wrote a short letter to the new Confederate Congress. Cooper insisted that the new nation must be able to defend itself; it would have to build an armory for half a million dollars or issue contracts for a full million. Cooper offered to sell the Confederacy his own business, "the most eligible in the South; or I can take the contract." In March, Cooper went directly to Montgomery and then wrote to Brown that he felt sure that Confederate president Jefferson Davis and the secretary of war were convinced "that we can have the Foundry & Armory for the Confederate States, in Georgia at Etowah—with the Power of supplying the Government & the States." Cooper laid out what he needed from Brown and the state of Georgia—now $300,000—and promised, "you will have the Property there quadrupled, & the whole Etowah Valley enriched." Cooper did not say it directly, but his implication was that Brown's own financial interests would benefit as a result. In Montgomery, though, other representatives with other interests got Cooper's proposal diverted to a committee on military affairs. Cooper's Etowah Iron Works did not become the site of a Confederate armory.[29]

Besides that disappointment, Cooper ran into a host of other difficulties. He got a contract within two weeks of the firing on Fort Sumter to provide arms to the Confederacy. But finding people who could actually set up the facilities to manufacture firearms and carry out the tasks was far more difficult. Cooper could not deliver on the contract within the four months he had been given, and his money problems were such that he wrote to the Department of War in September to explain why he needed an advance of a quarter million dollars in order to fulfill the contract.[30]

There were other iron makers in the Deep South also doing business, including Moses Stroup, Cooper's old partner. At Tannehill, Alabama, he built an iron furnace with two stacks, which was completed after the onset of the Civil War. When the operation sold in 1862, Stroup stayed on a few more months to superintend the furnace before traveling northeast about twenty miles to Oxmoor, where he built yet another furnace. In 1863, the Oxmoor furnace began producing ten tons of iron daily, which went directly into the Confederate effort.[31]

Other members of the crony network also changed positions. Within two months after Fort Sumter was fired upon, Ira Foster became quartermaster general for Georgia, responsible throughout the war for getting supplies to everyone the government had to equip. Changes also came to the Western & Atlantic Railroad. In 1861, Brown clashed with John W. Lewis over management of the Western & Atlantic, which resulted in Lewis's resignation as superintendent. Brown, pained by what had happened, reminded Lewis in a letter that "you were my early friend and helped me up in life. When I had secured position and power, I invited you to the highest position within my gift." Brown acknowledged that amid the stresses of his office he may have paid Lewis "too little respect," but Brown also "felt that you treated me with coldness and indifference" at times. This exchange is striking because most of these figures were not sentimental, at least in writing, yet the personal feelings revealed underscore the extent to which these high-level government and business relationships rested on mutual friendship. Following the resignation, Brown promptly chose Lewis's brother-in-law John S. Rowland to head the railroad. Rowland hired William Grisham as his secretary to handle the correspondence of the position. Despite their kerfuffle, Brown and Lewis resolved their differences, and when Brown asked Lewis in March 1862 to accept an interim appointment to the Confederate Senate, Lewis accepted.[32]

Two months later, in late May, Brown responded to a letter from Lewis, who wanted to help Georgia with a critical shortage of salt. Salt, of course, is a basic requirement of humans and other animals and an essential ingredient in the preservation of meat. The United States imported annually about twelve million bushels of salt, a great majority of it into the southern states. Lack of access to northern and international salt sources was a critical deficiency for parts of the Confederacy. Lewis, though, could have salt mined in southwestern Virginia at Saltville and shipped to Georgia, and Brown eagerly welcomed Lewis's aid. Lewis offered to make the arrangements and then sell the salt to the state, but Brown, worried that others would think there was cronyism involved or something untoward, said that "considering our former personal and social as well as our present official and political relations, I believe it will be better for both of us to have the salt made at State expense, and on State account." A few weeks later, from Canton, Brown announced that Lewis had arranged a lease for Georgia at the Virginia Salt Works that would benefit Georgia greatly: "Dr. Lewis has consented to take the control and direction of the works for the public benefit without compensation."[33]

Lewis's relevance continued. In November 1862, Lewis published a letter in Atlanta's *Intelligencer* explaining that the salt shortage was ending, and there was no reason to think salt would be in short supply in the future. But Lewis was concerned that "we are not making iron enough for war purposes." Because of the naval blockade, iron could not be imported and would have to be made domestically, and Lewis envisioned *"primitive forges."* He said there was enough waterpower and iron ore in northwestern Georgia to supply not just Georgia but the entire Confederacy. Lewis urged an immediate commencement of the work and thought that enslaved laborers, imported from coastal Georgia, could be the workforce. "I hope North-Western Georgia may soon have an hundred forges." Lewis offered his help as an expert. He said that aside from "one or two other persons in this State, I have perhaps the longest practical experience in iron making, and will cheerfully" answer questions about "ores, locations, necessary machinery, where it can be had, &c."[34] Lewis advocated changes that would build on the work he and others had been doing in northern Georgia since the late 1830s.

Lewis, Brown, and their compatriots were very organized people, but sometimes events outpace planners. War can change reality quickly, and warfare, of course, also means untimely deaths. By September 1861, one of Mark Cooper's three sons had died from wounds sustained at the First Battle of Bull Run (Manassas), and a second son in uniform died in December after being thrown from his horse. Smallpox swept through the Etowah area and killed some people. In December 1861, Governor Brown traveled to Cherokee County for the burial of his younger brother George

W. Brown, who had died in a Richmond hospital after serving with Hampton's Legion.[35]

The world looked very different by the end of 1862 than it had two years earlier. Joseph E. Brown and his Etowah Valley cronies—John W. Lewis, Ira Foster, Henry Hawley Waters, Eli McConnell, Mark A. Cooper, Eugene LeHardy, John S. Rowland, and William Grisham—had gone from being successful developers, miners, millers, and industrialists to running and working on behalf of the state of Georgia. Envisioning even brighter futures, they threw themselves wholeheartedly into secession. But as the death toll mounted, as U.S. armies drew closer, and as a terrible war entered its third year, there were serious questions about how it would all pan out.

CHAPTER 6

~~◦·◦~~

Destruction

THE POSSIBILITIES OF 1861, AS THE REPUBLIC OF GEORGIA became part of the Confederate States of America, became convoluted by problems soon after, and by late 1863 the situation was dire. The white people of the Etowah Valley had helped push out the Cherokee people who lived there and made astonishing changes in the ensuing years as they built towns, ran railroads, mined minerals, and forged iron. Now, everything they had built was vulnerable. Industry in the Etowah Valley went through three phases during the Civil War: first, a stage in which the problems of wartime production were paramount; second, a time during which Etowah Valley industries were imperiled by advancing federal forces; and third, a period of destruction as Union soldiers wrecked the Etowah Valley's industrial capacity. That destruction was followed by questions about what people would do in the aftermath of defeat, and where and how to reorient their lives.

In January 1862, a railroad developer wrote to President Jefferson Davis with advice; he suggested that the Confederate government purchase Mark A. Cooper's operation. Within days Davis got word that the quartermaster general of the Confederacy had contacted Cooper about obtaining sheet iron from his rolling mill, only to be informed that Cooper was not interested. Cooper told the Confederate government that he was earning too much money making bar iron and nails to justify altering his machinery. Cooper may have been speaking the truth, but he was also acting dangerously, because by spurning the Confederate government's desire for a contract he was turning down a party that not only wanted to do business with him but could also very easily ruin him. No matter whom Cooper

wished to do business with, he could only stay in operation with the cooperation of the Confederate government.[1]

Private industry in the Confederacy operated with very little independence. This situation was evident in the tug-of-war over labor. In a proclamation of September 1861, Governor Joseph E. Brown exempted from
Georgia military service various laborers, including "all persons employed
at furnaces in the making of iron, or in rolling mills." Brown encouraged
such workers not to join Confederate armies voluntarily. But those armies
needed soldiers, and in April 1862 Jefferson Davis and the Confederacy
began the conscription of almost all white males between eighteen and
thirty-five years old, which meant Cooper had to obtain exemptions from
the government in Richmond to retain his workers. This problem existed
throughout the Confederacy. As the secretary of the navy wrote to Davis
in 1862, "The want of expert workmen is felt in every workshop, public
and private." Many skilled workers were northerners or foreigners who
had quit their jobs and left when war began, and many southern workers
had joined the military. At the end of April, Cooper wrote to the secretary
of war and asked for the return of eight men who were serving in military
units. One was Ephram Jenkins, who had fifteen years of experience at
Etowah as both a collier who made charcoal and as a puddler who worked
with the rolling mill, making him doubly valuable. Some men were returned, but the Confederate government detailed at least one of them to
a different furnace. And men Cooper said he needed, who felled trees and
worked as teamsters, were not sent back; the Confederacy's insatiable de-
mands for soldiers outweighed Cooper's needs even in these integral aspects of his business.[2]

In 1861 and 1862, federal ships harassed the coast, but no major bat-
tles were fought on Georgia soil. One event that may have caused alarm
was a daring raid on the Western & Atlantic, which became known as
the Great Locomotive Chase. Because of the geography of the Confederate states and the railroad network in the Confederacy, the Western & Atlantic was a central and incredibly important railroad, constantly busy
with train traffic. In 1861, saboteurs disrupted rail transportation in eastern Tennessee as they burned numerous bridges, including two south of
Chattanooga. In June, a correspondent of Governor Brown reported new
threats to Western & Atlantic bridges and said, "Several suspicious persons (White & Black) have been caught by the Night Watch." Superintendent John W. Lewis had placed two watchmen at each longer bridge, but

they were unarmed. The next year, a Unionist civilian named James Andrews came up with an ambitious plan: infiltrate soldiers dressed as civilians into the Confederacy as far as Marietta or Atlanta, steal a train, and then run it northward along the route of the Western & Atlantic, destroying the track, bridges, and telegraph wires behind it all the way to Chattanooga, which would cut off Chattanooga from supply and make the city ripe for an attack by federal forces already operating in central Tennessee south of Nashville. Andrews and more than twenty soldiers made their way to Marietta, north of Atlanta; on the morning of April 12, 1862, at Camp McDonald, when the crew from the locomotive the *General* was eating breakfast at Mrs. Lacy's boardinghouse, they looked up from their eggs and biscuits to watch their train starting down the tracks. Andrews' Raiders cut telegraph wires so no messages could alert stations along the path to Chattanooga, and the raiders took their time moving northward. Their cover story was that they were taking three boxcars of munitions to General P. G. T. Beauregard at Corinth, which proved convincing. But because the busy railroad had only one track, they had to keep pace with the official schedule in order to move past southbound trains at stations with sidings. This meant slow progress since the average train on the Western & Atlantic traveled at sixteen miles per hour.[3]

Meanwhile, since Andrews and his men had taken the only locomotive in Marietta, the pursuers first ran after the train on foot a few miles before they encountered a work crew with a pole cart and began pushing themselves along, using the long poles; fortunately for them, the grade was downhill all the way to the Etowah River. After that, they would have serious problems making good time. The key for the pursuers, however, was the discovery of another locomotive with a full head of steam—the *Yonah*—at the Etowah River on Mark Cooper's spur, which ran to his ironworks. Andrews' Raiders had seen the *Yonah*, but there were many men around it; rather than blow their cover, they just kept going, and at certain points they put crossties over the track or wrecked a rail to slow or disable any pursuit. In the end, the crew from Marietta commandeered Cooper's engine and chased Andrews' Raiders several miles to Adairsville, where the Confederates switched to a much larger and newer engine, the *Texas*, which sped after the *General*. The Great Locomotive Chase ended near Chattanooga when the *General* finally ran out of wood and steam; its occupants scattered to the hills. Andrews' Raiders had briefly disrupted the Western & Atlantic but failed to burn the bridges that would have done serious damage.[4] While their failed mission became a footnote militarily, their efforts were a reminder that everyone recognized the importance of this key transportation route in the Confederate war effort. Without Cooper's railroad spur and his engine, the *Yonah*, sitting on the track, Andrews's raid might have turned out differently.

Cooper had problems that went far beyond Union saboteurs because the traffic on the Western & Atlantic Railroad, overloaded with necessary war dealings, prevented him from getting coal he required from the only place in Georgia he could obtain it: Dade County near Chattanooga. One result was that Cooper was unable to fulfill his contracts for various iron products, including bolt iron to be used in ship construction. Cooper foresaw an even more difficult future. He knew the Confederate government had the power to seize private enterprises necessary to the war effort. In May 1862, the Confederate government took over a nearby saltpeter mine used to manufacture gunpowder. In July, Cooper sold his entire ironworks and related landholdings for $400,000 in Confederate bonds to a partnership called Quinby and Robinson. William T. Quinby and William A. Robinson were iron makers from Memphis who worked exclusively with the Confederate government. Before Memphis fell to Union forces in June, they had looked for a new base of operations, and their correspondence with the Confederate government shows they were living in Richmond. Quinby and Robinson were insiders—they knew how to work with the Davis administration. The month after they purchased the Etowah Iron Works, Quinby and Robinson negotiated a contract to supply the Navy and War Departments with $1.5 million worth of "cannon, shot, shell, bolt, bar, rod, plate, boiler, and railroad iron and car springs" annually. They advertised in Atlanta and Chattanooga their desire to hire "one hundred able-bodied negroes" to perform the labor.[5]

In November 1862, William T. Quinby wrote to Governor Brown about their troubles at Etowah. Quinby explained that they were "greatly enlarging the facilities for manufacturing Iron," given their contract with the Confederate government. Freight rates for the Etowah facility were too high, though, and soon the works would be producing vastly more material. Quinby reminded Brown of the benefits to Georgia from this additional freight on the state-owned railroad, which Quinby thought "entitles us, we believe, to a few privileges or at least that we be placed on an equality with other manufacturers." Another problem was access to coal, the same problem Cooper had dealt with. Quinby complained that a competing Atlanta iron facility was able to obtain more coal than it needed, while the Etowah works were at a standstill because Quinby and Robinson could not get coal delivered from the mines in Dade County.[6]

Quinby and Robinson's problems worsened in the summer of 1863 when the U.S. Army, operating in Tennessee, targeted Chattanooga. Brown had warned in 1862 that if Chattanooga fell, then no coal could be shipped through the city, "and all our iron mills are stopped." The U.S. military strategists made the same calculation. As General William S. Rosecrans explained his strategy after the war, "The possession of Chattanooga would . . . cut off [the enemy's] use of the coal mines in the mountains on the south side of the Tennessee [River], from which he was supplying his furnaces at Etowah."[7] Furnaces could still use charcoal, but the crucial rolling mill could not.

Politically, Quinby and Robinson already had a good relationship with President Jefferson Davis and the Confederate government, but as their letter to Governor Brown indicated, they also needed a good relationship with Brown, and Brown and Davis did not get along well. Brown disagreed loudly and often publicly with Davis over numerous issues, including whether Georgia state arms could be carried outside the state; whether military units raised in Georgia were under Brown's control or the Confederate government's; the necessity of conscription; civil liberties, such as the suspension of the writ of habeas corpus; and who would control the Western & Atlantic.[8] Quinby and Robinson were politically adept, though; in 1863 they hired Gustav Smith, Brown's aide-de-camp, as president of their Etowah Iron Works and let Smith keep Governor Brown happy.

Gustavus Woodson Smith was a native Kentuckian and a West Point graduate who fought in the Mexican-American War but then left military life in 1854 and became a director of the Illinois Central Railroad. There, he undoubtedly became acquainted with another director, Leroy Wiley, who had joined in the late 1840s with Moses Stroup and Mark A. Cooper's Etowah iron-making operation. Gustav Smith also oversaw construction projects and wound up working for an iron company in Trenton, New Jersey. He then joined the Street Department of New York City and in 1858 became street commissioner, a powerful position in the largest city in the country. When the Civil War began in 1861, though, Smith left that employment and accepted a generalship in the Confederate army. His rejuvenated military career did not work out well for him; he fell out of favor with Jefferson Davis and resigned his commission in February 1863. But the people Davis did not like were sometimes people whom Joe Brown liked a lot. Soon Smith became an aide-de-camp to Governor Brown, helped with building fortifications in northern Georgia, and undoubtedly had Brown's blessing or maybe even was suggested by Brown for the presidency of the Etowah Manufacturing and Mining Company in May 1863.[9]

Smith walked into a mess. The previous year the Etowah Company had won a million-dollar contract from the Confederate government to deliver shell casings and ammunition, but illness and mechanical failures had prevented the company from delivering, and the Davis administration in Richmond was contemplating taking over the Etowah Company. Smith went right to work to improve the finances of the company and increase production. He renegotiated the main contract with the Confederate government in July 1863, though the contract spelled out that if the Etowah Company could not furnish what it promised and could not pay back its advance, then the Confederate government would have the right to take over the entire ironworks and operate it as the administration in Richmond pleased. Gustav Smith worked to fulfill the new contract but faced immediate problems. Union general William Rosecrans's army took Chattanooga in September 1863; Smith's supply of coal was gone. It was back to charcoal exclusively as a fuel, and Smith lamented charcoal as "slow, troublesome, and expensive."[10]

The nearby U.S. Army changed many things in the Etowah Valley. In September 1863, an Atlanta newspaper advertised "Rowland Springs for sale." The advertisement claimed a rare niche: "It will be found to be just the place for Refugees." Across the South, many families were fleeing battle lines, which sometimes shifted abruptly. The question was how long Rowland Springs would be a safe place for people fleeing from elsewhere. John S. Rowland died of chronic diarrhea that September, and his daughter-in-law said she could hear cannons booming sixty miles distant in the Battle of Chickamauga, south of Chattanooga, as he was being buried. Confederates used Cherokee Baptist College and Cassville Female College, closed since January, as hospitals in the weeks following.[11]

With Chattanooga in federal hands that winter, Confederates prepared to face an 1864 Union offensive in Georgia. The Union army, nearly a hundred thousand strong, commanded now by William Tecumseh Sherman, pushed into Georgia in 1864 along the path of the Western & Atlantic. On the Confederate side, Joseph E. Johnston and about sixty thousand soldiers stood in Sherman's path. They needed to be supplied from the south by the Western & Atlantic.[12]

In response to letters from Johnston about troubles getting supplies, Brown wrote on February 10, 1864, to Johnston about his problem with using the Western & Atlantic to supply Johnston's army because Georgia had so few engines and cars. Brown said he had answered many calls from President Davis to supply other railroad lines, and if he could only have returned a portion of the engines and cars he had lent out, he could answer all of Johnston's needs. Brown allowed that Georgia probably should have simply built new engines and cars, but doing so was an "impossibility" because "the Confederate Government has had control of all the iron mills and almost all the foundries in the Confederacy," and it "refused to let us get a supply of iron from the Etowah Works near the road for our ordinary repairs when we were hauling all the coal that kept the works going, and it has been with great difficulty that we could secure the supply." Brown said he would not even have been able to keep the railroad in decent repair without help from Gustav Smith, who had managed to provide the necessary iron.[13]

During the spring of 1864, the Confederate army in northern Georgia kept retreating ahead of the federal forces led by General William T. Sherman, who was no stranger to the Etowah Valley. In 1844, as a young lieutenant, Sherman had been posted briefly in Marietta. As Sherman recalled in his memoirs, "I had ridden the distance on horseback, and had noted well the topography of the country, especially that about Kenesaw, Allatoona, and the Etowah River. On that occasion I had stopped some days with a Colonel Tumlin, to see some remarkable Indian mounds on the Etowah River."[14] Sherman's visit with the Tumlins by the Mississippian mounds placed him within miles of the iron furnaces along the Etowah River, and his discussion of noting the topography around Allatoona indicates that he was nearly on top of the iron furnaces. Certainly, he knew all about them in 1864.

As Sherman's invading army drew closer, on May 20 Gustav Smith oversaw the evacuation of any machinery that could be moved, along with enslaved men, wagons, and livestock, all of which went to Macon, where Smith planned to rebuild. The furnaces, rolling mill, and much of the infrastructure, of course, could not be moved, and Sherman ordered his soldiers to destroy it. Two days after Smith finished the evacuation, on Sunday evening, May 22, Union soldiers wrecked the mills and furnaces. Furnaces that had produced untold tons of iron in the decades since Jacob Stroup first built a forge and furnace were ruined; the peak industrial period in the Etowah Valley was over.[15]

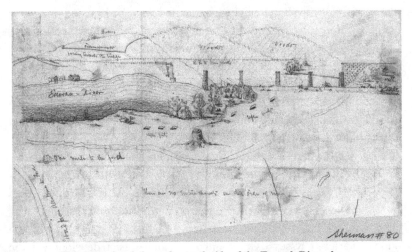

This **1864** sketch from the south side of the Etowah River shows
the stone supports of the burned Western & Atlantic bridge, as
well as the line of tracks marked "R.R. to Iron Works."
Courtesy of the Prints and Photographs Division, Library of Congress.

Confederates felt the loss. From Texas, Confederate politician Thomas
C. Reynolds wrote to General Sterling Price that it appeared the Union
army could not be held back by Joe Johnston. Johnston, wrote Reynolds,
"would surely not have given up the Etowah Iron-Works and the great
manufacturing region of North Georgia unless their defense had been desperate." Gustav Smith, now lacking a business to conduct, quickly resigned
from his position as president of the Etowah Manufacturing and Mining
Company in order to answer Governor Brown's request that he command
the Georgia militia. On June 5, General Sherman reported from Allatoona
Creek, "The wheat-fields of the country are our chief supply of forage." The
crops that in earlier years had fed Cooper's flour mill now fattened federal
horses and mules.[16]

Governor Brown suffered from Sherman's advances. In July 1864,
Brown and several other people finalized a new corporation, Fulton and
Company, which purchased John W. Lewis's iron furnace and more than
4,500 acres of land in Bartow County. Lewis remained a shareholder,
along with Georgia educator and politician M. C. Fulton, Joe Brown, and
several others. Beyond an existing iron furnace and another being built,
the property included a sawmill, a blacksmith shop, and all kinds of tools
and equipment.[17] The deed spelled out everything in detail, even though
by that time Sherman's armies had certainly wrecked much of what was

there. Perhaps the shareholders documented what had existed in hope of compensation at a later date, but in reality, all that probably remained was the acreage, though it was substantial and included numerous ore banks.

At the beginning of September, Sherman's army took Atlanta; in the wake of the army's passage, local government and stability collapsed, leaving a terrifying vacuum of power. Confederate and Unionist civilians, enslaved workers, deserters, draft dodgers, foraging Union soldiers, and Confederate home guard fighters all sought to stay alive and accomplish their goals. In August 1864, General Sherman had written to a subordinate, "If you send to Canton notify the people that if our [Western & Atlantic Rail]road is let alone we will feed ourselves, but if it be interrupted we will of necessity strip the country and destroy all things within reach." This demand that civilian populations be quiescent is consistent with the kind of warfare Ulysses S. Grant and Sherman had been developing in the western theater. Confederate civilians behind advancing Union lines were warned not to tolerate guerrilla fighters or bushwhackers in their midst; if they did, then the Union army would hold local civilians accountable.[18]

Confederate cavalry general Joseph Wheeler operated in the area, though, and had his mounted troops attacking Union supply trains, repeatedly wrecking portions of the Western & Atlantic. Some of his soldiers rested and received aid in Cassville, which was known by the U.S. Army. One raider during this time was a Canton man, Ben McCollum, who had fought with the Army of Northern Virginia, returned to Cherokee County, and become the head of a home guard unit. He and scores of men under his leadership ranged widely, especially across Cherokee and just to the north in Pickens County, and they struck terror wherever they went. As McCollum explained the situation, he had been sent to northern Georgia in the spring of 1864 by the Army of Northern Virginia to obtain horses. While at home, he had made a raid on the Union-controlled Western & Atlantic that so impressed General Wheeler that he asked McCollum to transfer out of the Army of Northern Virginia so he could stay and, in the words of McCollum, "operate in the line of the Western and Atlantic Railroad, tapping it at least once a week." Wheeler detailed some men from his command to work under McCollum.[19]

McCollum may have damaged the railroad, but he and his men were best known for attacking Unionist civilians. During this chaotic time, telling friend from foe was sometimes difficult. In fact, McCollum described wearing a Yankee uniform to trick a Unionist citizen into telling him information. On another occasion, McCollum and his men captured a fellow wearing "Yankee pants and the cap of a Confederate Colonel." McCollum's men soon hanged and shot to death this Pickens County resident, Milton Edwards. William Covington described five civilians McCollum and his men executed for aiding the Union; many more people may have died at their hands.[20]

McCollum and his men did not endear themselves to local inhabitants, not just Unionists. McCollum explained that his orders were "to subsist my Command on Government tithes." In other words, McCollum's Scouts, like the Union army foragers, would feed themselves and their horses and mules on provisions drawn from people in the area, many of whom were already in desperate circumstances. This provisioning did not increase McCollum's popularity, and not everyone accepted his legitimacy. Even before the war ended, in March 1865 a grand jury in Pickens County indicted McCollum on charges of both robbery and larceny.[21]

Crucially, though, the killing of ten U.S. soldiers accompanying a wagon train on the night of October 11, 1864, seems to have indicted Cassville. The soldiers' bodies were taken from where they were slain and dumped at the Cassville Female College, where Union soldiers were sleeping. Federal soldiers the next day burned both colleges in Cassville and a number of houses in town. A few weeks later, as Sherman's army prepared to evacuate Atlanta and head toward Savannah on its March to the Sea, the Union army ordered the burning of Canton and Cassville. On October 30, General John E. Smith sent orders to Colonel T. T. Heath of the Fifth Ohio Volunteer Cavalry to take his men to Canton, where he was to allow residents to empty their homes and businesses of anything they wanted, and then burn the town. Heath was then to move to Cassville and do the same thing there.[22]

When the federal soldiers arrived in Canton, Colonel Heath made his temporary headquarters in Governor Brown's home. Soldiers burned numerous businesses and homes; William and Susan Grisham's house was slated for burning. William was not home, but Susan went down the street to speak with Heath, who told her he had his orders. So Susan marshaled her enslaved people and those of her sister, who lived nearby, to pull out the furnishings from the house. But as soldiers looked through what was being put into the yard, one chanced upon William's Masonic apron in a chest of drawers. The soldier immediately took the apron to Colonel Heath, and the house went unmolested. Another Canton house was also saved because of Masonic membership. Heath finally left the Brown house, whereupon it was torched, and the soldiers moved on. The first Georgia newspaper to report the destruction, the *Macon Daily Telegraph and Confederate*, gave a brief, one-sentence notice: "The Yankees have burned most of Canton, Cherokee county, in retaliation for some tories who were hanged." In this context, "tories" would have been Unionist civilians, perhaps hanged by Ben McCollum and his men. Though some businesses, houses, and outbuildings were saved, the fires were damaging. Coming at the end of October, the burning of the town could not have made for a pleasant winter. In Cassville, the situation was more extreme. Three churches and three homes were all that stood when the soldiers finished. This burning effectively ended Cassville as a town, since much of the business of the county was moving already to Cartersville, which soon became the county seat.[23]

In November, Sherman's soldiers destroyed most of Atlanta and began the March to the Sea, leaving northern Georgia behind. One place they visited was Milledgeville, the capitol. Prisoners in the state penitentiary had long been building rolling stock for the Western & Atlantic and were also making rifles for the Confederates in their workshops. Before U.S. soldiers arrived, Brown paroled most of the prisoners as long as they agreed to fight for the Confederacy. Federal soldiers were not friends of Governor Brown, but they greatly advanced Brown's desire not to house prisoners in the state penitentiary, since it no longer existed after they burned it.[24]

Many people in the Etowah Valley were left with almost nothing. In January 1865, Governor Brown received a petition for aid from Bartow and Cherokee citizens, including ten "Solgers Wifes," who reminded the governor of the effects of the voracious armies, which left almost nothing behind. Weeks later, General William T. Wofford, a Bartow County native who had served in Virginia before being assigned to bring order in northern Georgia, wrote to Brown from Atlanta, "I find the country from here to Cartersville a perfect waste, worse than any portion of Virginia, the people are almost entirely destitute, women and children are beging for bread."[25]

Besides being concerned about ordinary people, Brown was also extremely interested in the Western & Atlantic. In December 1864, Brown had ordered an aide-de-camp, George W. Lee, to investigate the condition of the Western & Atlantic and also "to secure as far as practicable all property stolen or taken off improperly." Lee had a hard time; the weather was "the most disagreeable ever witnessed in this section," which slowed him, especially when he had to cross swollen streams. Lee's subsequent "Report of Examination into the Condition of the W. & A R. Road" was carefully detailed. Even before Lee reached Atlanta and the beginning of the Western & Atlantic, he spotted "the locomotive 'Etowah,' having been thrown from the track in a damaged condition." But Lee thought the engine was basically sound, so he had the engine put on the tracks and moved elsewhere temporarily. As Lee went along, for every mile of track he reported on the condition of the rails; how many were good, bent, ruined, and twisted; how many spikes and chairs (in which the rails rested) there were; and the condition of culverts and the road bed. He reported finding cow catchers, crank cars, and other materials as far as Calhoun, seventy-eight miles up the line, which was as far as he could safely travel.[26] That Lee's report went into Brown's personal papers, not the official papers of the governor's office, signals how much the railroad meant to Brown.

In February 1865, Brown sent a message to the legislators of Georgia, updating them on the miserable situation of Georgia and the Confederacy, defending Brown's efforts to protect the state, and asking them for more money with which to carry on the state's independence efforts. He also spoke directly about the destroyed penitentiary, estimating it would take $1 million to replace. Brown thought the penitentiary had not reformed its inmates but served as "a school for theft, lawlessness and villiany." People came out worse than when they went in. Brown advocated that the legislature let "other modes of punishment, such as hanging, whipping, branding, etc., be substituted."[27] Sherman's armies had done half of what Brown and Eli McConnell had advocated—end the penitentiary system. In time, Brown and his cronies would find a way to use prison labor outside the penitentiary walls.

During early 1865, destruction of the industrial capabilities built and maintained by former denizens of the Etowah Valley proceeded in Alabama. In March 1865, from the Tennessee River at the Mississippi and Alabama border, Union general James H. Wilson led almost fourteen thousand cavalry soldiers on a quick thrust into north-central Alabama, where Moses Stroup had been tending the fires first at Tannehill and then at Oxmoor. At the end of March, federal soldiers wrecked Stroup's ironworks at Oxmoor. A cavalry detachment attacked Tannehill briefly on its way to Tuscaloosa and, while returning, smashed the foundry and burned almost everything else that would aid in the making of iron. Moses Stroup was out of work—and left to ponder that of his six children, all three of his sons were dead because of the war. The Veitch brothers also were out of work.

Wilson's soldiers wrecked most of the remaining industry in Alabama as they took Selma and then made their way to Columbus, Georgia, and to Macon in the waning days of the war.[28]

In Macon, General Wilson met with Governor Joseph E. Brown, who was initially paroled, but Brown subsequently called the state legislature into session. Wilson interpreted Brown's action as hostile; he had Brown arrested and quickly on his way to Washington, D.C., where he spent two weeks in prison. While incarcerated, Brown received a letter from his wife, Elizabeth. She said that she had not yet been ousted from the governor's mansion and that Ira Foster had already stopped in to check on the family and offer help. Though their house in Canton had been burned, Elizabeth sent their son Julius, sixteen years old, to their farm in Cherokee County along the Etowah to see what was happening there. Elizabeth thought things might carry on much as they had before. Their former slaves in Milledgeville were still staying with Elizabeth, and she wondered whether the freedpeople at the farm would also remain. When Julius returned, he reported to his mother that "the negroes are all there yet; the crop is in very good order," but the situation was chaotic, with bandits stealing, bushwhackers threatening and shooting people, and arsonists burning a fence. In Canton, Elizabeth Brown's uncle William Grisham and his wife, Susan, already knew a new day was at hand. In March 1865, William Grisham duly noted in the family Bible under "Negroes births" that a couple he owned had named their new baby Sherman.[29]

Brown met personally with President Andrew Johnson while in the District of Columbia. Brown was eager to explain that his summoning of the legislature had not been meant to thwart federal control. The end of their meeting produced a second parole of Brown, and Brown not only pledged good behavior, but also agreed to encourage others to join in faithfully restoring and supporting the federal government. Brown returned to Georgia and soon was on his way to visit his farm and the burned homesite. At the end of June, Brown formally resigned his position as governor. In his farewell message, he said that while in some northern cities he had closely read the newspapers and talked with various people, and he wanted Georgians to know that slavery was dead, an "accomplished fact." Brown said Georgians should accept reality, be practical, and work out a labor system that would provide justice to everyone. Brown said he would immediately consider his former slaves to be free people and work out a crop-sharing or wage relationship with them. Brown believed that once the ill will created by the assassination of Abraham Lincoln subsided, most northerners would "exercise magnanimity," and Georgians would be best off taking an oath of allegiance to the United States and moving forward into the future.[30]

Brown practiced what he preached. That summer and fall he continually recommended to Georgians that they accept defeat in the war and that they array themselves as loyal citizens in service to the United States. He was careful, though, not to let the specific language of his parole be known. When it appeared that General Wilson did not know Brown had been paroled by Secretary of War Edwin Stanton and was interested in arresting him again, Brown was concerned that federal officials would just forward his second parole notice to Wilson. Brown worried that Wilson would use the language of the parole to damage Brown and suggest that his recommendations to the people of Georgia—that they accept the defeat of their rebellion and acquiesce to the federal government—were not Brown's genuine beliefs but a coercion created by the parole. Brown had been greatly sobered by the Confederacy's defeat and perhaps by his experience in prison, even if only for a few weeks, and he may well have worried that the loss of slavery would be followed by property seizure. Certainly Brown worried about whether he had a political future and about his financial prospects. As he wrote to his daughter Mary, who was in school in Athens, Georgia, "the future looks dark." Brown urged Mary, "I hope you will do all in your power to improve and secure a good education as it is uncertain whether you may have much else left." The daughter of the four-time governor could not count on her family connections and privilege to sustain her in the future, so she should improve her opportunities at school in the present. Brown said that paying the expenses of living, with three children away at school, was all he could manage. Brown was thinking, though, about possibilities. He instructed Mary, "If Col [M. C.] Fulton gets back tell him we [wish?] him here soon to have a meeting of the iron company."[31] Brown was hatching industrial plans for the future.

The Browns retained their close friends, notably Martha Fort, the widow of Tomlinson Fort, who died in 1859. When the Browns moved to Milledgeville, the Forts had befriended them. Martha Fort sent Elizabeth Brown peas from her garden, visited, and gave "a piece of sweet soap" and "oil cloth shoes" to the Browns' daughter Mary, who became a fast friend of Fannie, the youngest of the many Fort children. During the fall of 1865, Joe Brown bought a house in Atlanta, but it would be a few months until it was ready to live in; for a time it looked as though the Browns would move in with Martha Fort in Milledgeville temporarily.[32] Sympathetic feeling or similarity in outlook bound together the Forts and the Browns.

The Brown family would maintain ties to Cherokee County for a long time into the future—Joe Brown's parents still lived there, as did William and Susan Grisham and some other relatives—but Brown was finally taking John C. Calhoun's advice from twenty years earlier that Atlanta was the place to be. In 1867, William Grisham handed to the Inferior Court of Cherokee County "my receipts for the corn (and meal) sent by the Southern Relief Society of New York to this county." Grisham, in his usual fashion, had kept scrupulous records of hundreds of people, black and white, who had signed (often with an X, indicating their illiteracy) to receive charitable donations of food for the "destitute." In the column "Remarks," Grisham frequently wrote descriptions, such as "very old," "widow," "sickly," and "one arm."[33] Recovery, in the Etowah Valley, would be slow and painful for those who remained.

In 1873, a traveler passed through the area where the furnaces had been. He wrote, "The scenery along this route is unsurpassingly beautiful, but, it seems, is left to waste its beauty almost in solitude. The ruins of the old Etowah ironworks, scattered as they are for miles up the river and stamp Creek, to those who have seen them in full operation, in antebellum days, has a tendency rather to beget, than dispel, gloomy feelings." He recalled that "but a few short years ago the whole neighborhood for miles around these works was made resonant with the roaring of machinery, and the buzz and hum of industry," but now even the houses of the workers were almost all vacant, "or if occupied at all, by a thriftless, wandering, tenant, who is here today gone tomorrow." The writer regretted that "the furnace stacks all stand solitary and alone like a monument in a deserted graveyard, while the crumbling rock walls of the once stately flouring mill and the less pretending brick walls of the iron and brass foundry, have become the rendezvous of owls and bats. Three ponderous iron wheels which once, with electric speed, drove the machinery of the rolling mill, now stand as silent as so many tenants of the grave." The place had become overgrown with "briars, weeds and underbrush, and there is nothing left untouched by the fingers of decay to tell the story of their former greatness and grandeur, but the dashing, splashing and foaming waters of the Etowah and the craggy mountain peaks which surround the place like so many sentinels."[34]

The effort to make the Etowah Valley a central and industrialized part of a new nation, the Confederate States of America, had fallen apart, and the works that Joseph E. Brown, his network, and many others had built on the ruins of the Cherokee Nation were now thrown down and cast into ruin. Many of the people who had built the iron furnaces and the Western & Atlantic were dead: Jacob Stroup (1846), Ker Boyce (1854), Tomlinson Fort (1859), Charles McDonald (1860), Farish Carter (1861), John S. Rowland (1863), John W. Lewis (1865), and Stephen H. Long (1865). But Joseph E. Brown was only forty-four years old in 1865, with plenty of life and vigor. Though Brown and others were leaving or had already left the Etowah Valley behind, the values they formed and expressed there, and their insights into how to bring together forms of mining, industrialization, and transportation, in combination with the support of government, in order to realize their goals of development and wealth would remain, especially in three southeastern cities: Atlanta, Chattanooga, and Birmingham.

CHAPTER 7

Anew

THE DEFEAT OF THE CONFEDERACY, THE EMANCIPATION OF MORE than four million people, and the disbanding of Confederate armies, which sent soldiers back to often radically changed homes and communities, put people in new situations and often made existing plans obsolete. Even very talented and capable people were not sure what to do. Some people left, including Ira Foster, who abandoned the Etowah Valley and Georgia for opportunities elsewhere. Other people, such as Mark A. Cooper, tried unsuccessfully to stitch together a newly integrated industrial enterprise. Cooper's lasting effect on Georgia during this period lay in his advocacy for a convict labor system, which soon garnered state government approval. The person who took most advantage of that system was Joseph E. Brown, who struggled for years in the late 1860s with how to proceed before hitting on a winning formula that changed his life and shaped much of Georgia and the southeastern United States.

In the tumult of Reconstruction, Brown tried to figure out a pathway into the future for himself. Politically, he was comfortable with the conservative Republicans led by Andrew Johnson and anxious about the Radical Republicans, who he feared might force the people of the former Confederacy to pay the national debts accrued during the war. Brown, therefore, did everything in his power to allay northerners' fears of the South and to get southern whites to accept what had to be accepted and move on from the disastrous Civil War. Personally, Brown wished to improve his finances. He still owned thousands of acres of land, but in Reconstruction Georgia the value of that land was uncertain. And so Brown went in new directions that his political commitments of previous years would never have hinted at. The chief surprise is that a half year after he resigned as governor and the Confederacy ended, Brown became a secret informant for the U.S. Treasury Department.

It is hard to say how long this deal had been in the works. Conceivably, its origins were in Brown's meeting with President Johnson the previous June. Brown was implicitly under threat and also had useful information. The position of the United States was that everything owned by the Confederacy was now controlled by the federal government. But since records were sometimes burned or strewn, ownership could be hard to establish. Some businesses and individuals took advantage of the confusion to garner for themselves various commodities. Joe Brown knew better than most what belonged to whom. And so, in January 1866, Joe Brown and a Macon banker, Increase Cook Plant, reported that a railroad corporation had taken sixty miles of railroad iron that had belonged to the Confederate government. Brown and Plant also reported that the president or superintendent of the railroad bought five hundred bales of cotton with money he had received from the Confederate government, and they told where the cotton was stored. In return for their information, Brown and Plant were to receive one-quarter of the value of what the Treasury Department recovered. The agreement also stipulated that the Treasury Department was not to reveal Brown's or Plant's name.[1] One can understand why this secrecy was necessary for Brown since his future political opportunities would evaporate if word got out. But it also indicates perhaps how desperate Brown was to make money or the pressures that could be brought to bear on him by the federal government. While imprisoned in Washington, D.C., Brown was hardly in a position to refuse if President Johnson asked him to help the U.S. government to avoid pilfering in post-Confederate Georgia.

Brown also accepted a retainer of $5,000 to help four Augusta banks emerge from their financially embarrassed situations. Prior to the Civil War, Brown's criticism of banks as always taking advantage of the public had been a central calling card for him among the voting population. Now, Brown pocketed the bankers' money and went to work for them.[2]

Brown also tried, naturally, to use his existing connections. John W. Lewis had died in 1865, leaving behind his wife and seven children. One, Harriet, had married Joe Brown's younger brother James R. Brown. In 1866, the state legislature incorporated the Lewis Manufacturing and Mining Company, which was essentially the reconstituted Fulton and Company created in 1864, minus Lewis. The incorporators included M. C. Fulton, Joe Brown, and James Brown, whom Lewis had made the administrator of his estate. With the creation of this iron-manufacturing company, Brown was embracing his past. Brown and his fellow incorporators were taking the lands in the Etowah Valley once owned by Lewis and now controlled by his son and son-in-law (Joe Brown's brother James), adding in other people with money, and seeking to revive the iron furnace that Lewis had run. They thought the furnace might be repaired and put back into operation using the iron ore, limestone, and timber available on more than four thousand acres of land. But over the next few years, the company failed. Fulton apparently went into personal bankruptcy by 1868, and in 1870 all of the company's land was sold at a sheriff's sale in Bartow County for $8,600.[3] Was this failure caused not just by financial shakiness but also because the investing group lacked the expertise in iron production that Lewis had possessed? Whatever the reason, Joe Brown's investments were not panning out.

During the late 1860s, Brown consistently encouraged Georgians to accept what was necessary for full rehabilitation into the Union, and he worked for sectional reconciliation. Brown was the chair of a group that in early 1867 invited for a visit Henry Ward Beecher, the prominent abolitionist preacher and brother of the author of *Uncle Tom's Cabin*, Harriet Beecher Stowe. In March 1867, Brown published *An Appeal to the People of Georgia*, in which he wrote that he had grown up steeped in the political principles of John C. Calhoun, yet Brown had changed. Brown fell away so much from his earlier political beliefs that in 1868 he supported a Republican, Rufus Bullock, for governor. Brown envisioned that Bullock would win and keep the capital in Atlanta, where it had moved temporarily. Brown thought the state could have a new capitol building "hewn out of Stone Mountain with convict labor." Bullock won and appointed Brown to a twelve-year term as chief justice of the Georgia Supreme Court. Brown accepted the position rather than risk political invisibility, but he could not have wanted the job. It required him to give up his lucrative legal practice for a yearly salary of only $2,500. Brown did not abandon the things he cared about, however. Late in 1869 he joined the Atlanta Board of Education and served as chair for well over a decade. Meanwhile, Brown cast his eyes about, anticipating the future.[4]

That future was very uncertain. Talented, hardworking people lost their way. Ira R. Foster had business dealings in Georgia, including logging interests and a gold mine in Cherokee County. In 1866, he and some partners also incorporated the Island Manufacturing Company, located on the Etowah River in Bartow County. The manufacturing company was authorized to produce woolen and cotton goods, or be a gristmill, or manufacture things of wood or any metal, or tan leather, or produce shoes or paper. The unfocused business amounted to nothing. In late 1867 or 1868 Foster and several families from the Etowah Valley all moved to northern Alabama and created new lives there.[5]

Mark A. Cooper stayed in Georgia and tried to forge a future for himself and the state that would include convict labor. In 1866 Governor Charles Jenkins appointed Cooper, notable politician Howell Cobb, and John H. Fitten of Adairsville, a Bartow County stop on the Western & Atlantic, to recommend a new site for the Georgia penitentiary. Their report, submitted to the governor in November 1866, began with a blistering attack on teaching convicts skills to become mechanics, which the commissioners argued made mechanics feel degraded in their profession. The commissioners also focused on anticipated changes in the prison population, which they expected to be "filled to overflowing with the very worst portion of the Negro population." Therefore, the commissioners supported the abandonment of teaching convicts the skills they needed to work as mechanics.[6]

The commissioners said the location of a new penitentiary should be determined by how well it could be used to develop the resources of Georgia. The commissioners preferred Stone Mountain, just east of Atlanta, the largest natural outcropping of granite in the world. The prisoners could mine the materials to build the walls and buildings of the new penitentiary, greatly reducing the expenses of construction and transportation. Once built, the location would keep convicts busy for eternity. Stone Mountain was also desirable, said the commissioners, because of its proximity to the route of the Western & Atlantic. The commissioners envisioned a special "convict Train" that would carry the prisoners up and down the railroad line; they would be housed at night on the train cars and work daily in the various mines near its tracks or on the railroad itself. The commissioners thought that if Stone Mountain were rejected, the site of the new penitentiary ought to be on the Western & Atlantic, which would synergistically benefit the state.[7]

The report is remarkable for the way it echoed the ideas of Joseph E. Brown, though Cooper's own voice is also distinct. The authors advocated permanently getting rid of the Milledgeville state penitentiary and included Brown's and Eli McConnell's ideas of having convicts work on the

Western & Atlantic Railroad or in mining or industry connected to the Western & Atlantic. Soon, the legislature passed an act that allowed private entities to take on the prisoners of Georgia.[8]

One person who hoped to make use of this act, which had been prompted in part by his own recommendations, was Mark Cooper. In December 1866, Cooper incorporated the Bartow Foundry and Manufacturing Company, which was authorized to make metal castings at a foundry to be built near Cartersville. Perhaps Cooper imagined that convict labor could run the foundry. He was also one of four men who in 1866 incorporated the Iron and Mining Company of Dade County, Georgia. A few years later, Cooper involved himself with the Cartersville and Van Wert Railroad. In 1869, Cooper became head of this railroad, but financing was difficult to obtain, and the project went bankrupt. Cooper resigned his position as president late in 1870, having spent a year and a half unsuccessfully trying to make the railroad a reality.[9] Cooper had a plan that could have included a railroad, a foundry, his Dade County mining company, and perhaps convict labor, but he could not integrate these pieces nor make them work out. Even for someone as prominent and experienced as Cooper, there were no guarantees.

After Joe Brown's iron company in Bartow County went broke in June 1870, his big chance came later that year. The Western & Atlantic had become a political sore spot: Georgians complained that it was a source of patronage and vast corruption. Far too many employees who did not know anything about railroads held their jobs because they were related to state legislators or other public officials. The Western & Atlantic was no longer contributing to the state treasury, so the legislature considered leasing the railroad. In 1870, a legislator roughly drafted a bill to get it on the legislative calendar and then went to Chief Justice Brown and asked him to improve the legislation. Brown had just been gifted with the opportunity of a lifetime. He rewrote the bill, which promptly passed the legislature, leaving Brown in a perfect position to take advantage of the legislation he had written.[10] The new act authorized a lease of the state-owned railroad for twenty years to a company that would put up a bond worth $8 million and promise to pay to the state treasury at least $25,000 each month for the duration of the lease. A key clause required a majority of the lessees to have at least five years' residence in Georgia. Another important part dictated that the only people who could vote on matters related to the Western & Atlantic were the original lessees—in essence, a poison pill to prevent a later takeover of the lease.[11] Brown immediately resigned his position on the Georgia Supreme Court and worked to assemble a powerful group to bid to lease the railroad.

Another formidable group of Georgia railroaders, worried that an alliance of the Georgia Railroad and the Western & Atlantic would be detrimental to their interests, also lined up. These two strongest groups, rather than risk getting nothing, saw it in their interest to work together. Bids were due on Christmas Day, and the two sides negotiated right to the deadline. The combined alliance of twenty-three lessees bid the minimum per month, $25,000. Two other bids came in, each offering higher amounts monthly, more than $30,000. Whether through political shenanigans or based on a genuine belief that Brown's group could actually hold the lease successfully, Governor Rufus Bullock awarded it to Brown's group after he found one lease company bid to be invalid and the other lacking in its bonded guarantees.[12] Bullock may have anticipated that one of the lessees, his right-hand man, Hannibal I. Kimball, would lead the Western & Atlantic, but when the dust settled, the lessees made Brown the president. With twenty-three different people involved, it is debatable whether the railroad itself would have brought Brown much money directly, but Brown used his control over the railroad to assist with his projects in other areas, creating an integrated business empire that would keep costs low and bring back enormous profits.

One partner in this empire was Brown's eldest son, Julius. After his 1870 graduation from Harvard Law School, Julius became the chief attorney in his father's enterprises, including the Western & Atlantic, and his legal education undoubtedly helped bring the Brown family into a different era of corporate organization. In 1871, Julius connected the Brown family even more closely to the Fort family by marrying Frances G. "Fannie" Fort, the youngest of Tomlinson and Martha Fort's thirteen children. Julius and Fannie built their Atlanta home across the street from his parents, a symbol of the close family connections. But Julius was not a clone of his father. A child of privilege, he enjoyed collecting various things, including "bric-a-brac and curiosities." He joined the Young Men's Christian Association in Atlanta and hosted fancy dinners at which alcohol was served.[13]

Joe Brown also cultivated relationships at the other end of the Western & Atlantic, in Chattanooga and the surrounding area, where the efforts of the original investors still mattered. Ker Boyce's estate was controlled by his son James, who had good training. Before James went to college, his father had him work in Leroy M. Wiley's wholesale dry goods store in Charleston for six months. Wiley, of course, was a close associate of Farish Carter, and Ker Boyce was a partner in Wiley's Charleston firm years before Wiley joined with Mark A. Cooper and Moses Stroup in the iron business. James P. Boyce became highly religious; after college and seminary, his talents and connections took him up the ladder of Baptist leadership until he became head of the South Carolina State Convention in 1871. During this time he administered his father's estate, which required numerous trips to Chattanooga, where his brother, Samuel Johnston Boyce, lived.[14]

As high-powered Southern Baptists, Brown and James P. Boyce probably had known one another before they faced off in 1863 at a Baptist convention in Augusta in a debate over whether to pronounce their support for the Confederate government and lament the recent death of Stonewall Jackson. Boyce opposed the resolutions on the grounds that they mixed the church too much with politics, whereupon Governor Brown gave a speech in which he said, "All must admit that the institution of slavery is one of the prime causes of the war," and its continuation depended on Confederate military victories. "God in his providence has sent the heathen among us, and it is our duty to civilize and christianize them." Accordingly, all Christians needed to support the Confederate government in all of its constitutional efforts. Brown said that Southern Baptists should not make an idol of Stonewall Jackson but trust that God would send another person to take his place. He encouraged Boyce not to oppose the resolutions, which then went forward unanimously.[15]

In 1872, Boyce was in charge of finding a new home for the fledgling Southern Baptist Theological Seminary, begun in Greenville, South Carolina, which had suspended operations during the Civil War. Boyce prevailed on Brown, who was always interested in Baptist affairs and education, to join the seven-member relocation committee. Boyce traveled with the committee members as they visited the four chief cities vying for the seminary—Atlanta, Chattanooga, Memphis, and Louisville. Boyce liked Chattanooga very much but became concerned that his substantial landholdings there would open him to charges that he was favoring his personal and familial financial prospects. In the end, the seminary went to Louisville, as did Boyce, as its head.[16]

The same year Brown served on Boyce's committee, Brown and three other men leased thousands of acres of coal lands in far northwestern Georgia, another sign of Brown's ability to put together an integrated industrial juggernaut. The main family that controlled these coal lands, virtually the only coal in Georgia, was the Gordons. Beginning in the 1830s in

Eatonton, where his brother Charles had worked with Cooper on a railroad convention, Zachariah H. Gordon became a Baptist minister, ran Gordon Springs, and invested in coal property in Dade County. He bought his first Dade property in 1835 and by 1850 began purchasing several coal properties, mostly at high, difficult to access elevations. Gordon's original property was in an area called Castle Rock. In 1855 and 1856, the Gordons got charters from both Tennessee and Georgia to build a railroad that would run from the Shell Mound depot on the Nashville and Chattanooga Railroad southward to the coal beds. The Nickajack Railroad and Mining Company, running about eight miles up Nickajack Creek to the coal beds, began at the mouth, where Joseph E. Brown's kin had been killed in 1788.[17]

Zachariah's son John B. Gordon went into Confederate service in 1861 and became a celebrated general. In 1862, Zachariah and others incorporated the Castle Rock Coal Mining Company. The mines were damaged and closed before the end of the Civil War, but in 1867 John B. Gordon leased all the property of the company for five years. Every bushel of coal (about eighty pounds) would yield a royalty of one and a half cents to the Castle Rock Coal Company, and the lease detailed Gordon's obligation to build the partially completed Nickajack Railroad; the Castle Rock Coal Company already owned a locomotive engine and railroad iron, and the railroad line was graded. Gordon traveled to Pennsylvania, where he entered an agreement with four men from Lehigh County to finish the railroad and work the coal mines.[18]

Five years later, when the lease expired, John B. Gordon did not renew it. Rather, a group drawn from among the nine directors and president of the Castle Rock Coal Company, including Joe Brown, leased the approximately five thousand acres under the company's control on far better terms. Their lease ran for fifteen years, with another fifteen-year option, and they had to pay a royalty of only a half cent per bushel, one-third of what Gordon had contracted for. Plus they got the benefit of the Nickajack Railroad, which had been completed.[19]

How long Brown and the Gordon family had known each other, and when and how Brown became a director of the Castle Rock Coal Company are unknown.[20] Given Brown's connections to Cooper and their mutual interest in railroads, and given Brown's activity as a prominent lay Baptist, Brown had almost certainly met Zachariah Gordon much earlier. Brown would not have ignored a wealthy Baptist preacher who was mining coal and building a private railroad.

In February 1873, Brown and his fellow lessees of the Castle Rock en-

The *John W. Thomas*, belonging to the Dade Coal Company,
ran on the Nickajack Railroad to the coal beds.
Courtesy of the Hargrett Rare Book and Manuscript Library, University of Georgia.

terprise joined with Julius Brown and a few other investors and railroad men to incorporate the Dade Coal Company. Brown presided over and managed the company, and thus the ingredients for prosperity and power were coming together. Brown controlled the Western & Atlantic, leased mines in Dade County, and had access to a small railroad to get the coal to the Nashville and Chattanooga Railroad, from which it would soon be on the Western & Atlantic.

Brown could help people out, and he could damage his foes. In Atlanta, the Schofield rolling mills, which bought coal from Brown, complained about the quality. Louis Schofield said he had to mix Dade County coal with better coal from elsewhere. Schofield may have regretted his complaint, though, because in 1873 the Western & Atlantic, a major customer, ceased buying railroad iron from the Schofield mills, which went bankrupt the following year.[21]

In 1873 in the same session that chartered Dade Coal, the legislature also chartered the Rogers Iron Company of Bartow County, which ran an iron furnace at the Rogers station on the Western & Atlantic, north of Cartersville. The company was named after Robert L. Rogers, an enterprising man who ran lime kilns, a sawmill, and a wood and water station for the Western & Atlantic. People called his operation "BobRogersville." Begin-

ning in September 1872, after having seen iron ore lying on the surface in
the area, in two months Rogers built an iron furnace that was thirty-two
feet at the base and thirty-five feet high. It was a coal-fired furnace, and
Rogers was using 1,200–1,500 bushels of coal daily to burn iron ore into
six tons of iron product. Joseph E. Brown's name was not among the four
incorporators in 1873, but he was clearly an unnamed partner because the
day before the incorporation the state legislature passed an act prohibiting the sale of "spirituous or malt liquors" within a mile of the Rogers iron
furnace and the Castle Rock Coal Company and prohibiting the sale of any
intoxicating liquor within two miles of the works of the Dade Coal Company.[22] Obviously all three companies were connected, which made perfect sense. Rogers could not operate without a steady supply of coal, which
would virtually require him to work with Brown through the Dade Coal
Company and the Western & Atlantic. If Brown wanted to be a partner,
Rogers could not refuse him. For Brown, Rogers's furnace meant a market for his coal and additional tons of freight hauled daily on the Western
& Atlantic.

The other Brown family investment in Bartow County came the same
year—1873—when Julius Brown and four others incorporated the Georgia Iron and Coal Company. The company mined Bartow County iron ore,
much of it owned by James R. Brown, who repurchased in 1874 for $4,500
most of the property that had been part of John W. Lewis's holdings and
that had sold for $8,600 three years earlier.[23]

The final crucial ingredient in the business empire Brown was building
was labor. Who would do the work, and at what price? In 1866, one month
after Cooper and the other commissioners reported to the governor, the
legislature passed a law authorizing convict lease, though the first contract was not issued until 1868. The contract leased out a hundred black
convicts for one year to work on the Georgia and Alabama Railroad. The
lease was made to William A. Fort, a nephew of Tomlinson Fort who had
married a daughter of Zachariah Hargrove, the Cassville attorney who had
partnered with Fort, Farish Carter, and the Williams brothers in the development of Chattanooga.[24] Over and over again, the families that initi-
ated a developed Georgia of railroads, mills, furnaces, and banks were the
same families, decades later, still dedicated to these avenues of profit and
economic development. Eugene LeHardy, the Belgian engineer who was
stranded in Europe when he went to buy arms for the Confederacy, reap-
peared as the chief engineer on the Selma, Rome, and Dalton Railroad,
where he approved of convict lease workers as "efficient, effectual, [and]

reliable." LeHardy liked that convict labor brought revenue to the state government at the same time that it lowered the expenses of a penitentiary, and he believed it had deterrent effects on potential criminals.[25]

What Fort began in 1868 expanded the following year, when railroad contractors Grant, Alexander and Company were awarded every convict in the control of the state. So in 1870, when John T. Grant of Grant, Alexander and Company joined the Western & Atlantic lease group, and in 1873 when he partnered with Joe Brown in the Dade Coal Company, he not only brought extensive railroad construction and operation experience, he also brought the lessons of using convict labor. In 1874, the governor urged that the leases be lengthened from a maximum of two years to five. Brown, in partnership with John T. Grant and Grant's son William, leased convicts to work in the Dade Coal Company mines, the beginning of a powerful labor supply for Joseph E. Brown. Prisoners in Georgia had been leased for public works—mostly railroads—in Georgia, but an 1874 alteration to the law allowed convict lease "on any public or private works in the State of Georgia." Of the 616 available prisoners, by the end of 1874 Brown's Dade Coal controlled the labor of more than 150 at a cost to Dade Coal of under $800. By 1876, Dade Coal was guaranteed at least 300 convicts for the next twenty years. The state of Georgia liked leasing prisoners to Dade Coal in part because most prisoners worked underground and were even sometimes housed in the mines themselves, and the Dade mines were in such a mountainous, rugged, and isolated place there were almost no escapees.[26]

Prisoners in Georgia prior to the Civil War had almost always been white. There were few free black people, and enslaved black people who committed infractions were routinely dealt with outside of the legal system, mostly by their owners. After the Civil War, though, prisoners were overwhelmingly black. Some were violent criminals, but many people were convicted of crimes such as burglary and sentenced to ten years' imprisonment. Most prisoners were men, but some were women, and some were youths. Whites with political power set up the criminal justice system to provide a measure of the control over black labor that the slave system had once provided.[27]

The work in the Dade County coal mines was grueling. Men descended into the mines, and each went to a room off the main shaft, seeing by the light of his oil headlamp. During the day, each convict was responsible for between four and five tons of coal. An investigative committee sent by the state of Georgia in 1890 actually went into the mines and was appalled by what they discovered. Seams of coal could range from a foot and a half to four feet in height, which meant they found men who had to work on their stomachs, often in mud or water, with poor ventilation. Convicts dug underneath the coal seam and then blasted, using shot powder, which dislodged the coal. Then convicts gathered the coal, ideally separating it from slate or other debris, loaded it into a coal car on a track, and pushed it to the surface. If these black convicts failed to make their task for the day, they were whipped. Whipping was remarkably frequent; some men received a whipping before they even started working. Mine owners also tortured prisoners by strapping them to a board and then pouring water into their nostrils, which simulated the experience of drowning, inducing panic. One man's heart gave out, and he died from the experience, but the white men in charge came to prefer this terror-inducing form of discipline because workers could resume their labor after it was over without any physical marks or impairment.[28]

Like any mining operation in the late nineteenth century, the work was dangerous. Laborers tried to avoid being whipped by mining sufficient coal, but they were also responsible for safety work, such as timbering the roofs of the areas where they worked, which did not count toward their daily tonnage requirements. Inevitably, safety measures lagged, and workers were injured or killed as a result. Explosive blasts sometimes injured convicts, as did coal car accidents, pick wounds, and cave-ins in the mines. Between 1888 and 1894, the roughly five hundred workers at the Dade Mines experienced fifteen fatalities and more than a hundred injuries.[29]

Brown's mines were so terrifying and memorable that they entered into lore, including into African American music. In the 1920s a work song recorded in Georgia said:

> Joe Brown, Joe Brown,
> he's a mean white man
> he's a mean white man
> I know, honey he put
> them shackles around
> around my leg.[30]

In 1932, folklorist Lawrence Gellert heard a chain gang near Augusta, Georgia, singing a dreary ballad, "Joe Brown's Coal Mine." The convicts sang:

Sez ahm boun' to Joe Brown's coal mine
Sez ahm boun' to Joe Brown's coal mine
An' it's Lawdy me an' it's Lawdy mine
Sez ahm boun' to Joe Brown's coal mine.
Sez ahm goin' ef ah don' stay long
Sez ahm goin' ef ah don' stay long
An' it's Oh me, an' it's Oh mine
Sez ahm goin' ef ah don' stay long.
Dat's the train dat ah leave heah on
Sez dat's the train dat ah leave heah on . . .
Sez ahm boun' to dat Sundown job.[31]

That the mines made it into song in Georgia for decades afterward is one indication of the profound impression they made on the people who worked there and on the convicts' families and friends. Political investigations and newspapers chronicled and documented some of the realities of convict labor, but these songs capture elements missing from politics and mass media.

Certainly, the physical place itself was distinctive. One of the few unofficial visitors to Brown's Dade County mines was indefatigable evangelist Elizabeth R. Wheaton, who went to convict labor camps all across the South. She described the Dade coal mines district as "one of the most weird and desolate-looking places." Wheaton rode the Nickajack Railroad, which at first had a small passenger car, but during her later trips she rode on the engine since all the cars carried coal. Wheaton was determined to gain access to more convicts than just the ones who ran the train but "was often in great danger of my clothes taking fire as the fire blazed out of the engine when the men were shoveling in the coal. The railroad zig-zagged up the mountain, and once, a sister and myself were obliged to ride on the coal-box." In that instance, Wheaton kneeled in the coal box and held on for dear life: "As the engine twisted and turned, I was in danger of falling, and it was hundreds of feet down to the foot of the precipices in places where our train crept along."[32] Wheaton survived to tell her tale, and her account underscores the isolation of the Dade coal mines. Convicts were almost completely cut off from the rest of the world; the people Brown and his partners hired to run the mines were often entirely without oversight. State inspectors arrived now and then, but almost always with advance notice. The system that Joe Brown had advocated for in his twenties as a state legislator in 1849 and 1850 now had become an integral part

The Dade Coal Company roasted coal in beehive ovens
to produce coke, which fueled iron furnaces.
Courtesy of the Georgia Archives, RG50-2-33, ah01631.

of the criminal justice system of Georgia—to the personal enrichment of
Brown and his partners.

In 1876, Brown acquired one final ingredient in his budding empire—
the Rising Fawn iron furnace. Rising Fawn was in southern Dade County.
New York investors had built a massive iron furnace there in 1874, but the
company fell apart financially. Brown swooped in and acquired the furnace. Thereafter, coal drawn from the Dade mines went four miles via a
narrow-gauge railroad to Rising Fawn furnace, where workers loaded sixty
beehive coke ovens that turned the coal into coke, suitable for the furnace.
The pig iron produced in the furnace then traveled on a broad-gauge track
one mile to reach the Alabama and Chattanooga Railroad, from whence
it could be transported almost anywhere. The scale of iron production
had changed dramatically since Jacob Stroup built iron furnaces in the
Etowah Valley in the late 1830s and early 1840s. Yet Joe Brown was apply-
ing his antebellum knowledge in these postbellum ventures. Brown was
only six years removed from his failed Bartow County iron-making enterprise, but those six years had been a whirlwind of activity in which Brown
consistently came out on top, building an integrated extractive, industrial,
and transportation behemoth that would make Brown the most power-

The Rising Fawn iron furnace, massive in comparison to antebellum
furnaces, demonstrates the changing scale of iron production.
Courtesy of the Georgia Archives, RG50-2-33, ah01633.

ful man in Georgia until his death in 1894 and give him enormous control
over the economy of the state and participation in the growth of the entire
Southeast.[33]

Brown was not finished with state office, though he was very politically
unpopular in Georgia. Some Georgians were upset with Brown because
he had led them down the path of secession into disaster. Many more people, though, saw Brown as an unscrupulous opportunist who had left the
Democratic Party for the Republican Party after the war (and become
chief justice of Georgia as a result), only to return to the Democrats once
the Republicans were routed, telling people all the while to make their
peace with the federal government. Brown was powerful, but it was difficult to see how he could win elective office by appealing to the public for
their votes. So Brown took office in another way.

One of Georgia's senators in 1880 was John B. Gordon, the son of Zachariah Gordon of Dade County. Gordon's successful exploits as a Confederate general made him a very popular figure after the war, and yet Gordon
had trouble translating adulation into money. His business ventures generally fell flat. Immediately after the Civil War he started a lumber business, which failed in 1867. He took the Castle Rock coal lease and aban-

doned it after the five years was finished. He also ran unsuccessfully for governor as a Democrat against Rufus Bullock in the 1868 election. Next he became involved with two publishing companies and a central figure in the Southern Life Insurance Company. The publishing business turned out to be rocky, and Southern Life declared bankruptcy in 1876. With a wife and five children, and houses in both Atlanta and Washington, D.C., Gordon had trouble living on a senator's salary, which he had drawn since he was sent by the state legislature to Washington in 1873.[34]

Gordon's financial problems were Joe Brown's leverage, and the public in Georgia was shocked when in 1880 Gordon abruptly resigned his Senate seat, and Governor Alfred Colquitt immediately appointed Brown as the replacement. There were howls of protest, and most people thought the men had made secret deals. But the three main figures involved—Gordon, Colquitt, and Brown, often called the "Bourbon Triumvirate" because they were the leading politicians in Georgia for decades—all proclaimed their innocence; no evidence emerged at the time of their skullduggery, and the deed was done. Gordon and Brown were not fans of each other. Among other things, Brown had backed Gordon's Republican opponent in the 1868 gubernatorial race. Brown may have envied Gordon's popularity, while Gordon knew that Brown had taken the same coal lease (on far more favorable terms than Gordon had negotiated) and turned the Gordon family coal mines into wealth. Brown and Gordon were not enemies, though, and recognized ways they could work together. In the case of the Senate seat, Brown used Henry Grady, the New South proponent and editor of the *Atlanta Constitution*, as an intermediary. Grady even created code words they could use in their telegrams back and forth. Through Grady, Brown secretly arranged a position for Gordon as an attorney with the Louisville and Nashville Railroad with a substantially higher paycheck than his Senate post, and he busily negotiated how many thousands of dollars of Gordon's paycheck would be provided by the Western & Atlantic Railroad. Once the expected offer was tendered, Gordon took it. Colquitt was happy to gain Brown's support because Colquitt wanted to be reelected to the governorship. Brown spent the next decade as a senator, which meant he wielded significant power and could deflect attacks on the convict labor system and his operation of the Dade coal mines. Once again, Brown acted as a crony, utilizing secret deals with people he knew, inside and outside government, to get his way.[35]

Scholars uncovered Brown's secret political deal involving John B. Gordon many years ago. What has gone unmentioned is Brown's long connec-

tion to John's father, Zachariah Gordon, the Baptist minister who put together the coal lands and mines that became operated by Dade Coal, or
how John B. Gordon's uncle Charles P. Gordon worked with Mark A. Cooper in the 1830s to call a railroad convention that led to the first railroad
charter issued by the state. Brown was still working with a circle of Baptist
miners and railroad promoters, using associations and connections that
were long standing.

In the late nineteenth century the United States was a place in which
mining, railroads, iron, and steel construction played large roles. Brown
had been prepared for that world in the hills of northern Georgia as he
saw the gold rushers around him and saw the earth exploited in ever more
profound ways. Brown took notes, and as he married into Baptist fortune and earned the trust and mentorship of people like William and Joseph Grisham, John W. Lewis and Mark A. Cooper, he acquired slaves,
learned about the iron industry, sold land for a copper mine, and became
ardently attached to a railroad that sliced through what had once been the
home of the Cherokees. When Brown went to Milledgeville as governor,
he took many of these Etowah River friends along with him, but he did
not stop there. Brown acquired new cronies, people with national reach,
people with money in far-flung places. It took Brown a few years after the
Civil War, but he regained his footing and built an enormous business empire on the backs of convicts with the help of the state government he ran
for eight years. All in all, the gold rush, considering the iron industry it
spawned and the people it attracted to northern Georgia, had profound
effects on the subsequent development of the state and region.

EPILOGUE

THE EFFORTS OF JOSEPH E. BROWN AND HIS CRONIES HAD LONG-
range implications for the development of the Southeast. In February 1880, Brown wrote to James P. Boyce. The Southern Baptist Theological Seminary was having a rough time financially in Louisville; school
leaders were thinking of suspending operations, which might mean its de-
mise. The Panic of 1873 had erased the ability of some well-wishers to fund
the seminary as they had hoped, and Boyce had requested that someone
donate a major gift. Brown wrote that he was interested. He had apparently seen Boyce not long before, since he reported, "My health is about as
when I saw you last, though it is rather feeble at best." Boyce, unsurprisingly, wrote back to encourage Brown. Brown's next letter to Boyce implied
a substantial gift, and Brown wanted the money taken care of properly.
Most of the letter was about how various railroads were doing and which
ones Brown thought Boyce ought to avoid or invest in so that Brown's
gift would help the seminary in perpetuity. For Brown, investing in railroads seemed secure—and it was the arena Brown knew best. The correspondence is also a reminder of the relationship that Brown and Boyce
enjoyed, given the numerous things they talked about, including Baptist
matters and Chattanooga, where Boyce continued to manage his father's
estate. Brown did give a substantial gift—$50,000—which kept the South-
ern Baptist Theological Seminary from suspending and gave other potential donors confidence in the school. Brown had already served as a trustee
from 1872 to 1877. In 1880 he became chair of the board, and he served in
that position until his death in 1894.[1] Donations picked up after Brown's
gift, an event that changed the trajectory of the school to a path that made
it the most important Baptist seminary in the United States.

Boyce, living in Louisville as he ran the seminary, had an attorney in Chattanooga to manage his interests there: Tomlinson Fort Jr. Much like the children of Ker Boyce, the children of Tomlinson and Martha Fort had a huge interest in Chattanooga. Tomlinson Fort Jr. had joined the Confederacy and fought throughout the war. Rising to the rank of captain and wounded five times, he fell ill in North Carolina and was unconscious for two months, during which time the war ended. He made his way home wearing a buttonless Confederate jacket and secured mules to pull a wagon that he took to Chattanooga. Soon he was under arrest. He had gone to dine wearing his gray Confederate jacket, and a black waiter would not serve Fort and called him a "damn Rebel." A history of Chattanooga related that Fort "sprang from his chair and chased the waiter to the kitchen explaining as he went to all and sundry that he did not in the least mind being called a 'Rebel' but that the oath which accompanied the title could not go unpunished!" What Fort did to the waiter was unstated; the charges against Fort were later dropped.[2]

Fort soon obtained different clothes and became a civic leader. He served as Chattanooga's recorder, attorney, and mayor and served on the Board of Public Works for six years. He helped establish the Chattanooga Fire Department. And he carried on a law practice, through which he took care of his father's property, much of which stayed in the family's hands. In 1907, Tomlinson Fort Jr. was still administering the Boyce estate. The relationships created in the 1830s were still relevant. Other Forts also moved to Chattanooga, including his sisters Kate and Fannie. When Fannie's husband, Julius Brown, died in 1910, his will gave a portion of his estate to the Georgia Institute of Technology. Fannie contested the will, and her brother Tomlinson was her attorney.[3]

In 1887, Julius Brown still lived in Atlanta but was temporarily in Birmingham, where he gave his brother-in-law Tomlinson Fort Jr. power of attorney to act on his behalf in Tennessee. Why Brown was in Birmingham is unknown, but the Brown family certainly would have had reason to visit. Birmingham was a postwar city, founded in 1871. A key figure in the founding was a native Georgian, John T. Milner, who had helped to create Birmingham by deciding on the route of the South and North Railroad in Alabama, which crossed Jones Valley, where large amounts of iron ore were available. With the railroad, a boom in Jones Valley created a massive iron- and steel-making city.[4]

Milner, the grandson of a Baptist minister, grew up working in the gold fields of northern Georgia and building railroads. As part of the creation of Birmingham and the industrial development of Alabama generally, Milner advocated for convict labor, and he used such laborers by the hundreds in mines and other operations. Earlier, during the Civil War, Milner had created the Oxmoor furnace built by Moses Stroup, and when Birmingham emerged a few miles to the northeast because of his railroad, the Veitch brothers, Moses Stroup's protégés, were on hand. The Oxmoor furnace was rebuilt, and for years following 1873, John Veitch helped convert the Oxmoor furnaces to coke and helped shift from cold blast to hot blast furnaces. John Veitch knew furnace work. "In Cass County, Georgia," a biographical sketch of him explained, "he learned the practical work of a molder." John's eldest brother, Isaac, who also grew up in Cass County along the Etowah, also lived at Oxmoor and presumably worked there, apparently from 1865 until his death in 1881.[5]

The Veitch family was prominent in Birmingham's development. In 1875, the Veitch brothers made a record casting of six thousand pounds at Birmingham's Linn Iron Works, and in 1879 and 1880 John Veitch and C. E. Slade built Birmingham's first furnace. In 1883, a dozen years after Birmingham's creation, the first city directory listed ten Veitches— seven of them identified as molders, with a machinist, a boilermaker, and a foundry foreman rounding out the list. Today, traveling about Birmingham, Alabama, one notices the enormous cast-iron statue of Vulcan, the Roman god of fire, overlooking the city. Forged from iron ore drawn from the mountain on which he now perches, *Vulcan* was originally Birmingham's contribution to the 1904 world's fair in St. Louis, Missouri, a statement of how quickly this Alabama city, in existence for little more than three decades, had become a major producer of iron and steel. *Vulcan* is enormous—at fifty-six feet in height, weighing 126,000 pounds, it remains the largest cast-iron statue in the world. Yet despite the public excitement surrounding its creation, only a few people were present in the cramped space during the initial molding of the statue from the plaster casts of sculptor Giuseppe Moretti. One of these molders was Henry C. Veitch, whose presence signified a multigenerational tradition of iron making closely connected to Moses Stroup and the Etowah Valley.[6]

In Georgia, as Joseph E. Brown dominated the state and his eldest son, Julius, wielded powerful influence, a second son also emerged. Joseph Mackey Brown, named after both his father and grandfather, seemed determined to live a life entwined with the cronies and their legacies. Born in 1851 in Cherokee County, Joseph Mackey at first appeared to follow in the footsteps of his father and older brother. He read law in Julius's office, had

The cast-iron statue *Vulcan*, overlooking
Birmingham, reflects the Veitch family's expertise,
which was cultivated in Georgia's Etowah Valley.
George F. Landegger Collection of Alabama
Photographs in Carol M. Highsmith's America, Prints
and Photographs Division, Library of Congress.

some guidance from his father, and enrolled in Harvard Law School, but
eyestrain prevented the continuation of his studies. He returned to Georgia in 1874, unsure about his future. In Atlanta in 1877, he began work on
the Western & Atlantic Railroad, of which his father was president.[7]

Joseph Mackey Brown moved up the ladder. He began work as a clerk,
became a freight train conductor, went to the shipping department, became an assistant claim agent, and then was promoted to claim agent. He
worked as a ticket auditor and as a car accountant, and on his thirtieth
birthday was promoted to general freight agent for the railroad. Brown
was not involved in politics during these years, but he saw political mach-
inations all around him at a time of great consolidation in the American
railroad industry, and the high levels of competition in the industry affected even a state-owned railroad such as the Western & Atlantic.[8]

Three generations of the Brown family:
Joseph E. Brown, "Little Joe" Brown, and a baby.
Courtesy of the Hargrett Rare Book and Manuscript Library, University of Georgia.

In 1888, Joseph Mackey Brown purchased forty-nine acres in Marietta that had once belonged to Charles McDonald—the site where his father composed the letter accepting the gubernatorial nomination in 1857—and took up residence there, marrying in 1889. Brown and his bride, Cora Mc-Cord, left Augusta on their honeymoon in a special train pulled by a locomotive named after his father, the *Gov. Jos. E. Brown*. Symbolically and literally, Joseph Mackey was being pulled through life by the railroad his father presided over. The couple lived in Marietta, and Brown commuted to Atlanta, where he worked in his new position as the general traffic manager for the railroad.[9]

After Joseph Mackey Brown retired, in 1904 the governor appointed him to the first political position he had ever held, as one of the three members of a regulatory agency, the state's railroad commission. Commission members were to have no business in railroading to avoid conflicts of interest, but within months of his appointment Brown began receiving letters about the possibility of investing in a new railroad to run hundreds of miles from Atlanta to the Gulf of Mexico, probably ending at New Orleans. He also received a letter from former Alabama governor Joseph Forney Johnston, who explained the money to be made from purchasing large, mineral-rich tracts of land in Alabama along the path of the anticipated railroad (which was never built).[10] It was cronyism through and through.

As a railroad commissioner, Brown had public disagreements over railroad issues with a rising Georgia politician, Hoke Smith, whom Georgians elected as governor in 1906. Smith promptly abolished the convict lease system in Georgia. In 1907, Smith also suspended Joseph Mackey Brown from the commission, less than three months from the expiration of Brown's term. Following the ensuing kerfuffle, anti-Smith forces in the state, including men whose fortunes had been built through the lease of convicts, seized on Brown as the carrier of their interests. In the next gubernatorial election in 1908, they successfully ousted Smith in favor of Joseph Mackey Brown. The son of Joseph E. Brown had followed his father's footsteps into the governorship of the state. As governor, Brown was a friend to corporate and railroad interests in Georgia. Upon Brown's election, supporter James W. English, who had used convict labor extensively for decades at his Chattahoochee Brick Company, had thrown Brown a victory dinner. Two years later, when English had labor problems in a mine in northwestern Georgia, Brown immediately sent state troops to protect English's investments. Brown served a two-year term and lost his reelection bid to Smith in 1910. But when Smith left the governor's office for a Senate seat, Brown won the special election and served out the rest of the term, a year and a half in 1912–1913.[11]

In 1928, the state of Georgia unveiled on the capitol grounds a new statue of Joseph Emerson and Elizabeth Grisham Brown. The money had been allocated by Julius in his will. Giuseppe Moretti, who had sculpted *Vulcan* in Birmingham, created the statue. At the dedication ceremony, Joseph Mackey Brown was in attendance.[12] In one sense the statue clearly represented a familial sentimentality: the presence of Elizabeth Grisham Brown was unusual for grounds devoted to political statuary. And the money came from the family. Yet the statue belonged there if political importance was the criterion for inclusion. Joseph E. Brown was profoundly important in the political history of the state. A portion of his significance rested on Brown's background as an upcountry temperance Baptist who surrounded himself with a group of cronies likewise increasingly dedicated to building a modern future. Their vision included slavery and, after the Civil War, convict labor; a racial outlook colored their ventures. Their vision also rested on a diversified economy connected to other places; farming would be one part of an economy in which the riches in the soil and the waterpower on it could be mined and channeled into prosperity.

Railroads, land development, gristmilling, and iron making would all fuel that economic future. As these cronies took over Georgia's government and then dominated it, they not only remade their own fortunes, but recast large portions of the southeastern United States in their images in ways that still echo with their influence.

ACKNOWLEDGMENTS

IT IS A PLEASURE TO RECOGNIZE SOME OF THE MANY PEOPLE WHO have assisted in this project. At Reinhardt University, I have been fortunate to work with numerous supportive colleagues, including Provost Mark Roberts; Associate Provost Jacob Harney; Wayne Glowka, dean of the School of Arts and Humanities; and many faculty colleagues, especially Theresa Ast, Anne Good, Curt Lindquist, Donna Coffey Little, Philip Unger, and Pam Wilson. Our library staff, especially Joel Langford and Stephanie Olsen, consistently helped me. Reinhardt granted me sabbatical leave for a semester in 2017, allowing me precious time to write, for which I am thankful and appreciative.

Years ago, my former student Richard Wright and I worked together to investigate the iron industry in the Etowah Valley. We gave several academic and community talks and capped our collaborative efforts in 2009 with a coauthored article in the *Georgia Historical Quarterly* on Joseph E. Brown and the influence of the Etowah Valley on Brown's development. That research introduced me to Bill and Nell Galt Magruder, who welcomed me many times to their Canton home, gave me access to the papers of Nell's ancestors, including William and Susan Grisham, and helped me understand that family and their world. Their hospitality and generosity are greatly appreciated.

Special acknowledgment also goes to my Reinhardt colleague Jonathan Good, who read the entire manuscript and offered valuable feedback. In addition, Jeff Bishop, director of Reinhardt's Funk Heritage Center; Stefanie Joyner, head of the Cherokee County Historical Society; and my friend and colleague Russ Coil all read specific chapters and improved the manuscript with their comments. Matthew Davis, director of museums for Georgia College, promptly supplied helpful materials when asked. Lisa Tressler gave me a tour along the Etowah River that increased my knowledge. I also thank the Cherokee County Historical Society and its staff for friendly helpfulness and permission to draw from a chapter I published previously, "Joseph E. Brown and the Civil War in Cherokee County, Georgia," in *Cherokee County Voices from the Civil War* (2014). My friends Susan Ashmore and Mary Rolinson encouraged me on this project, as did Jeannine Rollins, who was quite helpful. In Athens, Peggy Galis introduced me to Pat Allen of the University of Georgia Press. Pat, Nate Holly, Jon Davies, Merryl A. Sloane, and two reviewers for the press who read the manuscript, gave me valuable advice and helped shepherd the project to completion. Scholarship is a communal endeavor, and I am appreciative of the many people who offered counsel and aid.

Throughout this project, I have appreciated the patience, support, and love of a wide variety of friends and family, especially my spouse, Amy Cottrill, and our daughters, Hannah and Lydia. They took it in stride when family vacations were interspersed with opportunistic research trips, indulged my soliloquies on research questions and discoveries, and generally acted as counterweights to single-minded behavior, for which I am exceedingly grateful.

NOTES

INTRODUCTION

1. See, for example, Nelson, *Iron Confederacies*; Morgan, *Planters' Progress*; Delfino and Gillespie, *Technology, Innovation, and Southern Industrialization*; Marrs, *Railroads in the Old South*; Thomas, *Iron Way*; Barnes, Schoen, and Towers, *Old South's Modern Worlds*; Majewski, *Modernizing a Slave Economy*; and Gagnon, *Transition to an Industrial South*. One illuminating work that effectively explains the interrelationships of various industries is Hall, *Mountains on the Market*.

2. On the gold rush, begin with Williams, *Georgia Gold Rush*; and Swanson, "From Georgia to California and Back."

3. Scholarship on iron making in the Etowah Valley includes Davis, "Story of a Community Once Called Etowah"; Mohr, *On the Threshold of Freedom*, 151–154; Bennett, *Tannehill*, 79–82; Pope, *Mark Anthony Cooper*; Wright and Wheeler, "New Men in the Old South"; and Knowles, *Mastering Iron*, 95–97, 188.

4. Taylor, "Convict Lease System in Georgia"; Lichtenstein, *Twice the Work of Free Labor*; Mancini, *One Dies, Get Another*; Blackmon, *Slavery by Another Name*; and LeFlouria, *Chained in Silence*.

CHAPTER 1. ARARAT

1. Price, *History of DeKalb County*, 65–66, 135–136; account of Charles Jordan, February–July 1825, Magruder Collection, Canton, Ga.; "License to Retail," December 7, 1824, ibid. For a letter about their arrangements, see Joseph Grisham to William Grisham, November 3, 1823, ibid., in which Joseph writes that he sent a wagonload of goods to William and gives advice about pricing ("You can sell goods higher than we do here") and credit ("Say you sell for cash & stick to it the money will come after a while.")

2. Lamar Roberts interview, Cherokee County Historical Society; Price, *History of DeKalb County*, 126–127; William Grisham to Melinda C. Grisham, January 13, 1825 (typescript), Magruder Collection, Canton, Ga. Philemon Bradford died in June 1824. His temperance views, which Joseph Grisham respected, can be inferred from an anecdote. When the young, enterprising Ker Boyce sought election from the South Carolina state legislators as the tax collector for the Newberry District, he devoted his "attentions, wit, and good sense" to acquiring Bradford's vote. Bradford, a few days later, observing

Boyce's "opponent mixing his morning toddy," said to him, "you drink too much, I can not vote for you, I intend to vote for my good friend Boyce." See O'Neall, *Annals of Newberry*, 118–119. Also on Bradford, see *Charleston (S.C.) City Gazette and Daily Advertiser*, October 31, 1812; "To the Editors," *Charleston City Gazette and Daily Advertiser*, December 7, 1816; "State Legislature," *Charleston City Gazette and Commercial Daily Advertiser*, November 1, 1820; B. F. Perry, "Reminiscences of the County of Greenville," *Greenville (S.C.) Enterprise*, September 6, 1871; and 1820 U.S. Census, Greenville, S.C., 96. In the National Archives, Washington, D.C., roll M33_120, image 157, shows that Bradford owned fifteen slaves in 1820.

3. William Grisham to Susan Bradford, June 19, September 10 and 18, 1825, Magruder Collection, Canton, Ga.; Young, *Collection of Upper South Carolina Genealogical and Family Records*, 157.

4. Garrett, *Atlanta and Environs*, 1:74; John McGinnis to William Grisham, Bill of Sale of Amy, February 24, 1830; John Kiser and Evan Howell to William Grisham, Bill of Sale of Tippoe, January 15, 1830; Kindred Blackstock to William Grisham, Bill of Sale of Rose, January 3, 1832; and Jackson H. Randal to William Grisham, Bill of Sale of Arminda, July 24, 1832, all in the Magruder Collection, Canton, Ga.

5. On the Cherokees, begin with McLoughlin, *Cherokee Renascence*; and Perdue and Green, *Cherokee Nation and the Trail of Tears*; on the Mississippian inhabitants centuries earlier, see King, *Etowah*. The Cherokees had traditionally lived to the north, in the Tennessee River Valley, but the tumult of the American Revolution pushed many Cherokees to the south, especially into the Etowah Valley.

6. Magrath, *Yazoo*; Wallace, *Long, Bitter Trail*, esp. 62–64. On the multiracial society the Cherokees created, see esp. Perdue, *"Mixed Blood" Indians*; and Miles, *Ties That Bind*.

7. On the Georgia gold rush, see esp. Williams, *Georgia Gold Rush*, which explains the effects on the Cherokee people; and Swanson, "From Georgia to California and Back." See also Young, "Southern Gold Rush"; Green, "Georgia's Forgotten Industry"; and Coulter, *Auraria*. The broad context is discussed well in Rozema, "Coveted Lands," esp. 110–180; and Rozema, "Science and Technology Awakened."

8. Watson, *Peacekeepers and Conquerors*, 106–113; Williams, *Georgia Gold Rush*, 26–36; Covington, "Letters from the Georgia Gold Regions."

9. Murray, *Whig Party in Georgia*, 16–25; see also Gilmer, *Sketches of Some of the First Settlers*, esp. 257–358.

10. Gardner, *Cherokees and Baptists in Georgia*, 37–40, 52–58, esp. n. 45 (quotation on 66); Walker, *Cherokee Footprints*, 2:39. On Cherokee buildings and improvements, see Wilms, "Cherokee Land Use in Georgia before Removal"; and Wilms, "Cherokee Indian Land Use in Georgia."

11. Gardner, *Cherokees and Baptists in Georgia*, 56–58, 85–90. Not all of O'Bryant's family went to Arkansas. His daughter Nancy began the trip, but her beau, Reuben Frank Daniel, a young local white man, caught up with the family at Charleston, Tennessee, where he asked Nancy to marry him. Nancy agreed, Duncan O'Bryant performed the ceremony, and Nancy returned with Daniel and became part of the settlement of Cherokee Court House, which became "Etowa" and then Canton. Gardner, *Cherokees and Baptists in Georgia*, 85n31.

12. Green, "Georgia's Forgotten Industry," 104.

13. Marlin, *History of Cherokee County*, 46; *Cherokee Intelligencer*, February 16, 1833; Sedgwick, *Tales and Sketches*, 309; John, *Spreading the News*, esp. 113–130. Grisham had tried to become a postmaster before. In 1825 he had written his sister from Decatur,

"I have gave out all hopes of being Postmaster here as the Postmaster General does not pay any attention to our Petition." William Grisham to Melinda C. Grisham, January 13, 1825 (typescript), Magruder Collection, Canton, Ga.

14. Cadle, *Georgia Land Surveying,* 279; *Acts of the General Assembly of the State of Georgia* (1833), 331–334; *Acts of the General Assembly of the State of Georgia* (1834), 263; Marlin, *History of Cherokee County,* 44–47. Grisham had not drawn his land through a lottery; he purchased it. Grisham may have been acquainted with Duncan O'Bryant and was possibly familiar with the area, as O'Bryant, like Grisham's brother Joseph, was a Baptist minister probably from upcountry South Carolina. Gardner, *Cherokees and Baptists in Georgia,* 39–40, esp. n. 6.

15. Cadle, *Georgia Land Surveying,* 267–283; "Gold and Land Lottery Register" pamphlets, Magruder Collection, Canton, Ga.; *Cherokee Phoenix,* December 9, 1832.

16. Young, "Exercise of Sovereignty," 61n40; *Acts of the General Assembly of the State of Georgia* (1834), 159–160; Taylor, *Cherokee County,* 1:62; "Reminiscences of Byron Waters," 6, Miscellaneous Collection, box 3, archives, Reinhardt University, Waleska, Ga.

17. Miles, *House on Diamond Hill,* 177–179, 181. Miles is silent about what happened to Vann's enslaved laborers on his Georgia plantation, but notes that the Vann family moved to a three-hundred-acre Tennessee plantation they owned, where at least some of their slaves worked, perhaps joined by others who moved with them from Georgia.

18. Joseph Grisham to William Grisham, June 8, 1834, Magruder Collection, Canton, Ga.; "Prospectus," reprinted in *Georgia Telegraph* (Macon), January 23, 1833. The journalist Cobb is not to be confused with his more famous namesake, who served as Georgia's governor, 1851–1853, and U.S. secretary of the treasury, 1857–1860. "From the Georgia Gazette," *Cherokee Intelligencer,* February 13, 1833; *Western Georgian* (Rome), January 19, 1838. Generally, see Ellis, *Union at Risk.*

19. *Cherokee Intelligencer,* March 9, 1833; "Celebration of the 4th of July, at Cherokee," *Cherokee Intelligencer,* July 13, 1833; "Celebration of the Fourth of July," *Cherokee Intelligencer,* July 13, 1833.

20. "Minutes of the Baptist Church of Christ, Canton, Ga.," August 23, 1833, Magruder Collection, Canton, Ga.

21. *Acts of the General Assembly of the State of Georgia* (1833), 17–20; Taylor, *Cherokee County,* 1:92.

22. *Cherokee Intelligencer,* February 16, April 20, and October 12, 1833; Cleveland and Cleveland, *Genealogy of the Cleveland and Cleaveland Families,* 3:2082–2083. *Acts of the General Assembly of the State of Georgia* (1833), 382–383, in reference to money that went missing when Bedney Franklin died, gives his year of death and his wealth at that time. See also Marlin, *History of Cherokee County,* 146–147; Mary G. Franklin, 1850 U.S. Census, Division 15, Cherokee, Ga., roll M432_65, 474A, image 150.

23. Inferior Court Minutes, April 15, 1835, and September 26, 1836, Cherokee County, Ga.

24. Letter from Elijah Hicks to Editor, *Cherokee Phoenix,* May 19, 1832; John Coffee to Wilson Lumpkin, May 13, 1832, box 1, folder 46, Telamon Cuyler Collection, Hargrett Rare Book and Manuscript Library, University of Georgia, Athens; *Cherokee Intelligencer,* February 13, 1833; Cunyus, *History of Bartow County,* 7–9, on one of the murderers, George Tooke; *Cherokee Intelligencer,* reprinted in *Columbian Register* (New Haven, Conn.), May 25, 1833; "Cherokees," *Cherokee Intelligencer,* May 11, 1833. It is unknown whether "Mr. Tait" was Samuel Tate, who purchased a tavern in 1834 not far away, along the federal road, and became an important figure in the early history of Cherokee and Pickens Counties. See Tate, *History of Pickens County,* 34–36, 304–305.

25. Lumpkin, *Removal of the Cherokee Indians*, 1:274–277.

26. Ibid., 1:278–288.

27. Joseph Grisham to William Grisham, June 8, 1834, Magruder Collection, Canton, Ga.; *The State v. Log-in-the-Water*, Superior Court Minutes, Cherokee County, Ga., September term, 1834.

28. *The State v. Edward Edwards*, Superior Court Minutes, Cherokee County, Ga., March term, 1835.

29. Hauptman, "General John E. Wool"; Watson, *Peacekeepers and Conquerors*, 144–162.

30. Latty, *Carrying Off the Cherokee*, 27–32, 77–79; Hill, "To Overawe the Indians," 484–485.

31. "Minutes of the Baptist Church of Christ, Canton, Ga.," August 26 and October 21, 1837, Magruder Collection, Canton, Ga.

32. Latty, *Carrying Off the Cherokee*, 94–95, 109–111; Watson, *Peacekeepers and Conquerors*, 162–163; Featherstonhaugh, *Canoe Voyage*, 2:229; diary of Nathaniel Reinhardt, quoted in Marlin, *History of Cherokee County*, 50. On the lack of standardized uniforms, see Hill, "To Overawe the Indians," 479.

33. Latty, *Carrying Off the Cherokee*, 115–116 (emphasis in original).

34. Lamar Roberts interview, Cherokee County Historical Society; Tocqueville, *Journey to America*, 200–201.

35. On the Trail of Tears, begin with Perdue and Green, *Cherokee Nation and the Trail of Tears*, 116–140; on death rates, see Thornton, "Cherokee Population Losses."

CHAPTER 2. A RAILROAD AND ROWLAND SPRINGS

1. "Western and Atlantic Rail Road," *Daily Constitutionalist* (Augusta, Ga.), February 22, 1838; "Rail Road," *Southern Banner* (Athens, Ga.), September 30, 1837.

2. Ford, "Public Career of Tomlinson Fort," 47, 50–51; Green, "Georgia's Board of Public Works," esp. 129–130.

3. Ford, "Public Career of Tomlinson Fort," 56. Kate Haynes Fort wrote that Calhoun and Tomlinson Fort, who did not agree on nullification, exchanged letters for years on the subject, and the two men sat up until two in the morning, while gathered for commencement at the University of Georgia years later, as Calhoun tried unsuccessfully to convert Fort to his ideas. See Fort, *Memoirs of the Fort and Fannin Families*, 32, 50–52; "Darien Bank," *Georgian* (Savannah), January 24, 1829; Murray, *Whig Party in Georgia*, 21–22, 26; Ford, "Public Career of Tomlinson Fort," 66. The best discussion of the Central Bank of Georgia is in Heath, *Constructive Liberalism*, 190–201, 211–223.

4. Fort, *Memoirs of the Fort and Fannin Families*, 34–36, 56. Fort's Central Bank salary is noted in Ford, "Public Career of Tomlinson Fort," 69. For the perspective of one of the people owned by the Fort family, see Nelson, "A 'Miserable Creature' or 'Remarkable Man.'"

5. "Rail Road Meeting," *Georgia Journal* (Milledgeville), September 8, 1831. Generally, see Pope, *Mark Anthony Cooper*, 73–80, 264–265. On Gordon, see Tankersley, "Zachariah Herndon Gordon," 234–235; on Gordon's tavern, see "4th of July Celebration in Eatonton," *Southern Recorder* (Milledgeville, Ga.), July 13, 1824; on Charles P. Gordon, see Miller, *Bench and Bar of Georgia*, 2:63–73; for the railroad charter, see *Acts of the General Assembly of the State of Georgia* (1831), 187–198. The state legislature later repealed the 1831 charter and replaced it with legislation that created, ultimately, one of Georgia's more powerful business interests, the Georgia Railroad Company. See also Phillips, *History of Transportation*, 225–231.

6. Wolmar, *Great Railroad Revolution*, esp. 1–87; Miner, *Most Magnificent Machine*, esp. 1–72; Gates, "Imitative Enterprise." See also Marrs, *Railroads in the Old South*.

7. On efforts in Charleston and more broadly in South Carolina to build railroads and connect the city and state to the interior of the country, see esp. Phillips, *History of Transportation*, 132–220; Marrs, *Railroads in the Old South*; and Grant, *Louisville, Cincinnati, and Charleston Rail Road*. The effort largely failed—even though enough railroad line was built to connect Columbia with Charleston—partly because South Carolina supported the potential railroad far more than other states did.

8. John C. Calhoun to Col. F. Carter, November 26, 1835, in Meriwether et al., *Papers of John C. Calhoun*, 12:566–569. Calhoun imagined that the railroad might run from Athens in a northwesterly direction, which would, not coincidentally, run near some of his lucrative gold mine investments. On Carter, see Flanders, "Farish Carter"; on his contractor experience, see, for example, the 1814 letters written by Carter in Miller, *Bench and Bar of Georgia*, 1:423.

9. Farish Carter to John C. Calhoun, November 14, 1836, in Meriwether et al., *Papers of John C. Calhoun*, 13:300–301. On Calhoun's involvement in Georgia gold mining, see Bartlett, *John C. Calhoun*, 203; and Cain, *History of Lumpkin County*, 92–94, 97.

10. *Acts of the General Assembly of the State of Georgia* (1836), 214–218.

11. DuBose, "Stephen Harriman Long," 169–171; Grant, *Louisville, Cincinnati, and Charleston Rail Road*, 53. Generally on Long, see Wood, *Stephen Harriman Long*.

12. DuBose, "Stephen Harriman Long," 171–175; for Long's survey, see "Report from the Secretary of War," December 29, 1837, 25th Cong, 2nd sess.; Johnston, *Western and Atlantic Railroad*, 24. The bond agreement Long made with Farish Carter and Thomas R. Huson is dated December 26, 1837, subser. 2.1.4, Farish Carter Papers, Southern Historical Collection, University of North Carolina, Chapel Hill; and see "Invoice of Real Estate Purchased for & on a/c of Messers Carter Boyce Long & Huson, [July 1840], ser. 2, ibid.

13. S. H. Long to Farish Carter, January 8 and 25, February 8 and 22, March 11, and April 30, 1838, Farish Carter Papers, Southern Historical Collection, University of North Carolina, Chapel Hill; and "Invoice of Real Estate Purchased," ibid. On the ground-breaking ceremony, see "Western and Atlantic Rail Road," *Daily Constitutionalist* (Augusta, Ga.), February 22, 1838. The Georgia Senate voted in 1849 to rescind the prohibition on engineers' land purchases. See *Journal of the Senate of the State of Georgia* (1849–1850), 122–123. See also Govan and Livingood, *Chattanooga Country*, 129n19.

14. S. H. Long to Farish Carter, April 30, 1838, Farish Carter Papers, Southern Historical Collection, University of North Carolina, Chapel Hill; "Darien Bank," *Georgian* (Savannah), January 24, 1829; *Acts of the General Assembly of the State of Georgia* (1831), 51–52.

15. Zachariah B. Hargrove, described as Fort's nephew in one source, married Malinda Fort Tate, a daughter of Robert Tate and Elizabeth Fort, in 1821. Tomlinson Fort had a sister Elizabeth, but she was born in 1789 and did not marry a Tate, thus it seems unlikely that Malinda was Tomlinson's niece. See "Genealogical Queries"; Fort, *Memoirs of the Fort and Fannin Families*, 7, 9; Ford, "Public Career of Tomlinson Fort," 71. On Hargrove, see Mahan, *History of Old Cassville*, 10, 12, 19, 21. Hargrove was also a receiver in Cassville in 1834 for the Bank of Macon. Cunyus, *History of Bartow County*, 269. One sign of Hargrove's prominence is that he had financial dealings with John C. Calhoun. See Meriwether et al., *Papers of John C. Calhoun*, 12:364–365, 510. An opponent of the Central Bank in 1836 accused Fort of being in collusion with Hargrove in speculating on land in the Cherokee country, which was either accurate (in which case, their collaboration commenced earlier than 1838) or prescient.

16. Govan and Livingood, *Chattanooga Country*; see also Wilson, *Chattanooga's Story*, 31. Historians of Chattanooga have been well aware that the city was a creation of the state of Georgia through the building of the Western & Atlantic Railroad and that the early land speculators were mostly Georgians, but the connection of these land speculators to the railroad itself and to Georgia's state government has not been noticed. See also the documents described in John Wilson, "The Samuel Williams Landholdings Stretched for over 40 Miles Up and Down the Tennessee River," March 20, 2019, Chattanoogan.com, https://www.chattanoogan.com/2019/3/20/384048/The-Samuel -Williams-Landholdings.aspx.

17. Stephen H. Long to Farish Carter, July 9 and 15, 1838, ser. 1, Farish Carter Papers, Southern Historical Collection, University of North Carolina, Chapel Hill; Tomlinson Fort [Jr.], "Some Early History Narrated," *Chattanooga News*, August 24, 1907; Stephen H. Long to Farish Carter, July 18, 1838, ser. 1, Farish Carter Papers, Southern Historical Collection, University of North Carolina, Chapel Hill; Z. B. Hargrove to Tomlinson Fort, December 31, 1838 (emphasis in original), Tomlinson Fort Family Papers, Stuart A. Rose Manuscript, Archives, and Rare Book Library, Emory University, Atlanta, Ga. On the streets named after Williams, Carter, and Boyce, see Wilson, *Chattanooga's Story*, 31; Stephen H. Long to Farish Carter, August 11, 1838, ser. 1, Farish Carter Papers, Southern Historical Collection, University of North Carolina, Chapel Hill. See also S. H. Long to Farish Carter, August 17, 1838, ser. 1, ibid. On the Carter and Vann landholdings in Murray County, see Miles, *House on Diamond Hill*, 209–210.

18. "Died," *Georgia Telegraph* (Macon), February 19, 1839; will of Zachariah B. Hargrove, January 20, 1839, in Wills, 1836–1922, Bartow County, Ga., Court of Ordinary; "Bank Reports: Western Bank of Georgia," *Augusta Chronicle*, July 6, 1840; *John H. Lumpkin and Wesley Shropshire, et al., v. Thomas H. Jones*, in Kelly, *Reports of Cases in Law and Equity . . . 1846*, 28; A. B. Fannin to Tomlinson Fort, July 2, 1839, and K. W. Hargrove to Tomlinson Fort, February 12, 1840, Tomlinson Fort Family Papers, Stuart A. Rose Manuscript, Archives, and Rare Book Library, Emory University, Atlanta, Ga.; Fort, "Some Early History Narrated."

19. On the economy in Georgia, see Heath, *Constructive Liberalism*, esp. 205–210; and Carey, *Parties, Slavery, and the Union*, 38–39. On Fort's economic difficulties, see the undated obituary of Martha Lowe Fannin Fort in the [*Atlanta?*] *Constitution*, box 2, folder 3, Tomlinson Fort Family Papers, Stuart A. Rose Manuscript, Archives, and Rare Book Library, Emory University, Atlanta, Ga. On his ownership of 140 shares of stock for which he had paid more than $4,500, see "Bank Reports: Western Bank of Georgia," *Augusta Chronicle*, July 6, 1840. On the loan, see Fort, *Memoirs of the Fort and Fannin Families*, 52.

20. *Georgian* (Savannah), January 23, 1829; "Bank of Darien," *Augusta Chronicle*, January 23, 1830.

21. *Acts Passed by the General Assembly of Georgia* (1835), 128–129. On the marriage, see Flanders, "Farish Carter," 144. The first interaction I have found between the two is a brief request to Carter from Charles McDonald on April 20, 1816, to pay McDonald's son ten dollars. Ser. 2.1.2, Farish Carter Papers, Southern Historical Collection, University of North Carolina, Chapel Hill. On the $1,000 loan, see Charles J. McDonald to Farish Carter, September 1 and 14, 1839, ser. 1, ibid. See also a note of the Bank of Milledgeville signed by Carter, "Pay to Charles McDonald" $2,711.33, dated December 24, 1836, and a note, "Cashier of Bank of Milledgeville. Pay to Charles J. McDonald on order one thousand dollars—9th March 1838," signed by Carter, ser. 2, ibid. As a fellow gold mine owner, Carter was, unsurprisingly, well acquainted with the Franklin family. See, for

example, the letter of November 17, 1833, from Leonidas Franklin (Ann's brother and Mary's son) to Farish Carter, ibid., advising Carter on how to build a lime kiln.

22. Fort, *Memoirs of the Fort and Fannin Families*, 28; Ford, "Public Career of Tomlinson Fort," 21, 72. Fort remained the head of the Central Bank of Georgia throughout the four years of his friend Governor McDonald's two terms. See "From Our Correspondent," *Augusta Chronicle*, December 2, 1842; and Fort, *Memoirs of the Fort and Fannin Families*, 140–141. On McDonald's life, see the biographical sketch in White, *Historical Collections of Georgia*, 239–245; Humphries, "Judges of the Superior Courts," 114–115; and Jackson, *Eulogy*.

23. On the economic troubles of the Central Bank, see Heath, *Constructive Liberalism*, 211–223; and Carey, *Parties, Slavery, and the Union*, 55–66. On the suspension in December 1841, see Heath, *Constructive Liberalism*, 270–271; on Long and the end of his work on the railroad, see Wood, *Stephen Harriman Long*, 189–202. Wood makes it seem as though the War Department asked for Long's resignation in February 1839 from his work on the railroad. Yet Long arranged a leave of absence from the War Department during the first half of 1840, and Governor McDonald wrote at the end of that time that he wished to retain Long, or to regain his services. Long was clearly working on the railroad during that leave of absence. See Wood, *Stephen Harriman Long*, 199, including n. 30; and a letter in April 1840 from Tomlinson Fort's father-in-law to Fort, which mentions that Long "was about to resign his Station as Chief Engineer." A. B. Fannin to Tomlinson Fort, April 27, 1840, box 1, folder 4, Tomlinson Fort Papers, Chattanooga Public Library, Chattanooga, Tenn. Long continued to reside in Marietta, Georgia, from 1837 until 1843, and when Wilson Lumpkin oversaw the railroad beginning in 1842, everything he wrote was about what Long had or had not done. Long may not have been overseeing the railroad construction through the end of 1841, yet his priorities evidently prevailed during that period. On Lumpkin's stint overseeing the Western & Atlantic Railroad, see Lumpkin, *Removal of the Cherokee Indians*, 2:267–290.

24. The cronyism notwithstanding, many economists would say the money spent on the railroad boosted the Georgia economy at a particularly vulnerable time. Long employed many laborers to grade the road, including fifty or sixty Cherokees until they were forced west in 1838. On the Cherokee laborers, whom Long tried to retain in 1838, see Wood, *Stephen Harriman Long*, 197.

25. Govan and Livingood, *Chattanooga Country*, 129–136; Cunyus, *History of Bartow County*, 23–24. On the naming of the Fort infant, see Eliza McDonald to Dr. and Mrs. Fort, August 10, 1846, box 1, folder 5, Tomlinson Fort Papers, Stuart A. Rose Manuscript, Archives, and Rare Book Library, Emory University, Atlanta, Ga. On the close ties between these families, see Eliza McDonald to Martha Fort, April 10, 1853, box 1, folder 6, ibid.

26. On the life of John S. Rowland, see Livingston, *American Portrait Gallery*, pt. 4, 3:266–268; "Obituary," September 30, 1863, in an unidentified newspaper, Rowland Springs Scrapbook, 2013.27.1, Bartow History Museum, Cartersville, Ga.; and Lewis, *Genealogy of the Lewis Family in America*, 247–248.

27. Brewster, *Summer Migrations and Resorts of South Carolina Low-Country Planters*; Lewis, *Ladies and Gentlemen on Display*.

28. "Western & Atlantic R. R.," *Augusta Chronicle*, October 11, 1845; [Boggs], *Alexander Letters*, 98–99.

29. "To the Editor of the Georgia Telegraph," *Georgia Telegraph* (Macon), May 25, 1847.

30. "A. B. Z. to Editors of the Charleston Courier," *Charleston Courier*, July 30, 1849;

Augusta Chronicle, September 3, 1849; "Georgia Correspondence," *Charleston Courier*, July 7, 1855.

31. *Charleston Courier*, July 30, 1849, and June 15, 1850; "Rowland Springs," *Charleston Courier*, July 18, 1851.

32. "Medicinal Springs," *Georgia Journal and Messenger* (Macon), July 12, 1848. See also "Medicinal Springs, Walker Co.," *Georgian* (Savannah), August 31, 1847; *Georgia Journal and Messenger* (Macon), August 29, 1849; "Gordon Springs for Sale," *Georgia Journal and Messenger* (Macon), February 25, 1852.

33. Armes, *Autobiography of Joseph Le Conte*, 122; *Federal Union* (Milledgeville, Ga.), August 24, 1847; *Savannah Daily Republican*, August 20, 1847.

34. "Rowland Springs," *Savannah Daily Republican*, July 31, 1847; *Savannah Daily Republican*, August 20, 1847.

35. *Charleston Courier*, July 30, 1849.

36. *Savannah Daily Republican*, September 18, 1846; "Rowland's Springs," *Georgian* (Savannah), June 12, 1847; "Watering Places," *Georgia Telegraph* (Macon), May 9, 1848; "Our City—The Watering Places," *Georgia Telegraph*, August 15, 1848; Simms, *Father Abbot*, 21. Simms scholar James E. Kibler believes that Simms visited Rowland Springs. See Dietrich, *History of Rowland Springs*, 25–26, 93–118.

37. The reward was posted in the *Tennessee Whig*, September 1, 1849, transcribed in the Rowland Springs Scrapbook, Bartow History Museum, Cartersville, Ga.

38. *Georgia Telegraph* (Macon), August 14, 1849.

39. "Capture of Four Runaway Negroes in Kentucky," *Keowee Courier* (Pickens Court House, S.C.), September 29, 1849.

40. "Rowland's Springs," *Columbus (Ga.) Times*, July 25, 1848.

CHAPTER 3. IRON

1. On the Stroups, see Hornsby and Stroupe, "History of the Stroup Ironmasters." For German American participation in the American Revolution, see esp. Nixon, *History of Lincoln County*. On the interconnections among iron-making families, see, for example, Cappon, "Iron-Making," 337.

2. For a list of iron-making occupations, see Ferguson and Cowan, "Iron Plantations," 133. See also Council, Honerkamp, and Will, *Industry and Technology in Antebellum Tennessee*, esp. 37–41.

3. On iron being used in place of money, see Nave, "History of the Iron Industry," 89–90, 92–93; and Cappon, "Iron-Making," 340.

4. Ferguson and Cowan, "Iron Plantations," 120–121; Lander, "Iron Industry," 342. On the integration of the Stroup and Fewell families, see the relevant gravestones in the Goodson family cemetery in Bartow County, Ga., and Deed Record Book G, 21, Clerk of Courts, Bartow County, where it is recorded that Jacob Stroup's purchase of a plot of land in 1840 was witnessed by Theodore M. and Monroe Fewell.

5. Jacob Stroup purchased 250 acres (lot number 4 in the Tenth District) from William Worley on December 20, 1829. Oversize box 1, folder 6, Benjamin Ryan Tillman Papers, Special Collections, Clemson University Libraries, Clemson, S.C. Jacob Stroup is consistently given credit for building the Habersham furnace, though the *Hancock Advertiser* reported in 1830 that it was Moses Stroup "erecting works for the manufacture of iron." Quoted in *Macon Telegraph*, July 24, 1830. Months later, the *Georgian* (Savannah), October 7, 1830, carried a report from a traveler who had "visited the Iron Works of Mr. Moses Stroup" in Habersham County. Williams, *Georgia Gold Rush*, 28, discusses

the gold finds in 1829, and the first documentation he found of a gold strike in Georgia is from Habersham County. See his reprint of a fragment of the *Georgia Journal* (Milledgeville), August 1, 1829, opposite page 48. For a description of the Shelton gold mine in Habersham, see Phillips, "Essay on the Georgia Gold Mines."

6. After his initial land purchase in 1829, Jacob Stroup acquired another parcel cheaply at a sheriff's sale in 1830, but his key land purchases occurred in 1832, when he bought more than 1,500 acres of land. Oversize box 1, folder 6, Benjamin Ryan Tillman Papers, Special Collections, Clemson University Libraries, Clemson, S.C. While a forge could have begun to operate very quickly, furnaces took time to build. His furnace was probably complete by 1832, which meant he needed ore, limestone, and timber lands. This matches J. P. Lesley's findings. Lesley reported in 1859 that Stroup's forge went into operation about 1830 and the furnace by 1832. Lesley, *Iron Manufacturer's Guide*, 76, 192. For a description of the works, see the 1837 offering of shares presented by the purchasers, Paul Rossignal, John R. Mathews, and Lewis Frederick E. Dugas. Oversize box 1, folder 8, Benjamin Ryan Tillman Papers, Special Collections, Clemson University Libraries, Clemson, S.C. Rossignal, Mathews, and Dugas were all incorporators in 1837 of both the Habersham Iron Works and Manufacturing Company, and the Blue Ridge Rail Road and Canal Company of Georgia. See *Acts of the General Assembly of the State of Georgia* (1837), 134–136, 193–200. Lesley, *Iron Manufacturer's Guide*, 76, noted that the works were abandoned about 1837 and were in ruins in 1859. The Habersham Ironworks Daybook, Georgia Archives, Morrow, shows that a commissary selling various items was operating at the place in 1840, but indicates no sign of iron manufacturing. A few more details about the financial failure of the ironworks can be found in *William W. Berry, et al., v. John R. Mathews, et al.*, in Kelly, *Reports of Cases in Law and Equity . . . 1846*, 1:519–524. An oral history claim that John C. Calhoun was a financial partner of Jacob Stroup is undocumented, though Calhoun's son-in-law Thomas Clemson bought the Habersham Iron Works and Manufacturing Company after Stroup sold his works and moved on. Wigginton, *Foxfire 5*, 88–90, and Lander, *Calhoun Family and Thomas Green Clemson*, 49.

7. On Nesbitt, see the brief biography in *Biographical Directory of the United States Congress*; and "Col. Wilson Nesbitt: Col. T. J. Moore Recalls Well Known Man," *State* (Columbia, S.C.), December 5, 1915. Nesbitt wrote to John C. Calhoun in 1819 or 1820 to offer "cannon shot," because "in a few weeks he will be putting his furnace in blast." Meriwether et al., *Papers of John C. Calhoun*, 4:343. See also "Claims of South-Carolina against the General Government," *Charleston City Gazette and Commercial Daily Advertiser*, February 7, 1822; and Nesbitt's advertisements to sell forges, furnaces, and thousands of acres of land rich in iron ore, limestone, and timber along the Broad River: "South Carolina Lands, &c. for Sale," *Daily National Intelligencer*, July 27, 1819; and "Valuable Property for Sale," *Daily National Intelligencer*, June 3, 1826. See also Ferguson and Cowan, "Iron Plantations," 122; generally, see Eelman, *Entrepreneurs in the Southern Upcountry*. A brother of Moses reported decades later that when his father "sold out his iron works in South Carolina to Colonel Nesbit, in 1827," he had left "my brother, Moses, with Nesbit." Jacob D. Stroup Jr., quoted in Armes, *Story of Coal and Iron in Alabama*, 65.

8. For the date of incorporation, see Richardson, *Reports of Cases in Equity*, 6:227; Lander, "Iron Industry," 343; Wilson Nesbitt, "President's Report," August 18, 1837, container 3, Franklin H. Elmore Papers, Library of Congress, Washington, D.C. As one sign of interest in new techniques, Nesbitt stockholder Dr. Thomas Cooper received a letter in March 1837 from a New York acquaintance answering Cooper's inquiries about

how to perform "the hot air blast," which promised to greatly reduce the fuel consumed in the firing of a furnace and the melting and purifying of iron ore. [Jno Mcannus?] to Thomas Cooper, March 5, 1837, container 2, Franklin H. Elmore Papers, Library of Congress, Washington, D.C.

9. Wilson Nesbitt, "President's Report," November 25, 1837, Franklin Harper Elmore Papers, South Caroliniana Library, University of South Carolina, Columbia.

10. Nesbitt, "President's Report," November 25, 1837.

11. Assorted receipts and legal papers, September and October 1837; Moses Stroup to President and Directors of the Nesbitt Manufacturing Co., November 17, 1837, all in container 3; and "M. Stroup Bill Expenses &c. at N. York & Boston, Nov. 1, 1837," container 8, all in the Franklin H. Elmore Papers, Library of Congress, Washington, D.C.

12. Receipts and contracts, October 1837, container 3, Franklin H. Elmore Papers, Library of Congress, Washington, D.C. The inference about Lawson's duties comes from a letter from Joseph Jones to Wilson Nesbitt, October 21, 1837, ibid., in which Jones offers his services to Nesbitt because he had heard "that you are in want of a Moulder to make Hot Blast pipes."

13. Nesbitt, "President's Report," November 25, 1837; Stroup to President and Directors, November 17, 1837; and "M. Stroup Bill Expenses."

14. Stroup to President and Directors, November 17, 1837.

15. Clemson, "Gold and the Gold Region"; Temin, *Iron and Steel*, 20. See also Knowles and Healey, "Geography, Timing, and Technology." Clemson for a time in 1842 ran his father-in-law's Obarr mine in Lumpkin County. He then purchased the Stroup-built iron furnace in Habersham County, intending to put it back into operation. Though unsuccessful, he still owned the furnace in the mid-1850s. Lander, *Calhoun Family and Thomas Green Clemson*, 46–58; Butler, "Thomas Green Clemson"; Kelly, "Scientist as Farmer," 148.

16. B. T. Elmore to F. H. Elmore, February 27, 1838, and January 8, 1839, container 3, Franklin H. Elmore Papers, Library of Congress, Washington, D.C.

17. "Memorandum of an Agreement by Moses Stroup on One Part and E. W. Harrison as Superintendent of the Nesbitt Manufacturing Company on the Other Part" [March 24, 1838], container 3, Franklin H. Elmore Papers, Library of Congress, Washington, D.C. More generally, see Lander, "Iron Industry," 343–347.

18. "Memorandum of an Agreement by Moses Stroup"; and an undated committee report signed by John G. Brown on slave valuations, container 3, Franklin H. Elmore Papers, Library of Congress, Washington, D.C.

19. The unavailability of credit is obvious from the international correspondence of Franklin H. Elmore, container 3, Franklin H. Elmore Papers, Library of Congress, Washington, D.C. On the level of indebtedness, see Lander, "Iron Industry," 346.

20. Memorial of Pierce M. Butler and others, "Praying the Establishment of a National Foundry," May 21, 1838, U.S. Congressional Serial Set, no. 330, House document 387, 25th Cong., 2nd sess. The petitioners also explained that they were in the midst of extensive ironworks in addition to their own. Directly across the river was the King's Mountain Company, which made iron well suited to small-arms manufacturing. The South Carolina Iron Company also operated nearby.

21. On contracts with the War Department, see G. Bomford to F. H. Elmore, January 20, 1841, and miscellaneous papers in Franklin Harper Elmore Papers, South Caroliniana Library, University of South Carolina, Columbia. On the failure of the Nesbitt Iron Manufacturing Company, see Lander, "Iron Industry," 346–348.

22. The land deeds for early Cass County are not complete. For Stroup's 1833 pur-

chase, see Deed Record Book H, 236, Clerk of Courts, Bartow County. The next recorded land purchases of Jacob Stroup occurred in 1837: the two pivotal lots where he would build his forge and furnace. See Deed Record Book C, 262–263, Clerk of Courts, Bartow County. On the gold rush in Cherokee County, see Marlin, *History of Cherokee County*, esp. 143–149. For a contemporary notice of gold in both Cherokee and Cass Counties, see "Extent of the Gold Region in Georgia," *Western Herald* (Auraria, Ga.), reprinted in *Family Lyceum* (Boston), July 13, 1833. See also the Stroup ledger (erroneously called the Reinhardt store ledger), photocopy, archives, Reinhardt University, Waleska, Ga., which has a notation "commenced building furnace Stack Oct 8th 1839." Stephen H. Long to Farish Carter, February 8, 1838, Farish Carter Papers, Southern Historical Collection, University of North Carolina, Chapel Hill. Jacob D. Stroup, a son of Jacob, quoted in Armes, *Story of Coal and Iron in Alabama*, 65. Long did not forget about the possibilities of iron manufacture. He wrote to Carter in 1843, when Stroup had just one furnace built and Long and Carter and their associates still owned quite a bit of land along the Etowah, to remind him that "the establishment of iron works on the Etowah, on a scale sufficiently large for the preparation of rails for the road, is a matter that ought not to be overlooked." S. H. Long to Farish Carter, March 1, 1843, ser. 1, Farish Carter Papers, Southern Historical Collection, University of North Carolina, Chapel Hill.

23. Hodge, "Manufacture of Iron in Georgia," 507–511.

24. See 25th Cong., 2nd sess., Senate doc. 57, 3–40. See also Wood, *Stephen Harriman Long*, 189–198.

25. When Moses Stroup came to Georgia is unclear. His brother claimed decades later that Moses arrived at the Etowah operation in 1843. Armes, *Story of Coal and Iron in Alabama*, 65. But Moses purchased his first land in Bartow County in November 1842. Deed Record Book G, 8–9, Clerk of Courts, Bartow County; "Georgia Iron Ware," *Georgia Telegraph* (Macon), March 11, 1845 (quotation).

26. Cooper quoted in Pope, *Mark Anthony Cooper*, 93; "Iron Works, Cass Co., Ga.," *Georgia Telegraph and Republic* (Macon), May 27, 1845. In his memoir, reprinted in Pope, *Mark Anthony Cooper*, 263–280, Cooper recalled that he had purchased half of Moses Stroup's iron business "about the year 1842" (266). Aside from the fact that Sophronia, Cooper's wife, gave birth to a child in Cartersville in 1844 (99), there is no evidence of Cooper in the area, and the first evidence of Cooper and Stroup as partners comes from 1845. See also "Iron Works," *Augusta Chronicle*, August 12, 1843, which presents Moses Stroup as a sole proprietor; and "Cass Co. Iron Works—The State Road," *Augusta Chronicle*, August 19, 1845, which says Moses Stroup "has recently sold a half interest to the Hon. Mark A. Cooper." Cooper's first land transaction in Cass County occurred in December 1845. Deed Record Book G, 275, Clerk of Courts, Bartow County.

27. On Mark Anthony Cooper, see esp. Pope, *Mark Anthony Cooper*; and "Death of Mark A. Coope[r]," *Christian Index*, March 26, 1885.

28. Mark A. Cooper to Mr. Camak, February 2, 1846, reprinted in *Georgia Telegraph* (Macon), March 24, 1846, in *Southern Patriot* (Charleston, S.C.), March 31, 1846, and in *Southern Cultivator* (Atlanta, Ga.), March 1846. Pope, *Mark Anthony Cooper*, 111–113, discusses the flour mill output; see also "Etowah Mills," *Georgia Telegraph*, January 18, 1848. On Western & Atlantic purchases of Cooper's rails, chairs, and other iron products, see Charles F. M. Garrett to Mssrs. Cooper and Stroup, May 28, 1845; William L. Mitchell to Messrs. Cooper, Stroup and Wiley, October 21, 1848; William L. Mitchell to Messrs Cooper Wiley & Co., May 30, 1850; and W. L. Mitchell to Mark A. Cooper, July 23, 1851, all in Western and Atlantic Railroad—Chief Engineer—Outgoing Correspon-

dence, Record Group 18, Records of the Western & Atlantic Railroad, Georgia Archives, Morrow. The Georgia Railroad also purchased iron rails from Etowah. *Sun* (Baltimore, Md.), September 23, 1848.

29. Western and Atlantic Railroad, Chief Engineer's Report (1848), 3, Georgia Archives, Morrow; Pope, *Mark Anthony Cooper*, 267. Beginning in 1848, advertisements for flour from the "Etowah Mills" appeared in Macon, Savannah, and Augusta, Georgia, and in Charleston, South Carolina. See *Georgia Telegraph* (Macon), February 29, 1848; *Charleston Courier*, September 13, 1848; *Savannah Daily Republican*, February 20, 1849; *Augusta Chronicle*, March 6, 1849; and "Editorial Correspondence," *Charleston Courier*, October 13, 1849. On wheat production in northern Georgia, see Gates, "Impact of the Western & Atlantic Railroad," esp. 181–182.

30. As late as February 1846, the governor of Georgia granted a forty-acre lot of land to just Cooper and Stroup. The document is reproduced in Pope, *Mark Anthony Cooper*, 94. The earliest mention of Cooper, Stroup, and Wiley being associated together comes from a land purchase they made in June 1846. *Silva, et al. v. Ranklin, et al.*, in *Reports of Cases in Law and Equity, Argued and Determined in the Supreme Court of Georgia*, 80:82. On Wiley, see the biographical vignette in Ackerman, *Historical Sketch of the Illinois-Central Railroad*, 25–27. His lengthy letters to Carter are in the Farish Carter Papers, Southern Historical Collection, University of North Carolina, Chapel Hill. On Wiley as a director of the Bank of Milledgeville, see "Bank of Milledgeville," *Georgia Telegraph* (Macon), September 15, 1836 (in which Wiley is apparently misidentified as "Leroy M. Wilson"); and "Bank Reports," *Augusta Chronicle*, April 30, 1840. On Wiley's connections to the Bank of Macon, see "To the Public," *Georgian* (Savannah), September 25, 1832; Leroy M. Wiley to Farish Carter, August 18, 1839, ser. 1, Farish Carter Papers, Southern Historical Collection, University of North Carolina, Chapel Hill; Pope, *Mark Anthony Cooper*, 103–104. The $15,000 amount is mentioned in the land deeds recording Wiley's new partnership. See Deed Record Book G, 277–280, Clerk of Courts, Bartow County.

31. Lewis, *Transactions of the Southern Central Agricultural Society*, vi. This society should be seen in the context of broader agricultural improvement efforts. See esp. Rossiter, "Organization of Agricultural Improvement"; Rosengarten, "Southern Agriculturist in an Age of Reform"; and Faust, "Rhetoric and Ritual of Agriculture."

32. Lewis, *Transactions of the Southern Central Agricultural Society*, 257–261.

33. Ibid., 276–278.

34. Ibid., 280–297. On the connection of agricultural fairs to technological progress, see, for example, Gates, "Modernization as a Function of an Agricultural Fair"; more generally, see Neely, *Agricultural Fair*.

35. Tonnage reported in "Etowah Manufacturing and Mining Company," *Georgia Telegraph* (Macon), April 27, 1858.

36. "Memoirs of Mark Anthony Cooper," reprinted in Pope, *Mark Anthony Cooper*, 267; *Exposition of the Property of the Etowah Manufacturing and Mining Co.*, 4; *Chattanooga Advertiser*, quoted in "Department of Manufactures," *DeBow's Review of the Southern and Western States*, January 1852; Pope, *Mark Anthony Cooper*, 108–109, 116.

37. Agreement dated December 26, 1836, container 2, Franklin H. Elmore Papers, Library of Congress, Washington, D.C.; on the dispute and the valuation of slaves, see the undated committee report signed by John G. Brown, container 3, Franklin H. Elmore Papers, Library of Congress, Washington, D.C. Elmore describes the slaves in a letter from Washington City, December 1838, ibid. On the withdrawal of the Earles, see the meeting minutes of the Nesbitt Manufacturing Company in Columbia, December 18, 1838, and the accompanying agreement, ibid.

38. Cunyus, *History of Bartow County*, 78–79, 176; Meynard, *Venturers*, 636, 651–652; Deed Record Book BB, 697–698, Clerk of Courts, Bartow County.

39. Knowles, "Labor, Race, and Technology," 7. Knowles notes that in 1851 Joseph Reid Anderson, who oversaw the Tredegar Iron Works, wrote to Mark A. Cooper, offering "to help train slaves for the new Etowah rolling mill." The obvious inference is that he felt Cooper relied too much on free labor (12). *Scientific American*, May 31 and November 15, 1851. Ison exhibited his machine for forming railroad chairs at the 1851 Southern Central Agricultural Fair, where the judging committee concluded that his machine "is a valuable improvement, and that its use will very much reduce the price of Rail-Road Chairs, and recommend it to a premium." Lewis, *Transactions of the Southern Central Agricultural Society*, 15.

40. "Etowah Iron Works," *Daily Picayune* (New Orleans, La.), October 5, 1849. The situation along the Etowah contrasted sharply, for example, with the ironworks at Buffalo Forge, Virginia, which relied heavily on enslaved laborers. Dew, *Bond of Iron*.

41. On markets for iron products, see Knowles and Healey, "Geography, Timing, and Technology," 627; and Pope, *Mark Anthony Cooper*, 118. For lists of furnaces, forges, and rolling mills, see Lesley, *Iron Manufacturer's Guide*, 76–78, 193, 246. During the Civil War, another furnace was partially constructed, though it was never finished nor fired. See Joseph and Reed, *Ore, Water, Stone and Wood*.

42. Dew, "Slavery and Technology in the Antebellum Southern Iron Industry," 112. On the railroad car axle capability, see Black, *Railroads of the Confederacy*, 23; Lesley, *Iron Manufacturer's Guide*, 76–78. On consumer products made of iron, see *Georgia Telegraph* (Macon), August 1, 1848. On the number of employees, see "Etowah Manufacturing and Mining Company," *Georgia Telegraph*, April 27, 1858. On the population, see "Mill," *Cassville Standard*, December 1, 1859. On the brewery, see "Dissolution," *Southern Confederacy*, April 10, 1862.

The only mention of a house of prostitution comes from Davis, "Story of a Community Once Called Etowah," 13. His 1989 article did not include documentation. In 2003, Dunaway, *Slavery in the American Mountain South*, 127, used Davis's description and expanded on it without additional evidence by saying it was "a bordello staffed by enslaved women." Since then, Hébert, *Long Civil War*, 16, citing Dunaway, elaborated even further: "Slaves were in such number at Etowah that its owner Mark A. Cooper reportedly opened a bordello run by enslaved females who provided sex to workers, enslaved and free, in exchange for the company town script." These inferences are groundless. Davis almost certainly relied on the 1860 Cass County Census. Among the "free inhabitants in Stamp Creek," family number 1017 was a household led by J. Thompson, female, in which four free white women, ranging in age from nineteen to fifty, all had occupations listed as "Whore." The fifty-year-old woman evidently had a son, sixteen, whose occupation was listed as "a damn vagabond." While the census taker listed only free inhabitants, there was no evidence that enslaved women were forced to work as prostitutes.

43. The exact date that Stroup sold out to Cooper is unclear. Cooper, Stroup, and Wiley were still presented as a going partnership at the August 1848 agricultural fair. On the Round Mountain furnace, see Armes, *Story of Coal and Iron in Alabama*, 65–66; Act Incorporating the Alabama Mining and Manufacturing Company, in *Acts of the Second Biennial Session of the General Assembly of Alabama* (1850), 292–294; 1850 U.S. Census, Cherokee County, Ala. Moses's father, Jacob Stroup, had already overseen the building of an early iron furnace in eastern Alabama on Cane Creek in Calhoun County in the early 1840s. Armes, *Story of Coal and Iron in Alabama*, 65, 90–91.

44. For the family background of Henry F. Veitch, see the family records of Edward T. Veitch, Sumiton, Ala., and John Brigman, Vestavia, Ala. See Armes, *Story of Coal and*

Iron in Alabama, 136; "Nesbitt Mang. Co. Balance Sheet, Nov. 1, 1837," and "Ac/s Disbursement of Cash by E. W. Harrison Supt. Nesbitt Manufacturing Company," both in container 8, folder: Bills and Receipts, 1837, Franklin H. Elmore Papers, Library of Congress, Washington, D.C.; and a receipt for payment of $90.72 to Henry F. Veitch for his "labour at Ellen Furnace," May 1, 1838, container 3, Franklin H. Elmore Papers, Library of Congress, Washington, D.C. I have inspected the gravestones at the Goodson cemetery, also known as the furnace cemetery, in Bartow County. See ledger, Allatoona Iron Works, Cass County, Ga., 1845, Georgia Miscellany, Stuart A. Rose Manuscript, Archives, and Rare Book Library, Emory University, Atlanta, Ga.

45. On Stroup at Tannehill, see Bennett, *Tannehill*, 83–87; and Armes, *Story of Coal and Iron in Alabama*, 66–67; on John Alexander, see Bennett, *Tannehill*, 217–230. A John Alixander, Moses Stroup, and Henry F. Veitch all appear in "Nesbitt Mang. Co. Balance Sheet, Nov. 1, 1837," container 8, Franklin H. Elmore Papers, Library of Congress, Washington, D.C.

46. "North East and South West Alabama Railway," *American Railway Times*, April 9, 1859.

CHAPTER 4. THE EDUCATION OF JOSEPH E. BROWN

1. "Early History of the South-West," 11.

2. Ibid., 11–12, 74.

3. Ibid., 12–16, 73.

4. Ibid., 74–78. The quotation about the enslaved people Brown reacquired comes from a subsequent telling of Brown's story that mostly follows Brown's original account but includes some additional information. See Putnam, *History of Middle Tennessee*, 308. For the genealogical connections and history of the Brown family, see Martha Galt to Mrs. Barton, December 1956, Joseph Brown subject file, Cherokee County Historical Society, Canton, Ga.; genealogical materials, box 7, folder 9, Joseph E. Brown Papers, Atlanta History Center, Ga.; and Joseph Brown to Joseph E. Brown, April 22, 1859, box 1, folder 1, Joseph E. and Elizabeth Grisham Brown Collection, Hargrett Rare Book and Manuscript Library, University of Georgia, Athens.

5. On the Brown family, the farm in South Carolina, the move to Georgia, and the gristmill, see Martha Galt to Mrs. Barton, December 1956; and Brown, "Courtship and Marriage," 11. On Auraria's law offices, see "Georgia Gold Region," *Niles' Weekly Register* (Baltimore, Md.), May 4, 1833. Ira Foster quoted in Avery, *History of the State of Georgia*, 10. Generally, see Williams, *Georgia Gold Rush*; and Young, "Southern Gold Rush." The arguments and descriptions in this paragraph and elsewhere in this chapter sometimes follow closely an article I coauthored: Wright and Wheeler, "New Men in the Old South."

6. "Dahlonega, or Georgia Gold Region" 112 (emphasis in original).

7. Williams, *Georgia Gold Rush*, 107–108; Head and Etheridge, *Neighborhood Mint*; Birdsall, *United States Branch Mint*.

8. Speer, "Life and Times of Joseph Emerson Brown," 231; "Hon. J. E. Brown," in *Representative Men of the South*, 158–159.

9. Avery, *History of the State of Georgia*, 10; W. Leverett recommendation, October 6, 1843, box 1, folder 1, Brown Family Papers, Hargrett Rare Book and Manuscript Library, University of Georgia, Athens. On the job at the Etowah Academy, see "Hon. J. E. Brown," 159. Brown, "Courtship and Marriage," 11, 15, mentions the friendship between Joseph Grisham and Mackey Brown, and Joe Brown's baptism; Brown joined

the Canton Baptist Church in January. "Minutes of the Baptist Church of Christ, Canton, Georgia," January 27, 1844, Magruder Collection, Canton, Ga. On Brown's living arrangements with the Lewis family, see "Hon. J. E. Brown," 159; and Martha Galt to Mrs. Barton, December 1956.

10. On Lewis, see the biographical sketches in Boykin, *History of the Baptist Denomination*, 2:332–333; and Cunyus, *History of Bartow County*, 78–79; Joseph Grisham to William Grisham, October 9, 1837, and "Minutes of the Baptist Church of Christ, Canton, Ga.," August 26, 1837, both in Magruder Collection, Canton, Ga. Lewis was called to serve the Canton Baptist church in late November 1840. "Minutes of the Baptist Church of Christ, Canton, Ga.," November 27, 1840, ibid.; "Pickens R. Lewis Accidentally Kills Himself," *Cherokee Advance* (Canton, Ga.), July 29, 1892. As one sign of Lewis's wealth, in 1850 he owned sixty-four slaves. See 1850 U.S. Census, Slave Population Schedules, Cherokee County, Ga., reel 89, 206–207.

11. "Hon. J. E. Brown," 159. A notice that Brown had been admitted to the bar in Cherokee County is dated August 20, 1845, box 1, folder 1, Brown Family Papers, Hargrett Rare Book and Manuscript Library, University of Georgia, Athens; Avery, *History of the State of Georgia*, 13. On Brown's trip to Washington and his meeting with Calhoun, see Martha Galt to Mrs. Barton, December 1956; and Brown, "Courtship and Marriage," 11. Calhoun was saying the same thing in published speeches; see Johnston, *Western and Atlantic Railroad*, 28. On Brown's earnings, see Avery, *History of the State of Georgia*, 14.

12. Joseph Grisham to William Grisham, January 18, 1838; March 25, 1839; and April 13, 1840, all in Magruder Collection, Canton, Ga.; Birdsall, *United States Branch Mint*, 81.

13. See, for example, Geo. S. Hoyle to William Grisham, November 22, 1844, Magruder Collection, Canton, Ga.

14. Guidry, "Elizabeth Grisham Brown," 6–7, 12; Brown, "Courtship and Marriage," 10–11.

15. Brown, "Courtship and Marriage," 10–11.

16. Ibid., 10–12, 14; Joseph Grisham to William Grisham, May 10, 1842, Magruder Collection, Canton, Ga.

17. Rorabaugh, "Sons of Temperance," 263, 265, 268.

18. Meynard, *Venturers*, 954–955; Cunyus, *History of Bartow County*, 79. On Elias Earle and the Earle family's involvement with the Nesbitt Company, see Lander, "Iron Industry"; and Ferguson and Cowan, "Iron Plantations," 119–120.

19. Joseph Grisham to William Grisham, October 15, 1840, Magruder Collection, Canton, Ga.; Lesley, *Iron Manufacturer's Guide*, 77–78. On Lewis selling his furnace to his brother-in-law, see Meynard, *Venturers*, 636, 651–652. The transaction is recorded in Deed Record Book BB, 697–698, Clerk of Courts, Bartow County Courthouse, Cartersville, Ga. The lot given by Lewis to Brown is described in a typescript of the legal document, May 26, 1848, box 2, folder 1, Joseph E. Brown Papers, Kenan Research Center, Atlanta History Center, Ga.

20. For the dates of construction, see the 1870 case of *B. G. Pool[e] and O. H. Lufburrow v. P. R. and B. J. Lewis*, in *Reports of Cases in Law and Equity, Argued and Determined in the Supreme Court of Georgia*, 41:163; Lewis, *Transactions of the Southern Central Agricultural Society*, 258–259; account book, 1846–1854, 1868–1871, box 1, folder 4, Joseph E. Brown Papers, Kenan Research Center, Atlanta History Center, Ga.

21. The act of incorporation is reprinted in *Exposition of the Property of the Etowah Manufacturing and Mining Co.*, 12–14.

22. "Tunnell," *Federal Union* (Milledgeville, Ga.), November 6, 1849.

23. *Journal of the Senate of the State of Georgia* (1849–1850), esp. 33–36, 101, 274–286, 490.

24. *Journal of the Senate . . . 1849*, 22, 49–50, 164–166. For Brown's chairmanship, see Joseph E. Brown to William Grisham, November 24, 1849, Magruder Collection, Canton, Ga. Brown also mentioned that he had intended to call on Tomlinson Fort, but "Dr Fort has been lying very sick ever since the Commencement of the session and I have not thought it proper to trouble him especially as I was not acquainted with him."

25. *Journal of the Senate . . . 1849*, 184, 365, 388–397 (quotations on 396–397).

26. *Journal of the Senate . . . 1849*, 20–21, 217–218, 232, 292. Brown also introduced legislation to charter both the Dalton Female College and the Southern Central University of Georgia, which would be located in Dalton (175).

27. *Journal of the Senate . . . 1849*, 182, 234–235.

28. John W. Lewis, Eli McConnell, Samuel Tate, and J. P. Brooke, "To the People! of Cherokee County, Georgia," box 1, Grisham Family Papers, Stuart A. Rose Manuscript, Archives, and Rare Book Library, Emory University, Atlanta, Ga. See also Wright and Wheeler, "New Men in the Old South," 375–376. Cherokee County voters elected four different representatives instead. *Journal of the State Convention, Held in Milledgeville*, 3.

29. "Land and Mills," circular, box 5, folder 2, Joseph E. and Elizabeth Grisham Brown Collection, Hargrett Rare Book and Manuscript Library, University of Georgia, Athens; account book, 1846–1854, 1868–1871; "Minutes of the Baptist Church of Christ, Canton, Ga.," August 23 and September 27, 1851, May 22 and June 26, 1852, all in Magruder Collection, Canton, Ga.

30. Elizabeth Grisham Brown diary, January 5, 1856, box 8, folder 1, Joseph Emerson Brown Family Papers, Hargrett Rare Book and Manuscript Library, University of Georgia, Athens.

31. On the colleges, see Cunyus, *History of Bartow County*, 141–147; Mahan, *History of Old Cassville*, 41–67; "List of Subscribers to Cherokee Baptist College," October 24, 1854, box 1, folder 4, Ira Roe Foster Papers, Alabama Department of Archives and History, Montgomery; Elizabeth Grisham Collins to Susan Grisham, April 6, 1858, Magruder Collection, Canton, Ga.

32. Mary G. Franklin Account Books, 1842–1855, Cherokee County, Ga., part of the microfilm "Slavery in Ante-bellum Southern Industries," ser. A, Duke University, Durham, N.C.

33. Maysilles, *Ducktown Smoke*, esp. 24–32; Davis, *Where There Are Mountains*, esp. 157–159; Krueger, "Canton Copper Mine, 1854–1919" (1996), 2, 4–5, unpublished paper, Cherokee County Historical Society, Canton, Ga. Brown's permit for W. F. and S. Harris, October 7, 1854, and the one-eighth option are in box 2, folder 1, Joseph E. Brown Papers, Kenan Research Center, Atlanta History Center, Ga. See also Joel L. Galt to William Grisham, October 28, 1854, Magruder Collection, Canton, Ga.

34. Julien Deby, "Canton Copper Mine, Cherokee Co., Georgia," *Mining Magazine* (New York), 5 (November 1855): 395–397. On Deby, see his obituary in *Journal of the Iron and Steel Institute* 47 (1895): 260–261.

35. On Shepard, see Robinson, "Charles Upham Shepard," esp. 87–89, 92–94, 96; his obituary is in *Appleton's Annual Cyclopaedia and Register*, 700.

36. Shepard, *Report on the Copper and Silver-Lead Mine*, 7, 9, 11, 12, 16.

37. Ibid., 19–20; Krueger, "Canton Copper Mine," 5–6. Abraham Lincoln, one of the most prominent attorneys in Illinois in the mid-1850s, made about $5,000 annually. Oates, *With Malice toward None*, 98.

38. "In the Harvest Field," *Macon Telegraph and Messenger*, July 30, 1880; on sending wheat to Etowah gristmills, see Elizabeth Grisham Brown diary, July 31 and December 21, 1855, box 8, folder 1, Joseph Emerson Brown Family Papers, Hargrett Rare Book and Manuscript Library, University of Georgia, Athens.

39. "Sweetwater—the Factory," *Georgia Journal and Messenger* (Macon), March 6, 1850; Lewis, *Transactions of the Southern Central Agricultural Society*, 258–259; Cooper, *Cotton States and International Exposition*, 303; on the Browns' meals and lodging with McDonald, see Elizabeth Grisham Brown diary, April 5, May 5, and August 24, 1854; April 3, October 3 and 26, 1855; and June 9, 1856, box 8, folder 1, Joseph Emerson Brown Family Papers, Hargrett Rare Book and Manuscript Library, University of Georgia, Athens.

CHAPTER 5. THE REPUBLIC OF GEORGIA

1. Parks, *Joseph E. Brown*, 40–42.

2. Ibid., 67–68; "Solicitor General's Appointment," *Cassville Standard*, July 22, 1858; "Right Tune Just in Time," *Augusta Dispatch*, n.d., in Frank Brown's scrapbook, box 7, folder 1, Joseph E. and Elizabeth Grisham Brown Collection, Hargrett Rare Book and Manuscript Library, University of Georgia, Athens.

3. On Foster, see Smith, *History of the Georgia Militia*, 1:292; and Owen, *History of Alabama and Dictionary of Alabama Biography*, 3:603. For Foster's stance on temperance, see his speech to the Cumming Temperance Society, box 1, folder 1, Ira Roe Foster Papers, Alabama Department of Archives and History, Montgomery. Though unsigned, the speech is written in Foster's hand and compares to Ira Foster to R. Taylor, July 3, 1842, box 1, folder 3, ibid. For Foster's investment in gold, see "Copy of Agreement between Joseph Dunigan, John Deavours, and Ira R. Foster," March 20, 1843, box 1, folder 2, ibid.; Ira R. Foster to General Eli McConnell, June 19, 1850, box 1, folder 4, ibid.; Page & Smith to Messrs. Foster and Galt, August 26, 1851, ibid.

4. "List of Subscribers to Cherokee Baptist College," October 24, 1854, box 1, folder 4; "Ira R. Foster Treasurer," April 23, 1855, box 1 folder 4; I. R. Foster to Maj. M. A. Cooper, February 3, 1860, box 1, folder 6; Lewis and Poole Acct., box 1, folder 13, all in Ira Roe Foster Papers, Alabama Department of Archives and History, Montgomery.

5. Joseph E. Brown to "Dear Genl" [Ira Foster], June 30, 1857, Joseph E. Brown Letters, Hoole Library, University of Alabama, Tuscaloosa; "Ratification Meeting in Cherokee County" [July 7, 1857], unidentified newspaper clipping, n.d., box 5, folder 2, Joseph E. and Elizabeth Grisham Brown Collection, Hargrett Rare Book and Manuscript Library, University of Georgia, Athens; Joseph E. Brown to Howell Cobb, February 15, 1859, Joseph E. Brown Letters, Hoole Library, University of Alabama, Tuscaloosa. Also see Joseph E. Brown to J. Holt, postmaster general, April 13, 1859, Ira R. Foster Papers, Hargrett Rare Book and Manuscript Library, University of Georgia, Athens.

6. Waters was born in 1819 in Rensselaer County, New York. Gifted with "inventive ability," he worked "as a mechanic and assisted in the construction of . . . one of the first steam road locomotives ever operated" in that state, and then came to Georgia as a young man. Like Brown, he taught school for a time before he became an attorney practicing in Canton. Waters had a position as treasurer of Cherokee County before he headed to California in 1849 by way of Cuba and Mexico to dig for gold. His descendants remembered Waters's oft-told story of how "all the men of his party who drank whisky while on the trip . . . were attacked by disease that soon terminated their lives." Waters arrived in San Francisco "and thence made his way to the original placer mines in Tuolumne County." After two years Waters returned to Georgia and resumed his legal prac-

tice. Brown and Boyd, *History of San Bernardino and Riverside Counties*, 3:1118–1119. On his mill ties, see the financial claim made against Waters by William McConnell, a carpenter who worked on the mills, in Deed Book G, 369, Superior Court, Cherokee County. On his work as county treasurer, see *Reports of Cases in Law and Equity, Arrived and Determined in the Supreme Court of Georgia*, 9:185–188. On the location of his mills and for an extensive description and defense of Waters's career, see "Gov. Brown, Col. Waters and the Cassville Meeting," *Weekly Intelligencer* (Atlanta, Ga.), June 2, 1859. On the bridge, see "Reminiscences of Byron Waters," unpublished manuscript, box 3, Miscellaneous Collection, archives, Reinhardt University, Waleska, Ga.

7. McConnell, born in 1801 in Hall County, was one of the earliest white settlers of Cherokee County and served in the state legislature and as a brigadier general, like Ira Foster, in the state militia. His ties to gold, education, and railroads included service as a director of the Auraria branch of the Bank of Darien in 1835, trustee of the Etowah Academy (with William Grisham), and an incorporator in the mid-1850s of the North-Eastern Railroad, a planned railroad intended to pass through Rabun Gap at the far northeastern corner of the state. See Smith, *History of the Georgia Militia*, 1:320; and Marlin, *History of Cherokee County*, 36, 38–39, 192. On his mill connections, see *History of Texas*, 450–451; and *Heritage of Cherokee County*, 56. On the Bank of Darien, see "From the Darien Telegraph," *Augusta Chronicle*, January 25, 1835; on the Etowah Academy, see *Acts of the General Assembly of the State of Georgia* (1834), 14; on the railroad, see *Acts of the General Assembly of the State of Georgia* (1855–1856), 178–179. On his appearances for meals at the Brown home, see Elizabeth Grisham Brown diary, January 2, 1854; January 2, July 15, August 25, and October 3, 1855; and April 8, 1856, box 8, folder 1, Joseph Emerson Brown Family Papers, Hargrett Rare Book and Manuscript Library, University of Georgia, Athens. See also Annual Report of the Principal Keeper and Book Keeper of the Georgia Penitentiary, for the Fiscal Year Ending 1st Oct., 1858, 2–3, Georgia Archives, Morrow.

8. *Southern Education for Southern Youth*, 3–4 (emphasis in original). Stiles was prominent in Georgia politics, served a term in the U.S. Congress, and was a diplomat in Austria during the late 1840s. See Hébert, *Long Civil War*, 47.

9. *Southern Education for Southern Youth*, 5–13 (emphasis in original).

10. Ibid., 15–28 (quotations on 17, 21, 24, 26, 28; emphasis in original).

11. *Address, Delivered by Rev. C. W. Howard, before the Mnemosynean Society of the Cassville Female College, Commencement Day, July 21st, 1858* (N.p., n.d.) is quoted and summarized in *Russell's Magazine* 4 (1858): 92–93; and the passages on Washington are quoted in the *Southern Literary Messenger* (Richmond, Va.), new ser., 6 (September 1858): 231–232. Charles W. Howard, originally from Charleston, became a minister in the French Protestant (Huguenot) Church. In 1842 he entered into a hog-raising agreement with Tomlinson Fort and Fort's relative Joseph D. Fannin. In 1850, Howard discovered "hydraulic limestone," a natural cement, on land he owned, and some of his eleven enslaved laborers began mining and selling it. Like so many up-and-coming people in the Etowah Valley, he believed in a diversified agricultural economy and in 1858 announced that he would publish a new agricultural journal, the *South Countryman*. On Howard's South Carolina background, see "New Agricultural Journal," *Charleston Courier*, April 29, 1858. The agreement with Fort and Fannin is dated November 1, 1842, in box 1, folder 10, Tomlinson Fort Papers, Stuart A. Rose Manuscript, Archives, and Rare Book Library, Emory University, Atlanta, Ga. On Howard's hydraulic limestone quarry, see "Valuable Discovery," *Augusta Chronicle*, July 31, 1853; and Cummings, *American Cements*, 21. On the short-lived journal, which soon merged with the *Southern Cultiva-*

tor, which Howard joined as an editor, see "New Agricultural Journal"; and "Southern Cultivator for August," *Augusta Chronicle*, July 23, 1859. On Howard as a slaveholder, see the Slave Schedule for Cass County, Ga., in the 1850 U.S. Census.

12. *Augusta Constitutionalist* and *Cartersville Express* quoted in "Maj. Cooper's Rail Road Completed," *Cassville Standard*, October 28, 1858.

13. "Eugene LeHardy, Viscount De-Braulieu," *Augusta Chronicle*, January 3, 1875; Battey, *History of Rome and Floyd County*, 355–356. On LeHardy's acquaintance with Rowland, see Eugene LeHardy diary, 27, Hargrett Rare Book and Manuscript Library, University of Georgia, Athens; on Eugene LeHardy Stroup, see Stroup family genealogical records in my possession and the 1860 U.S. Census for Rocky Run Township, Hancock County, Ill., where the Stroup family had moved within the previous few years. In that 1860 Census, Eugene's middle initial is listed as H, but every other census and official record has his middle initial as L. See also *Rome Courier*, April 17, 1855; Reports of the Superintendent and Treasurer of the Western and Atlantic Rail-Road, 1858, 6, Georgia Archives, Morrow.

14. The railroad charter is included in *Exposition of the Property of the Etowah Manufacturing and Mining Co.*, 12–14; *Acts of the General Assembly of the State of Georgia* (1858), 194. See Eugene LeHardy to Gov. Joseph E. Brown, January 5, 1859, Governor's Incoming Correspondence, Civil War—Governor Joseph E. Brown, Georgia Archives, Morrow (available as Georgia, Civil War Correspondence, 1847–1865, Ancestry.com).

15. Pope, *Mark Anthony Cooper*, 141–147; Mark A. Cooper to Joseph E. Brown, May 10, 1860, box 3, folder 1, Telamon Cuyler Collection, Hargrett Rare Book and Manuscript Library, University of Georgia, Athens. See Mark A. Cooper to Joseph E. Brown, August 10, 1860, box 3, folder 1, ibid., in which Cooper enclosed an itemized bill from the Ames Manufacturing Company; and Candler, *Confederate Records*, 2:3–5.

16. Joseph E. Brown to Ira Foster, May 14, 1860, in Georgia, Civil War Correspondence, 1847–1865, Ancestry.com.

17. Ira R. Foster, John W. Anderson, and P. H. Colquitt to Joseph E. Brown, "Report of Com[missioners] on Military, 1860," box 55, folder 15, Telamon Cuyler Collection, Hargrett Rare Book and Manuscript Library, University of Georgia, Athens.

18. Joseph E. Brown to William S. Grisham, May 28, 1860, box 1, folder 2, Brown Family Papers, Hargrett Rare Book and Manuscript Library, University of Georgia, Athens; Elizabeth Grisham Brown diary, March 11 and 15, 1855; July 4, 1856, box 8, folder 1, Joseph Emerson Brown Family Papers, Hargrett Rare Book and Manuscript Library, University of Georgia, Athens; Parks, *Joseph E. Brown*, 106–107; see also the statement by Joseph E. Brown from "Rowland's Springs," June 28, 1860, in *Exposition of the Property of the Etowah Manufacturing and Mining Co.*, 7–8; and "Gov. Brown," *Federal Union* (Milledgeville, Ga.), August 7, 1860. On the location of Lewis's house, see "Most Desirable Places in Upper Georgia," *Georgia Weekly Telegraph* (Macon), January 18, 1870.

19. Candler, *Confederate Records*, 1:19–47 (quotations on 21, 47).

20. Ibid., 1:48–57 (quotations on 53, 56, 57).

21. *Journal of the House of Representatives of the State of Georgia* (1860), 11, 17–18, 23.

22. Ibid., 20–21 (quotation on 21).

23. Joseph Barbier to Joseph E. Brown, November 1860, box 55, folder 13, images 57–59, Telamon Cuyler Collection, Hargrett Rare Book and Manuscript Library, University of Georgia, Athens. For context, see "Direct Trade with Europe," *Augusta Chronicle*, October 3, 1860; and Kearns, "Secession Diplomacy," esp. 56–57.

24. Brown's December 7 letter was published in *Federal Union* (Milledgeville, Ga.),

December 11, 1860, and appears in Freehling and Simpson, *Secession Debated*, 145–159 (quotations on 153–154). On Brown's crucial role in Georgia's secession decision, see Coleman, *History of Georgia*, 149–152.

25. Battey, *History of Rome and Floyd County*, 356; "Eugene LeHardy, Viscount De-Braulieu." Mark Cooper, who was in a position to know, wrote to Brown in March 1861 and mentioned in his letter that "some time ago you appointed a man to go to Europe to buy Arms." Mark A. Cooper to Joseph E. Brown, March 14, 1861, Governor's Incoming Correspondence, Civil War—Governor Joseph E. Brown, Georgia Archives, Morrow (available as Georgia, Civil War Correspondence, 1847–1865, Ancestry.com). LeHardy discovered that because of the Union blockade of the southern coast, he could not return to his home. He stayed in Europe and built a railroad in Spain, then returned to Georgia after the end of the war. On secession, see Freehling and Simpson, *Secession Debated*, vii–xxi; and Johnson, *Toward a Patriarchal Republic*. For Brown's involvement, see esp. Parks, *Joseph E. Brown*, 110–128.

26. On the secession crisis, begin with Potter, *Impending Crisis*.

27. Skid Harris to Joseph E. Brown, February 16, 1861, Governor's Incoming Correspondence, Civil War—Governor Joseph E. Brown, Georgia Archives, Morrow (available as Georgia, Civil War Correspondence, 1847–1865, Ancestry.com).

28. The speech, held by the Cherokee County Historical Society, is written in William Grisham's hand.

29. Mark A. Cooper to Joseph E. Brown, November 14 and December 21, 1860, box 3, folder 1, Telamon Cuyler Collection, Hargrett Rare Book and Manuscript Library, University of Georgia, Athens; Cooper's February letter was published in "Provisional Congress of the Confederate States!: Ninth Day," *Macon Daily Telegraph*, February 15, 1861. The proceedings were also printed in the *New York Herald*, February 23, 1861. Mark A. Cooper to Gov. Joseph E. Brown, March 14, 1861, Governor's Incoming Correspondence, Civil War—Governor Joseph E. Brown, Georgia Archives, Morrow (available as Georgia, Civil War Correspondence, 1847–1865, Ancestry.com). Cooper was far from the only businessman who saw the creation of the Confederacy as a business opportunity. See DeCredico, *Patriotism for Profit*.

30. Pope, *Mark Anthony Cooper*, 172–173; Mark A. Cooper to Secretary of War, September 12, 1861, Etowah Manufacturing & Mining Co., Confederate Papers Relating to Citizens or Business Firms, War Department Collection of Confederate Records, Record Group 109, National Archives, Washington, D.C.

31. Armes, *Story of Coal and Iron in Alabama*, 161–164.

32. Joseph E. Brown to "Genl" [Ira Foster], June 9, 1861, Joseph E. Brown Letters, Hoole Library, University of Alabama, Tuscaloosa; Parks, *Joseph E. Brown*, 164–165, 181, 192 (Brown's letter quoted on 165). Confederate senators were elected by state legislatures, but in this case the elected senator, Robert Toombs, turned down the offer, which placed the decision in Governor Brown's hands. For Grisham's appointment, see Reports of the Superintendent and Treasurer of the Western and Atlantic Rail-Road, 1862, 8, 15, Georgia Archives, Morrow.

33. Joseph E. Brown to John W. Lewis, May 26, 1862, Governor's Letter Books, Georgia Archives, Morrow (available as Georgia, Civil War Correspondence, 1847–1865, Ancestry.com); Candler, *Confederate Records*, 2:223; Lonn, *Salt as a Factor*, esp. 13–18, 26, 96–97.

34. John W. Lewis to Editor, *Intelligencer* (Atlanta, Ga.), November 2, 1862 (emphasis in original), box 6, folder 1, Joseph E. and Elizabeth Grisham Brown Collection, Hargrett Rare Book and Manuscript Library, University of Georgia, Athens.

35. Hébert, *Long Civil War*, 85–89, 93–94; Pope, *Mark Anthony Cooper*, 174–179;

"Sad Visit," *Cherokee Mountaineer*, January 18, 1862, in the scrapbook in box 6, folder 1, Joseph E. and Elizabeth Grisham Brown Collection, Hargrett Rare Book and Manuscript Library, University of Georgia, Athens.

CHAPTER 6. DESTRUCTION

1. Pope, *Mark Anthony Cooper*, 180. On the developer, Walter L. Goodman, see Armes, *Story of Coal and Iron in Alabama*, 165; Morgan, "Public Nature of Private Industry"; Morgan, *Planters' Progress*.

2. "Proclamation," *Augusta Chronicle*, September 24, 1861; *Official Records of the Union and Confederate Navies*, vol. 2:243; Pope, *Mark Anthony Cooper*, 181, 183. Cooper also had two "free persons of color" leave his employ with soldiers under the command of Colonel William T. Wofford. Cooper complained to Governor Brown that the men had been "kidnapped" from Cooper's guardianship, but Wofford said there was no legal arrangement to that effect in Cass County and that the men had exercised their rights as free people and hired themselves voluntarily as cooks with a Captain Ford, who served under Wofford's command. Pope, *Mark Anthony Cooper*, 177–178.

3. G. D. Phillips to Joseph E. Brown, June 7, 1861, box 56, folder 2, images 26–27, ser. 1, Historical Manuscripts, Telamon Cuyler Collection, Hargrett Rare Book and Manuscript Library, University of Georgia, Athens; Bonds, *Stealing the General*, 3–123.

4. Bonds, *Stealing the General*, 113–200.

5. On the saltpeter cave, see Donnelly, "Bartow County Confederate Saltpetre Works." On the sale, see Pope, *Mark Anthony Cooper*, 185. On Quinby and Robinson and their Memphis operation, see Davis, "Story of a Community Once Called Etowah"; and Quinby and Robinson to Stephen R. Mallory, [April 4], 1862, "Amt of Capital Required to Make the 'Etowah Iron Works' Capable of Producing 10.000 Tons of Wrought Iron per Annum," Confederate Papers Relating to Citizens or Business Firms, War Department Collection of Confederate Records, Record Group 109, National Archives, Washington, D.C. The contract stipulations come from *War of the Rebellion*, ser. 2, 2:244. On bolt iron, see "Col. Tift's Marine Ram," *Macon Daily Telegraph*, April 9, 1862. For the advertisement, see *Chattanooga Daily Rebel*, October 8, 1862. The ad copy has a note indicating that the advertisement ran also in the *Atlanta Confederacy* and the *Memphis Appeal*.

6. William T. Quinby to Gov. Joseph E. Brown, November 11, 1862, Governor's Incoming Correspondence, Civil War—Governor Joseph E. Brown, Georgia Archives, Morrow (available as Georgia, Civil War Correspondence, 1847–1865, Ancestry.com).

7. Joseph E. Brown to Sec. of War George W. Randolph, May 1 and 2, 1862, *War of the Rebellion*, ser. 1, vol. 10:480, 483; Rosecrans, "Mistakes of Grant," 583.

8. On the public disagreements between Brown and Davis, see Niven, "Joseph E. Brown, Confederate Obstructionist."

9. Hudson, *Odyssey of a Southerner*, 35–152. On Wiley's association with the Illinois Central, see Ackerman, *Historical Sketch of the Illinois-Central Railroad*, 25–27.

10. Contract, July 1, 1863, Confederate Papers Relating to Citizens or Business Firms, War Department Collection of Confederate Records, Record Group 109, National Archives, Washington, D.C.; Hudson, *Odyssey of a Southerner*, 161–162 (quotation on 162). On Smith's trouble obtaining coal, see General Beauregard's letter of reply to Smith on October 29, 1863, *War of the Rebellion*, ser. 1, vol. 28, pt. 2:456.

11. *Daily Intelligencer* (Atlanta, Ga.), September 17, 1863; Dietrich, *History of Rowland Springs*, 8; Mahan, *History of Old Cassville*, 80–82.

12. McPherson, *Battle Cry of Freedom*, 743–750.

13. Joseph E. Brown to Joseph E. Johnston, February 10, 1864, *War of the Rebellion*, ser. 1, 52:616–617.

14. *Memoirs of William T. Sherman*, 729–730.

15. Hudson, *Odyssey of a Southerner*, 162; Pope, *Mark Anthony Cooper*, 187.

16. *War of the Rebellion*, ser. 1, vol. 41:1011–1012; vol. 38, pt. 4:408–409.

17. John W. Lewis to Fulton & Co., Deed Record Book P, 730–731, Clerk of Courts, Superior Court, Bartow County.

18. *War of the Rebellion*, ser. 1, vol. 38, pt. 5:607. On local conditions, see Hébert, *Long Civil War*, 117–170. The best work on the topic of federal military policy is Grimsley, *Hard Hand of War*, esp. 111–119, 142–225.

19. Mahan, *History of Old Cassville*, 104. McCollum wrote about his war experiences; some of his writing appears in *Heritage of Cherokee County*, 407–411 (quotation on 410); see also McCollum, "Second Battle of Big Shanty."

20. *Heritage of Cherokee County*, 410. On other killings committed by McCollum and his Scouts, see Marlin, *History of Cherokee County*, 73–77.

21. *Heritage of Cherokee County*, 410; Superior Court Minutes, March 1865 (microfilm), Pickens County Library, Jasper, Ga.

22. Mahan, *History of Old Cassville*, 104–105; *War of the Rebellion*, ser. 1, vol. 39, pt. 3:513.

23. Lamar Roberts interview, Cherokee County Historical Society; Marlin, *History of Cherokee County*, 76; "Fight at Rough and Ready," *Macon Daily Telegraph and Confederate*, November 15, 1864; "Governor Brown's House Burned [by] Vandals," *Southern Banner* (Athens, Ga.), November 23, 1864 (reprinted from the Atlanta *Intelligencer*; a briefer reprinting appears in *Daily Constitutionalist* [Augusta, Ga.], November 19, 1864); "From Cherokee Georgia," *Macon Daily Telegraph and Confederate*, April 5, 1865. In June 1864, Union soldiers had burned the bridge at Canton over the Etowah River. See *War of the Rebellion*, ser. 1, vol. 38, pt. 3:866; Mahan, *History of Old Cassville*, 106–111.

24. Coleman, *History of Georgia*, 191, 203; see also Bonner, "Sherman at Milledgeville," esp. 286, 288. Bonner contended that the few remaining prisoners began to burn the penitentiary even before U.S. soldiers arrived. In Georgia, inmates had been performing labor since 1817. Derbes, "Origins of the Prison-Industrial Complex," 49.

25. Petition, January 18, 1865, box 59, folder 14, images 12–14, Telamon Cuyler Collection, Hargrett Rare Book and Manuscript Library, University of Georgia, Athens; William T. Wofford to Governor Joseph E. Brown, February 8, 1865, box 59, folder 15, images 9–11, ibid. See also Hébert, *Long Civil War*, 166–170.

26. "Report of Examination into the Condition of the W. & A R. Road," April 18, 1865, and "Tabular Statement of the Condition of the Western and Atlantic Rail Road," April 1, 1865, box 1, folder 3, Brown Family Papers, Hargrett Rare Book and Manuscript Library, University of Georgia, Athens.

27. Candler, *Confederate Records*, 2:818–855 (quotations on 830–831).

28. Jones, *Yankee Blitzkrieg*, esp. 63, 151; Bennett, *Tannehill*, 127; Armes, *Story of Coal and Iron in Alabama*, esp. 187–201.

29. *Intelligencer* (Atlanta, Ga.), quoted in "Ex-Governor Joseph E. Brown," *Macon Daily Telegraph*, July 25, 1865; Elizabeth G. Brown to Joseph E. Brown, May 26, 1865, box 1, folder 4, Brown Family Papers, Hargrett Rare Book and Manuscript Library, University of Georgia, Athens; Grisham family Bible, Magruder Collection, Canton, Ga.

30. Parole terms in Nichols, "Political Career of Joseph E. Brown," 17–18; Candler, *Confederate Records*, 2:885–892 (quotations on 887, 888, 889).

31. Parks, *Joseph E. Brown*, 333–339; Joseph E. Brown to Mary Brown, [?] 2, 1865,

October 3 and 12, 1865, all in box 1, folder 3, Joseph E. and Elizabeth Grisham Brown Collection, Hargrett Rare Book and Manuscript Library, University of Georgia, Athens.

32. Elizabeth G. Brown to "My dear son," April 27, 1862, box 1, folder 2, Brown Family Papers, Hargrett Rare Book and Manuscript Library, University of Georgia, Athens; Frank P. Brown to Mary Brown, April 28, 1864, box 1, folder 3, Joseph E. and Elizabeth Grisham Brown Collection, Hargrett Rare Book and Manuscript Library, University of Georgia, Athens; Mary V. Brown to Elizabeth G. Brown, January 28, 1864, box 1, folder 3, ibid.; diary of Joseph M. Brown, February 16, 1869, box 3, folder 2, Brown Family Papers, Hargrett Rare Book and Manuscript Library, University of Georgia, Athens; Joseph E. Brown to "My dear daughter" [Mary V. Brown], October 12, 1865, Joseph E. and Elizabeth Grisham Brown Collection, Hargrett Rare Book and Manuscript Library, University of Georgia, Athens; Mary V. Brown to Frank P. Brown, November 19, 1865, box 1, folder 3, ibid. See Fort, *Memoirs of the Fort and Fannin Families*, 57, on Tomlinson Fort's friendship with Joseph E. Brown.

33. William Grisham ledger, submitted May 21, 1867, Magruder Collection, Canton, Ga. Almost certainly these donations came from the New York Ladies' Southern Relief Association. See Holmes, *New York Ladies' Southern Relief Association*. Grisham spent most of the summer of 1867 dispensing more aid, including bacon, from the South Western Commission of Louisville, Kentucky, and from Maryland Quakers.

34. "Trip to Cherokee County," *Cartersville Standard and Express*, May 29, 1873. The description fits well with the general interest in and love of ruins. See Nelson, "Pleasures of Civil War Ruins"; and Swanson, "Rhetoric of Ruin."

CHAPTER 7. ANEW

1. Agreement, Baldwin County, January 18, 1866, box 1, folder 5, Brown Family Papers, Hargrett Rare Book and Manuscript Library, University of Georgia, Athens. See also Parks, *Joseph E. Brown*, 357. Plant was born in New Haven, Connecticut, in 1814 and moved to Georgia as a teenager. Hall, *America's Successful Men of Affairs*, 2:632.

2. Joseph E. Brown to Alfred Baker, January 22, 1866, box 1, folder 5, Brown Family Papers, Hargrett Rare Book and Manuscript Library, University of Georgia, Athens. The banks were the Bank of Augusta, Mechanics Bank of Augusta, the City Bank of Augusta, and Union Bank of Augusta. On Brown's relationship to banks while he was governor, see Parks, *Joseph E. Brown*, 69–71.

3. *Acts of the General Assembly of the State of Georgia* (1866), 117–119. The other incorporators were William L. High, E. Waitzfelder, M. Waitzfelder, and Thomas Lewis. On Fulton's financial troubles, see M. C. Fulton to Joseph E. Brown, June 20, 1868, box 2, folder 2, Brown Family Papers, Hargrett Rare Book and Manuscript Library, University of Georgia, Athens; Record Book W, 294–295, Clerk of Courts, Bartow County Courthouse, Cartersville, Ga.

4. Beecher replied that his schedule precluded a visit, but he fully supported "promoting that entire cordiality and good will, which ought to exist between every part of our widely spread land." Henry Ward Beecher to Joseph E. Brown, February 1, 1867, box 1, folder 3, Brown Family Papers, Hargrett Rare Book and Manuscript Library, University of Georgia, Athens; [Brown], *Appeal to the People of Georgia*, box 1, folder 7, ibid.; Parks, *Joseph E. Brown*, 350–433 (quotation on 410, from the Atlanta *Daily New Era*, March 11, 1868); Roberts, *Joseph E. Brown and the Politics of Reconstruction*, 43–69. See also Nelson, *Iron Confederacies*, 78.

5. On Foster's lumber interests, see various letters in box 1, folder 6, Ira Roe Foster Papers, Alabama Department of Archives and History, Montgomery. *Acts of the General*

Assembly of the State of Georgia (1866), 116–117, shows Foster incorporating the Kellogg gold mine, which was presumably in Cherokee County. Foster's mills were near Kellogg Creek, and one of his fellow incorporators was Miles G. Dobbins, who lived across the line in Bartow County. On Dobbins, see Cunyus, *History of Bartow County*, 200–201; *Acts of the General Assembly of the State of Georgia* (1866), 89–91; Duncan and Smith, *History of Marshall County*, 46–47. Foster was apparently still in Cherokee County in October 1867. See Joseph E. Brown to "Dear Gen'l" [Ira R. Foster], October 7, 1867, Joseph E. Brown Letters, Hoole Library, University of Alabama, Tuscaloosa.

6. Howell Cobb, Mark A. Cooper, and John H. Fitten, "Report of the Committee on the Removal of the Penitentiary," November 2, 1866, 1–2, box 53, Governor's Incoming Correspondence, Executive Department Papers, Georgia Archives, Morrow.

7. Ibid., 4–17.

8. Taylor, "Convict Lease System in Georgia," 6.

9. *Acts of the General Assembly of the State of Georgia* (1866), 81, 115–116; Conway, *Reconstruction of Georgia*, 204–208; Pope, *Mark Anthony Cooper*, 87–91.

10. Parks, *Joseph E. Brown*, 450.

11. Ibid.

12. The most complete rendering of these events, except for the information about Brown's involvement with the writing of the lease legislation, is Thompson, *Reconstruction in Georgia*, 238–254. See also Parks, *Joseph E. Brown*, 450–466, which describes Brown's involvement in drafting the legislation; Duncan, *Entrepreneur for Equality*, 112–117; Conway, *Reconstruction of Georgia*, 192–197; and Johnston, *Western and Atlantic Railroad*, 62–66. Johnston also includes the actual lease legislation and the 1870 lease in an appendix, 224–229.

13. *Atlanta Constitution*, November 10, 1871 (the marriage); "Handsome Residence," *Atlanta Constitution*, March 5, 1872; "Major's Roll-Call," unidentified newspaper clipping, n.d., box 6, Julius L. Brown Papers, Atlanta History Center, Ga.

14. Broadus, *Memoir of James Petigru Boyce*, 22, 213; Nettles, *James Petigru Boyce*; Kelly, "Portrait Painting in Tennessee," 232.

15. "Speech of Gov. Brown in the Baptist Biennial Convention at Augusta, Ga., May 11th, 1863," reprinted from the *Christian Index* in an unidentified newspaper, n.d., scrapbook, box 6, folder 1, Joseph E. and Elizabeth Grisham Brown Collection, Hargrett Rare Book and Manuscript Library, University of Georgia, Athens.

16. On the history of the seminary, see Mueller, *History of Southern Baptist Theological Seminary*; and Wills, *Southern Baptist Theological Seminary*; for the membership of the relocation committee, see Broadus, *Memoir of James Petigru Boyce*, 223.

17. The lease is mentioned in *Acts and Resolutions of the General Assembly of the State of Georgia* (1873), 185–186; and Roberts, "Joseph E. Brown, and His Georgia Mines," 286, gives the acreage. Generally, on Zachariah Gordon, see Boykin, *History of the Baptist Denomination*, 2:228–229; and Tankersley, "Zachariah Herndon Gordon." On his first Dade property, see Record Book D, 151, Superior Court, Dade County, Ga. Gordon was interested in development. In 1847 the state legislature considered the petitions of several Cass County residents on behalf of Zachariah Gordon and Elias King, who applied for permission to build a mill dam across the Oostanaula River, which joined with the Etowah at Rome to form the Coosa. On the attempted Oostanaula dam, which was postponed and then failed to pass, see *Journal of the House of Representatives of the State of Georgia, 1847*, 82–83, 222. Gordon's 1850 and 1851 lot purchases are in Record Book C, 135–137, 216–217, Superior Court, Dade County, Ga. The U.S. Census of 1850 found Zachariah Gordon; his wife, Malinda; their seven children; and two

boarders living in the East Chickamauga District of Walker County. On the Nickajack Railroad and Mining Company, incorporated by Z. H. Gordon and Co., and James H. and Andrew G. Gordon & Co., see *Acts of the State of Tennessee* (1855–1856), 28–29; and *Acts of the General Assembly of the State of Georgia* (1855–1856), 177–178.

18. 1860 U.S. Census, District 1, Jackson County, Ala.; Zachariah Gordon was listed as a farmer; John B. Gordon, twenty-eight years old, was listed as a miner. The incorporation of the Castle Rock Coal Mining Company is in *Acts of the General Assembly of the State of Georgia* (1862), 73–74. For the transfer of about 3,600 acres of Dade County lands from Zachariah H. Gordon to the Castle Rock Coal Company, see Record Book F, 32–34, Superior Court, Dade County, Ga. On the damage to the mines and their closure, see Eckert, *John Brown Gordon*, 128. The 1867 lease is in Record Book F, 243–244, Superior Court, Dade County, Ga.; the Lehigh agreement is in Record Book F, 244–245, ibid. Gordon's partners were Peter [Horner?], Levi Line, Jessie M. Line, and Eli J. Sagar.

19. Record Book G, 357–361, Superior Court, Dade County, Ga.

20. Tankersley, "Zachariah Herndon Gordon," 234.

21. *Acts and Resolutions of the General Assembly of the State of Georgia* (1873), 185–186. Elizabeth Grisham Brown's brother William S. Grisham (not to be confused with her uncle), set up as a coal dealer in Atlanta. See Grisham's advertisement from 1874 in an unidentified newspaper clipping, box 1, folder 7, Julius L. Brown Papers, Atlanta History Center, Ga.; Grisham's obituary in an unidentified newspaper clipping, n.d., box 9, folder 2, Joseph E. and Elizabeth Grisham Brown Collection, Hargrett Rare Book and Manuscript Library, University of Georgia, Athens; Roberts, "Joseph E. Brown and His Georgia Mines," 288–289.

22. *Acts and Resolutions of the General Assembly of the State of Georgia* (1873), 180–182, 179–180. On Brown's involvement with the Rogers Iron Company, see Cunyus, *History of Bartow County*, 198.

23. *Acts and Resolutions of the General Assembly of the State of Georgia* (1873), 186–189; Record Book S, 495–496, Clerk of Courts, Bartow County Courthouse, Cartersville, Ga. See "Rehabilitating the Rising Fawn Plant."

24. On the 1868 lease, see Lichtenstein, *Twice the Work of Free Labor*, 42, 47; and Taylor, "Convict Lease System in Georgia," 7–9. On William A. Fort's relationship to Tomlinson Fort, see Fort, *Memoirs of the Fort and Fannin Families*, 213; and the William A. and Eudocia Fort grave marker in Myrtle Hill Cemetery in Rome, which confirms his birthdate. On Eudocia, see Battey, *History of Rome and Floyd County*, 303.

25. "Report of the Chief Engineer on the Present Condition of the Selma Rome & Dalton [Railroad]," April 9, 1868, Selma, Rome and Dalton Railroad Company letter book, Hargrett Rare Book and Manuscript Library, University of Georgia, Athens.

26. Taylor, "Convict Lease System in Georgia," 9–10, 22–25; Lichtenstein, *Twice the Work of Free Labor*, 65, 68–69. On John T. Grant, see esp. Nelson, *Iron Confederacies*, 78–79.

27. Lichtenstein, *Twice the Work of Free Labor*, 59, 70; LeFlouria, *Chained in Silence*.

28. Lichtenstein, *Twice the Work of Free Labor*, 122, 128–134. See also Blackmon, *Slavery by Another Name*; and Mancini, *One Dies, Get Another*.

29. Lichtenstein, *Twice the Work of Free Labor*, 134–135.

30. Ibid., 105.

31. Mancini, *One Dies, Get Another*, 81.

32. Wheaton, *Prisons and Prayer*, 198–199.

33. Janes, *Hand-book of the State of Georgia*, 45.

34. Eckert, *John Brown Gordon*, 125–175.

35. Ibid., 201–238; Parks, *Joseph E. Brown*, 508–520.

EPILOGUE

1. Joseph E. Brown to James P. Boyce, February 3, 1880, "Correspondence from Joseph E. Brown to James P. Boyce in Regard to the Sum of $50,000 Given to the Southern Baptist Theological Seminary . . . May 21, 1879–May 6, 1880," Southern Baptist Theological Seminary, Louisville, Ky.; Mueller, *History of Southern Baptist Theological Seminary*, 46–47.

2. For the connection between James P. Boyce and Tomlinson Fort Jr., who worked for Boyce at least in 1877 and 1885, see *J. P. Boyce, Executor, etc., v. J. C. Stanton et al., and Other Consolidated Causes*, in *Reports of Cases Argued and Determined in the Supreme Court of Tennessee*, 15:274–325, esp. 276, 286. On Fort, see the biographical sketch of him in Armstrong, *History of Hamilton County and Chattanooga, Tennessee*, 1:411–412 (quotation on 411).

3. "Julius L. Brown's Bequest to Tech Is Attacked in Court," unidentified newspaper clipping, n.d., Julius L. Brown personality file, Atlanta History Center, Ga.; Sam Flemings to Tomlinson Fort [Jr.], October 26, 1907, box 4, folder 2, Tomlinson Fort Papers, Chattanooga Public Library, Chattanooga, Tenn.

4. Julius L. Brown to Tomlinson Fort [Jr.], power of attorney, March 31, 1887, box 3, folder 6, Tomlinson Fort Papers, Chattanooga Public Library, Chattanooga, Tenn; Armes, *Story of Coal and Iron in Alabama*, 109–120; and DuBose, *Jefferson County and Birmingham, Alabama*, esp. 136–145.

5. Blackmon, *Slavery by Another Name*, 51–53, 70–78; Armes, *Story of Coal and Iron in Alabama*, 238–242, 253–261; DuBose, *Jefferson County and Birmingham, Alabama*, 466; Veitch family records in possession of John Brigman, Vestavia, Ala.

6. Rowell, *Vulcan in Birmingham*, 23; Armes, *Story of Coal and Iron in Alabama*, 284–285; *First City Directory*, 172–173. On the ubiquity of the Veitches in early Birmingham, see DuBose, *Jefferson County and Birmingham, Alabama*, 282; *Iron Molders' Journal* (Cincinnati, Ohio) 32 (December 1896): 395; Morris, *Vulcan and His Times*, esp. 12. Generally, see Lewis, *Sloss Furnaces and the Rise of the Birmingham District*.

7. Gabard, "Joseph Mackey Brown," 16–19, 21–27.

8. Ibid., 27–30.

9. Ibid., 41–45.

10. Ibid., 60–73.

11. Ibid., 73–245, esp. 111 and 136 on the labor problems of J. W. English. On English as a beneficiary of convict leases, see LeFlouria, *Chained in Silence*.

12. Gabard, "Joseph Mackey Brown," 304–305.

BIBLIOGRAPHY

MANUSCRIPT COLLECTIONS AND UNPUBLISHED GOVERNMENT DOCUMENTS

Alabama Department of Archives and History, Montgomery

Ira Roe Foster Papers

Bartow County Courthouse, Cartersville, Ga.

Court of Ordinary
Superior Court, Clerk of Courts

Bartow History Museum, Cartersville, Ga.

Rowland Springs Scrapbook

John Brigman, Vestavia, Ala.

Veitch family records

Chattanooga Public Library, Chattanooga, Tenn.

Tomlinson Fort [Jr.] Papers

Cherokee County Courthouse, Canton, Ga.

Inferior Court
Superior Court, Clerk of Courts

Cherokee County Historical Society, Canton, Ga.

Joseph E. Brown subject file
William Grisham farewell speech
Krueger, Thomas H. "The Canton Copper Mine, 1854–1919." 1996.
Lamar Roberts interview, June 4, 2014

Dade County Courthouse, Trenton, Ga.

Superior Court, Clerk of Courts

Duke University, Durham, N.C.

Mary G. Franklin Account Books, 1842–1855

Georgia Archives, Morrow

Annual Report of the Principal Keeper and Book Keeper of the Georgia Penitentiary, for the Fiscal Year ending 1st Oct., 1858.
Etowah, Ga., mill journal, 1855–1858
Executive Department Papers
Foster and King's Mill Account Book, Cherokee County, Ga., 1857–1858.
Governor's Incoming Correspondence
Habersham Ironworks Daybook
Records of the Western & Atlantic Railroad, Record Group 18
Reports of the Superintendent and Treasurer of the Western and Atlantic Rail-Road

Hargrett Rare Book and Manuscript Library,
University of Georgia, Athens

Joseph E. and Elizabeth Grisham Brown Collection
Joseph Emerson Brown Family Papers
Brown Family Papers
Telamon Cuyler Collection
Ira R. Foster Papers
Eugene LeHardy diary
Selma, Rome and Dalton Railroad Company letter book

Hoole Library, University of Alabama, Tuscaloosa

Joseph E. Brown Letters

Kenan Research Center, Atlanta History Center, Ga.

Joseph E. Brown Papers
Julius L. Brown Papers
Julius L. Brown personality file

Library of Congress, Washington, D.C.

Franklin H. Elmore Papers
"Memorial of Pierce M. Butler and Others, Praying the Establishment of a National Foundry." U.S. Congressional Serial Set no. 330, House document no. 387, May 21, 1838, 25th Cong., 2nd sess.
"Report from the Secretary of War." December 29, 1837, 25th Cong., 2nd sess.

William and Nell Galt Magruder, Canton, Ga.

Magruder Collection

National Archives and Records Administration, Washington, D.C.

Confederate Papers Relating to Citizens or Business Firms, War Department Collection of Confederate Records, Record Group 109

Pickens County Library, Jasper, Ga.

Superior Court Minutes of Pickens County

Reinhardt University, Waleska, Ga.

Miscellaneous Collection
Reinhardt store ledger

South Caroliniana Library, University of South Carolina, Columbia

Pierce Mason Butler Papers
Elmore Family Papers
Franklin Harper Elmore Papers

Southern Baptist Theological Seminary, Louisville, Ky.

Correspondence from Joseph E. Brown to James P. Boyce

*Southern Historical Collection,
University of North Carolina, Chapel Hill*

Farish Carter Papers

Special Collections, Clemson University Libraries, Clemson, S.C.

Benjamin Ryan Tillman Papers

*Stuart A. Rose Manuscript, Archives, and Rare Book Library,
Emory University, Atlanta, Ga.*

Georgia Miscellany
Grisham Family Papers
Tomlinson Fort Family Papers

Edward T. Veitch, Sumiton, Ala.

Veitch family records

PUBLISHED PRIMARY SOURCES

Acts and Resolutions of the General Assembly of the State of Georgia, 1842. Milledgeville, Ga.: William S. Rogers, 1843.
———. *1873.* Atlanta, Ga.: W. A. Hemphill, 1873.
Acts of the General Assembly of the State of Georgia, 1831. Milledgeville, Ga.: Prince and Ragland, 1832.
———. *1833.* Milledgeville, Ga.: Polhill and Fort, 1834.
———. *1834.* Milledgeville, Ga.: P. L. and B. H. Robinson, 1835.
———. *1836.* Milledgeville, Ga.: P. L. Robinson, 1837.
———. *1837.* Milledgeville, Ga.: P. L. Robinson, 1838.
———. *1855–1856.* Milledgeville, Ga.: Boughton, Nisbet and Barnes, 1856.
———. *1858.* Columbus, Ga.: Tennent Lomax, n.d.
———. *1862.* Milledgeville, Ga.: Boughton, Nisbet and Barnes, 1863.
———. *1866.* Macon, Ga.: J. W. Burke, 1867.
Acts Passed by the General Assembly of Georgia, 1835. Milledgeville, Ga.: John A. Cuthbert, 1836.
Acts of the Second Biennial Session of the General Assembly of Alabama. Montgomery, Ala.: Brittan and De Wolf, 1850.
Acts of the State of Tennessee, 1855–1856. Nashville, Tenn.: G. C. Torbett, 1856.

Armes, William Dallam, ed. *The Autobiography of Joseph Le Conte*. New York: D. Appleton, 1903.

[Boggs, Marion Alexander, selector and arranger]. *The Alexander Letters, 1787–1900*. Savannah, Ga.: George J. Baldwin, 1900.

[Brown, Joseph E.]. *An Appeal to the People of Georgia*. Atlanta, Ga.: n.p., 1867.

Brown, Mrs. Joseph Emerson. "Courtship and Marriage of a Georgia First Lady." *Atlanta Historical Bulletin* 12 (June 1967): 8–15.

Candler, Allen D., comp. *The Confederate Records of the State of Georgia*. Atlanta, Ga.: Chas. P. Byrd, 1909.

Clemson, Thomas G. "Gold and the Gold Region." *Orion: A Monthly Magazine of Literature and Art* (April 1844): 57–66.

Cleveland, Edmund Janes, and Horace Gillette Cleveland, comps. *The Genealogy of the Cleveland and Cleaveland Families*. 3 vols. Hartford, Conn.: Case, Lockwood & Brainard, 1899.

Covington, James W., ed. "Letters from the Georgia Gold Regions." *Georgia Historical Quarterly* 39 (1955): 401–409.

"Dahlonega, or Georgia Gold Region." *Merchants' Magazine and Commercial Review* (New York) (July 1848): 112–113.

"Early History of the South-West." *South-Western Monthly* (Nashville, Tenn.) 1 (1852): 10–16, 72–78.

An Exposition of the Property of the Etowah Manufacturing and Mining Co. at Etowah, Cass County, Georgia, and Testimonials of Its Value. New York: George F. Nesbitt, 1860.

Featherstonhaugh, G. W. *A Canoe Voyage up the Minnay Sotor*. 2 vols. London: Richard Bentley, 1847.

First City Directory of Birmingham and County Gazetteer, for 1883–84. Atlanta, Ga.: H. H. Dickson, 1883.

Fort, Kate Haynes, ed. and comp. *Memoirs of the Fort and Fannin Families*. Chattanooga, Tenn.: Macgowan and Cooke, 1903.

Hodge, J. T. "The Manufacture of Iron in Georgia." *Merchants' Magazine and Commercial Review* (May 1849): 507–511.

Jackson, Henry R. *Eulogy upon the Life and Character of the Honorable Charles J. McDonald*. Atlanta, Ga.: Franklin Printing House, 1861.

Jones, Thomas G., comp. *Reports of Cases Argued and Determined in the Supreme Court of Alabama*. Montgomery: Joel White, 1877.

Journal of the House of Representatives of the State of Georgia, 1847. Milledgeville, Ga.: Miller Grieve, 1848.

———. *1860*. Milledgeville, Ga: Boughton, Nisbet and Barnes, 1860.

Journal of the Senate of the State of Georgia, 1849–1850. Milledgeville, Ga.: Richard M. Orme, 1849.

Journal of the State Convention, Held in Milledgeville, in December, 1850. Milledgeville, Ga.: R. M. Orme, 1850.

Kelly, James M., comp. *Reports of Cases in Law and Equity, Argued and Determined in the Supreme Court of the State of Georgia, in the Year, 1846*. 2 vols. New York: Edward O. Jenkins, 1847.

Lewis, David W., ed. *Transactions of the Southern Central Agricultural Society*. Macon, Ga.: Benjamin F. Griffin, 1852.

Lewis, William Terrell. *Genealogy of the Lewis Family in America, from the Middle of the Seventeenth Century Down to the Present Time*. Louisville, Ky.: Courier-Journal, 1893.

Lumpkin, Wilson. *The Removal of the Cherokee Indians from Georgia*. 2 vols. New York: Dodd, Mead, 1907.

McCollum, Ben F. "The Second Battle of Big Shanty." *Georgia Magazine* 5 (February–March 1962): 31–33.

Memoirs of William T. Sherman: By Himself. New York: D. Appleton, 1875.

Meriwether, Robert L., W. Edwin Hemphill, Clyde N. Wilson, Shirley B. Cook, and Alexander Moore, eds. *The Papers of John C. Calhoun*. 28 vols. Columbia: University of South Carolina Press, 1959–2003.

Official Records of the Union and Confederate Navies in the War of the Rebellion. 30 vols. Washington, D.C.: Government Printing Office, 1894–1922.

Phillips, William. "Essay on the Georgia Gold Mines." *American Journal of Science and Arts* (July 1833): 1–18.

Reports of Cases Argued and Determined in the Supreme Court of Tennessee, 1886; rpt., Louisville, Ky.: Fetter Law Book, 1902.

Reports of Cases in Law and Equity, Arrived and Determined in the Supreme Court of Georgia. 82 vols. New York: Edward O. Jenkins, 1847–1890.

Richardson, J. S. G. *Reports of Cases in Equity, Argued and Determined in the Court of Appeals and Court of Errors, South-Carolina*. Charleston, S.C.: McCarter, 1855.

Rosecrans, W. S. "The Mistakes of Grant," *North American Review* 141 (December 1885): 580–599.

Sedgwick, Catherine Maria. *Tales and Sketches: Second Series*. New York: Harper & Brothers, 1844.

Shepard, Charles Upham. *Report on the Copper and Silver-Lead Mine at Canton, Cherokee County, Georgia*. 2nd ed. New Haven, Conn.: Ezekiel Hayes, 1856.

Simms, William Gilmore. *Father Abbot; or, The Home Tourist: A Medley*. Charleston, S.C.: Miller and Brown, 1849.

Southern Education for Southern Youth: An Address before the Alpha Pi Delta Society of the Cherokee Baptist College, Delivered at the Commencement on the 14th July, 1858, by Hon. William H. Stiles. Savannah, Ga.: Power Press of George N. Nichols, 1858.

Taylor, Wyndell O., comp. *Cherokee County, Georgia, Land Records*. 7 vols. Powder Springs, Ga.: Bot's Books, 1992–1996.

Tocqueville, Alexis de. *Journey to America*. Edited by J. P. Mayer. New Haven, Conn.: Yale University Press, 1960.

The War of the Rebellion: A Compilation of the Official Records of the Union and Confederate Armies. 128 vols. Washington, D.C.: Government Printing Office, 1880–1901.

Wheaton, Elizabeth R. *Prisons and Prayer; or, A Labor of Love*. Tabor, Iowa: M. Kelley, 1906.

PUBLISHED SECONDARY SOURCES

Ackerman, William K. *Historical Sketch of the Illinois-Central Railroad*. Chicago, Ill.: Fergus Printing, 1890.

Appleton's Annual Cyclopaedia and Register of Important Events of the Year 1886. New York: D. Appleton, 1887.

Armes, Ethel. *The Story of Coal and Iron in Alabama*. 1910; rpt., Birmingham, Ala.: Book-keepers Press, 1972.

Armstrong, Zella. *The History of Hamilton County and Chattanooga, Tennessee*. 2 vols. Chattanooga, Tenn.: Lookout, 1940.

Avery, I. W. *The History of the State of Georgia from 1850 to 1881*. New York: Brown & Derby, 1881.

Barnes, L. Diane, Brian Schoen, and Frank Towers, eds. *The Old South's Modern Worlds: Slavery, Region, and Nation in the Age of Progress*. New York: Oxford University Press, 2011.

Bartlett, Irving H. *John C. Calhoun: A Biography*. New York: Norton, 1993.

Battey, George Magruder, Jr. *A History of Rome and Floyd County*. Atlanta, Ga.: Webb & Vary, 1922.

Bennett, James R. *Tannehill and the Growth of the Alabama Iron Industry including the Civil War in West Alabama*. Saline, Mich.: McNaughton & Gunn, 1999.

Biographical Directory of the United States Congress, 1774 to 1903. Washington, D.C.: U.S. Government Printing Office, 1903.

Birdsall, C. M. *The United States Branch Mint at Dahlonega, Georgia: Its History and Coinage*. Easley, S.C.: Southern Historical Society Press, 1984.

Black, Robert C., III. *The Railroads of the Confederacy*. 1952; rpt., Chapel Hill: University of North Carolina Press, 1998.

Blackmon, Douglas A. *Slavery by Another Name: The Re-enslavement of Black Americans from the Civil War to World War II*. New York: Doubleday, 2008.

Bonds, Russell S. *Stealing the General: The Great Locomotive Chase and the First Medal of Honor*. Yardley, Pa.: Westholme, 2007.

Bonner, James C. "Sherman at Milledgeville in 1864." *Journal of Southern History* 22 (August 1956): 273–291.

Boykin, Samuel, comp. *History of the Baptist Denomination in Georgia*. 2 vols. Atlanta, Ga.: Jas. P. Harrison, 1881.

Brewster, Lawrence Fay. *Summer Migrations and Resorts of South Carolina Low-Country Planters*. Durham, N.C.: Duke University Press, 1947.

Broadus, John A. *Memoir of James Petigru Boyce, D.D., LL.D.* New York: A. C. Armstrong and Son, 1893.

Brown, John, Jr., and James Boyd. *History of San Bernardino and Riverside Counties*. 3 vols. Chicago, Ill.: Lewis, 1922.

Butler, Chalmers M. "Thomas Green Clemson: Scientist and Engineer." In *Thomas Green Clemson*, edited by Alma Bennett, 103–136. Clemson, S.C.: Clemson University Digital Press, 2009.

Cadle, Farris W. *Georgia Land Surveying History and Law*. Athens: University of Georgia Press, 1991.

Cain, Andrew W. *History of Lumpkin County for the First Hundred Years, 1832–1932*. 1932; rpt., Spartanburg, S.C.: Reprint Company, 1978.

Cappon, Lester J. "Iron-Making: A Forgotten Industry of North Carolina." *North Carolina Historical Review* 9 (1932): 331–348.

Carey, Anthony Gene. *Parties, Slavery, and the Union in Antebellum Georgia*. Athens: University of Georgia Press, 1997.

Coleman, Kenneth, ed. *A History of Georgia*. 2nd ed. Athens: University of Georgia Press, 1991.

Conway, Alan. *The Reconstruction of Georgia*. Minneapolis: University of Minnesota Press, 1966.

Cooper, Walter G. *The Cotton States and International Exposition and South, Illustrated*. 1895; rpt., Atlanta, Ga.: Illustrator, 1896.

Coulter, E. Merton. *Auraria: The Story of a Georgia Gold-Mining Town*. Athens: University of Georgia Press, 1956.

Council, R. Bruce, Nicholas Honerkamp, and M. Elizabeth Will. *Industry and Technol-*

ogy in Antebellum Tennessee: The Archaeology of Bluff Furnace. Knoxville: University of Tennessee Press, 1992.

Cummings, Uriah. *American Cements*. Boston: Rogers and Manson, 1898.

Cunyus, Lucy Josephine. *History of Bartow County, Georgia, Formerly Cass*. 1933; rpt., Easley, S.C.: Southern Historical Press, 1971.

Davis, Donald Edward. *Where There Are Mountains: An Environmental History of the Southern Appalachians*. Athens: University of Georgia Press, 2000.

Davis, Robert S., Jr. "The Story of a Community Once Called Etowah." In *A North Georgia Journal of History*, edited by Olin Jackson, 12–15. Woodstock, Ga.: Legacy Communications, 1989.

DeCredico, Mary A. *Patriotism for Profit: Georgia's Urban Entrepreneurs and the Confederate War Effort*. Chapel Hill: University of North Carolina Press, 1990.

Delfino, Susanna, and Michelle Gillespie, eds. *Technology, Innovation, and Southern Industrialization: From the Antebellum Era to the Computer Age*. Columbia: University of Missouri Press, 2008.

Derbes, Brett J. "Origins of the Prison-Industrial Complex: Inmate Labor in the Deep South, 1817–1865." In *Reconsidering Southern Labor History: Race, Class, and Power*, edited by Matthew Hild and Keri Leigh Merritt, 47–62. Gainesville: University Press of Florida, 2018.

Dew, Charles B. *Bond of Iron: Master and Slave at Buffalo Forge*. New York: Norton, 1994.

———. *Ironmaker to the Confederacy: Joseph R. Anderson and the Tredegar Iron Works*. Richmond: Library of Virginia, 1999.

———. "Slavery and Technology in the Antebellum Southern Iron Industry: The Case of Buffalo Forge." In *Science and Medicine in the Old South*, edited by Ronald L. Numbers and Todd L. Savitt, 107–126. Baton Rouge: Louisiana State University Press, 1989.

Dietrich, Paul Henry. *The History of Rowland Springs, Cartersville, Georgia: In Prose and in Poetry*. Cleveland, Tenn.: Carroll Printing, 2014.

Donnelly, Ralph W. "The Bartow County Confederate Saltpetre Works." *Georgia Historical Quarterly* 54 (Fall 1970): 305–319.

DuBose, Beverly M. "Stephen Harriman Long." *Atlanta Historical Bulletin* 3 (July 1938): 169–178.

DuBose, John Witherspoon. *Jefferson County and Birmingham, Alabama: Historical and Biographical*. Birmingham, Ala.: Teeple & Smith, 1887.

Dunaway, Wilma A. *Slavery in the American Mountain South*. New York: Cambridge University Press, 2003.

Duncan, Katherine McKinstry, and Larry Joe Smith. *The History of Marshall County, Alabama*, vol. 1: *Prehistory to 1939*. Albertville, Ala.: Thompson, 1969.

Duncan, Russell. *Entrepreneur for Equality: Governor Rufus Bullock, Commerce, and Race in Post–Civil War Georgia*. Athens: University of Georgia Press, 1994.

Eckert, Ralph Lowell. *John Brown Gordon: Soldier, Southerner, American*. Baton Rouge: Louisiana State University Press, 1989.

Eelman, Bruce W. *Entrepreneurs in the Southern Upcountry: Commercial Culture in Spartanburg*. Athens: University of Georgia Press, 2008.

Ellis, Richard E. *The Union at Risk: Jacksonian Democracy, States' Rights, and the Nullification Crisis*. New York: Oxford University Press, 1987.

Faust, Drew Gilpin. "The Rhetoric and Ritual of Agriculture in Antebellum South Carolina." *Journal of Southern History* 45 (November 1979): 541–568.

Ferguson, Terry A., and Thomas A. Cowan. "Iron Plantations and the Eighteenth- and

Nineteenth-Century Landscape of the Northwestern South Carolina Piedmont." In *Carolina's Historical Landscapes: Archaeological Perspectives*, edited by Linda F. Stine et al., 113–144. Knoxville: University of Tennessee Press, 1997.

Flanders, Ralph B. "Farish Carter, a Forgotten Man of the Old South." *Georgia Historical Quarterly* 15 (June 1931): 142–172.

Freehling, William W., and Craig M. Simpson, eds. *Secession Debated: Georgia's Showdown in 1860*. New York: Oxford University Press, 1992.

Gagnon, Michael J. *Transition to an Industrial South: Athens, Georgia, 1830–1870*. Baton Rouge: Louisiana State University Press, 2012.

Gardner, Robert G. *Cherokees and Baptists in Georgia*. Atlanta: Georgia Baptist Historical Society, 1989.

Garrett, Franklin M. *Atlanta and Environs: A Chronicle of Its People and Events*. 3 vols. New York: Lewis Historical Publishing, 1954.

Gates, Frederick B. "The Impact of the Western & Atlantic Railroad on the Development of the Georgia Upcountry, 1840–1860." *Georgia Historical Quarterly* 91 (Summer 2007): 169–184.

Gates, Warren J. "Modernization as a Function of an Agricultural Fair: The Great Grangers' Picnic Exhibition at Williams Grove, Pennsylvania, 1873–1916." *Agricultural History* 58 (July 1984): 262–279.

"Genealogical Queries." *William and Mary Quarterly* 5 (January 1925): 53–60.

Gilmer, George R. *Sketches of Some of the First Settlers of Upper Georgia, of the Cherokees, and the Author*. 1855; rpt., Baltimore, Md.: Genealogical Publishing, 1970.

Govan, Gilbert E., and James W. Livingood. *The Chattanooga Country, 1540–1951: From Tomahawks to TVA*. New York: Dutton, 1952.

Grant, H. Roger. *The Louisville, Cincinnati, and Charleston Rail Road: Dreams of Linking North and South*. Bloomington: Indiana University Press, 2014.

Green, Fletcher M. "Georgia's Board of Public Works, 1817–1826." *Georgia Historical Quarterly* 22 (June 1938): 117–137.

——. "Georgia's Forgotten Industry: Gold Mining." *Georgia Historical Quarterly* 19 (June 1935): 93–111, (September 1935): 210–228.

Grimsley, Mark. *The Hard Hand of War: Union Military Policy toward Southern Civilians, 1861–1865*. New York: Cambridge University Press, 1995.

Hall, Henry, ed. *America's Successful Men of Affairs: An Encyclopedia of Contemporaneous Biography*. 2 vols. New York: New York Tribune, 1896.

Hall, Randall L. *Mountains on the Market: Industry, the Environment, and the South*. Lexington: University Press of Kentucky, 2012.

Hauptman, Laurence M. "General John E. Wool in Cherokee County, 1836–1837: A Reinterpretation." *Georgia Historical Quarterly* 85 (Spring 2001): 1–26.

Head, Sylvia, and Elizabeth W. Etheridge. *The Neighborhood Mint: Dahlonega in the Age of Jackson*. Macon, Ga.: Mercer University Press, 2000.

Heath, Milton Sydney. *Constructive Liberalism: The Role of the State in Economic Development in Georgia to 1860*. Cambridge, Mass.: Harvard University Press, 1954.

Hébert, Keith S. *The Long Civil War in the North Georgia Mountains: Confederate Nationalism, Sectionalism, and White Supremacy in Bartow County, Georgia*. Knoxville: University of Tennessee Press, 2017.

The Heritage of Cherokee County, Georgia, 1831–1998. Waynesville, N.C.: Walsworth Publishing, 1998.

Hill, Sarah H. "'To Overawe the Indians and Give Confidence to the Whites': Preparations for the Removal of the Cherokee Nation from Georgia." *Georgia Historical Quarterly* 95 (Winter 2011): 465–497.

History of Texas, Together with a Biographical History of Tarrant and Parker Counties. Chicago, Ill.: Lewis Publishing, 1895.

Holmes, Anne Middleton. *The New York Ladies' Southern Relief Association, 1866–1867.* New York: Mary Mildred Sullivan Chapter, United Daughters of the Confederacy, 1926.

Hudson, Leonne M. *The Odyssey of a Southerner: The Life and Times of Gustavus Woodson Smith.* Macon, Ga.: Mercer University Press, 1998.

Humphries, John D. "Judges of the Superior Courts of Fulton and DeKalb Counties." *Atlanta Historical Bulletin* 4, no. 17 (April 1939): 112–132.

Janes, Thomas P. *Hand-book of the State of Georgia.* 2nd ed. Atlanta, Ga.: S. W. Green, 1876.

John, Richard R. *Spreading the News: The American Postal System from Franklin to Morse.* Cambridge, Mass.: Harvard University Press, 1998.

Johnson, Michael P. *Toward a Patriarchal Republic: The Secession of Georgia.* Baton Rouge: Louisiana State University Press, 1977.

Johnston, James Houstoun. *Western and Atlantic Railroad of the State of Georgia.* 1931; rpt., Atlanta, Ga.: Stein Printing, 1932.

Jones, James Pickett. *Yankee Blitzkrieg: Wilson's Raid through Alabama and Georgia.* Athens: University of Georgia Press, 1976.

Joseph, J. W., and Mary Beth Reed. *Ore, Water, Stone and Wood: Historical and Architectural Investigations of Donaldson's Iron Furnace, Cherokee County, Georgia.* Mobile, Ala.: U.S. Army Corps of Engineers, 1987.

Kelly, James C. "Portrait Painting in Tennessee." *Tennessee Historical Quarterly* 46 (Winter 1987): 195–276.

Kelly, John W. "The Scientist as Farmer." In *Thomas Green Clemson*, edited by Alma Bennett, 137–158. Clemson, S.C.: Clemson University Digital Press, 2009.

Kemp, Kathryn W. *God's Capitalist: Asa Candler of Coca-Cola.* Macon, Ga.: Mercer University Press, 2002.

King, Adam. *Etowah: The Political History of a Chiefdom Capital.* Tuscaloosa: University of Alabama Press, 2003.

Knowles, Anne Kelly. "Labor, Race, and Technology in the Confederate Iron Industry." *Technology and Culture* 42 (January 2001): 1–26.

———. *Mastering Iron: The Struggle to Modernize an American Industry, 1800–1868.* Chicago, Ill.: University of Chicago Press, 2013.

Knowles, Anne Kelly, and Richard G. Healey. "Geography, Timing, and Technology: A GIS-Based Analysis of Pennsylvania's Iron Industry, 1825–1875." *Journal of Economic History* 66 (September 2006): 608–634.

Lander, Ernest M., Jr. *The Calhoun Family and Thomas Green Clemson: The Decline of a Southern Patriarchy.* Columbia: University of South Carolina Press, 1983.

———. "The Iron Industry in Ante-Bellum South Carolina." *Journal of Southern History* 20 (August 1954): 337–355.

Latty, John W. *Carrying Off the Cherokee: History of Buffington's Company; Georgia Mounted Militia.* Self-published, 2011.

LeFlouria, Talitha L. *Chained in Silence: Black Women and Convict Labor in the New South.* Chapel Hill: University of North Carolina Press, 2015.

Lesley, J. P. *The Iron Manufacturer's Guide.* New York: John Wiley, 1859.

Lewis, Charlene M. Boyer. *Ladies and Gentlemen on Display: Planter Society at the Virginia Springs, 1790–1860.* Charlottesville: University Press of Virginia, 2001.

Lewis, W. David. *Sloss Furnaces and the Rise of the Birmingham District: An Industrial Epic.* Tuscaloosa: University of Alabama Press, 1994.

Lichtenstein, Alex. *Twice the Work of Free Labor: The Political Economy of Convict Labor in the New South*. New York: Verso, 1996.

Livingston, John. *American Portrait Gallery, Containing Portraits of Men Now Living, with Biographical and Historical Memoirs of Their Lives and Actions*. New York: n.p., 1854.

Lonn, Ella. *Salt as a Factor in the Confederacy*. Tuscaloosa: University of Alabama Press, 1965.

Magrath, C. Peter. *Yazoo: Law and Politics in the Early Republic: The Case of Fletcher v. Peck*. Providence, R.I.: Brown University Press, 1966.

Mahan, Joseph B., Jr. *A History of Old Cassville, 1833–1864*. Cartersville, Ga.: Etowah Valley Historical Society, 1994.

Majewski, John. *Modernizing a Slave Economy: The Economic Vision of the Confederate Nation*. Chapel Hill: University of North Carolina Press, 2009.

Mancini, Matthew J. *One Dies, Get Another: Convict Leasing in the American South, 1866–1928*. Columbia: University of South Carolina Press, 1996.

Marlin, Lloyd G. *The History of Cherokee County*. Atlanta, Ga.: Walter W. Brown, 1932.

Marrs, Aaron W. *Railroads in the Old South: Pursuing Progress in a Slave Society*. Baltimore, Md.: Johns Hopkins University Press, 2009.

Maysilles, Duncan. *Ducktown Smoke: The Fight over One of the South's Greatest Environmental Disasters*. Chapel Hill: University of North Carolina Press, 2011.

McLoughlin, William G. *Cherokee Renascence in the New Republic*. Princeton, N.J.: Princeton University Press, 1986.

McPherson, James M. *Battle Cry of Freedom: The Civil War Era*. New York: Oxford University Press, 1988.

Meynard, Virginia G. *The Venturers: The Hamptons, Harrison, and Earle Families of Virginia, South Carolina, and Texas*. Easley, S.C.: Southern Historical Press, 1981.

Miles, Tiya. *The House on Diamond Hill: A Cherokee Plantation Story*. Chapel Hill: University of North Carolina Press, 2010.

———. *Ties That Bind: The Story of an Afro-Cherokee Family in Slavery and Freedom*. Berkeley: University of California Press, 2005.

Miller, Stephen F. *The Bench and Bar of Georgia: Memoirs and Sketches*. 2 vols. Philadelphia, Pa.: Lippincott, 1858.

Miner, Craig. *A Most Magnificent Machine: America Adopts the Railroad, 1825–1862*. Lawrence: University Press of Kansas, 2010.

Mohr, Clarence L. *On the Threshold of Freedom: Masters and Slaves in Civil War Georgia*. Athens: University of Georgia Press, 1986.

Morgan, Chad. *Planters' Progress: Modernizing Confederate Georgia*. Gainesville: University Press of Florida, 2005.

———. "The Public Nature of Private Industry in Confederate Georgia." *Civil War History* 50 (March 2004): 27–46.

Morris, Philip. *Vulcan and His Times*. Birmingham, Ala.: Birmingham Historical Society, 1995.

Mueller, William A. *A History of Southern Baptist Theological Seminary*. Nashville, Tenn.: Broadman Press, 1959.

Murray, Paul. *The Whig Party in Georgia, 1825–1853*. Chapel Hill: University of North Carolina Press, 1948.

Neely, Wayne Caldwell. *The Agricultural Fair*. New York: Columbia University Press, 1935.

Nelson, Megan Kate. "The Pleasures of Civil War Ruins." In *Weirding the War: Stories from the Civil War's Ragged Edges*, edited by Stephen Berry, 36–53. Athens: University of Georgia Press, 2011.

Nelson, Scott Reynolds. *Iron Confederacies: Southern Railways, Klan Violence, and Reconstruction*. Chapel Hill: University of North Carolina Press, 1999.

Nettles, Thomas J. *James Petigru Boyce: A Southern Baptist Statesman*. Phillipsburg, N.J.: P. & R. Publishing, 2009.

Niven, Alexander C. "Joseph E. Brown, Confederate Obstructionist." *Georgia Historical Quarterly* 42 (September 1958): 233–257.

Nixon, Alfred. *A History of Lincoln County*. 1901; rpt., N.p.: Lincoln County Historical Society, 1978.

Oates, Stephen B. *With Malice toward None: A Life of Abraham Lincoln*. New York: Harper & Row, 1977.

O'Neall, John Belton. *The Annals of Newberry: Historical, Biographical, and Anecdotal*. Charleston, S.C.: Courtenay, 1859.

Owen, Thomas McAdory. *History of Alabama and Dictionary of Alabama Biography*. 4 vols. Chicago, Ill.: S. J. Clarke, 1921.

Parks, Joseph H. *Joseph E. Brown of Georgia*. Baton Rouge: Louisiana State University Press, 1977.

Perdue, Theda. *"Mixed Blood" Indians: Racial Construction in the Early South*. Athens: University of Georgia Press, 2003.

Perdue, Theda, and Michael D. Green. *The Cherokee Nation and the Trail of Tears*. New York: Viking, 2007.

Phillips, Ulrich Bonnell. *A History of Transportation in the Eastern Cotton Belt to 1860*. New York: Columbia University Press, 1908.

Pierce, Alfred M. *Giant against the Sky: The Life of Bishop Warren Akin Candler*. Nashville, Tenn.: Abingdon-Cokesbury Press, 1948.

Pope, Mark Cooper, III. *Mark Anthony Cooper: The Iron Man of Georgia: A Biography*. Atlanta, Ga.: Graphic, 2000.

Potter, David. *The Impending Crisis, 1848–1861*. New York: Harper & Row, 1976.

Price, Vivian. *The History of DeKalb County, Georgia, 1822–1900*. Fernandina Beach, Fla.: Wolfe Publishing, 1997.

Putnam, A. W. *History of Middle Tennessee; or, Life and Times of General James Robertson*. Nashville, Tenn.: Author, 1859.

"Rehabilitating the Rising Fawn Plant." *Age of Steel* 92, no. 17 (October 25, 1902): 23.

Representative Men of the South. Philadelphia, Pa.: Chas. Robson, 1880.

Roberts, Derrell. "Joseph E. Brown and His Georgia Mines." *Georgia Historical Quarterly* 52 (September 1968): 285–292.

———. *Joseph E. Brown and the Politics of Reconstruction*. Tuscaloosa: University of Alabama Press, 1973.

Robinson, Gloria. "Charles Upham Shepard." In *Benjamin Silliman and His Circle: Studies on the Influence of Benjamin Silliman on Science in America*, edited by Leonard G. Wilson, 85–103. New York: Science History Publications, 1979.

Rorabaugh, W. J. "The Sons of Temperance in Antebellum Jasper County." *Georgia Historical Quarterly* 64 (Fall 1980): 263–279.

Rosengarten, Theodore. "The Southern Agriculturist in an Age of Reform." In *Intellectual Life in Antebellum Charleston*, edited by Michael O'Brien and David Moltke-Hansen, 279–294. Knoxville: University of Tennessee Press, 1986.

Rossiter, Margaret W. "The Organization of Agricultural Improvement in the United States, 1785–1865." In *The Pursuit of Knowledge in the Early American Republic:*

American Scientific and Learned Societies from Colonial Times to the Civil War, edited by Alexandra Oleson and Sanborn C. Brown, 279–298. Baltimore, Md.: Johns Hopkins University Press, 1976.

Rowell, Raymond J., Sr. *Vulcan in Birmingham*. N.p.: n.p., 1972.

Rozema, Vicki Bell. "Science and Technology Awakened: Resource Exploitation and the Cherokee Removal." *Journal of East Tennessee History* 85 (2013): 3–23.

Shadburn, Don L. *Cherokee Planters in Georgia, 1832–1838: Historical Essays on Eleven Counties in the Cherokee Nation of Georgia*. Roswell, Ga.: W. H. Wolfe Associates, 1990.

Smith, Gordon Burns. *History of the Georgia Militia, 1783–1861*. 4 vols. Milledgeville, Ga.: Boyd, 2000.

Speer, Emory. "The Life and Times of Joseph Emerson Brown, War Governor of Georgia." In Speer, *Lincoln, Lee, Grant and Other Biographical Addresses*, 227–269. New York: Neale, 1909.

Stone, R. C. *The Gold Mines, Scenery and Climate of Georgia and the Carolinas*. New York: National Bank Note, 1878.

Swanson, Drew A. "From Georgia to California and Back: The Rise, Fall, and Rebirth of Southern Gold Mining." *Georgia Historical Quarterly* 100 (2016): 160–186.

———. "A Rhetoric of Ruin: Imagining and Reimagining the Georgia Coast." In *Coastal Nature, Coastal Culture: Environmental Histories of the Georgia Coast*, edited by Paul S. Sutter and Paul M. Pressly, 175–207. Athens: University of Georgia Press, 2018.

Tankersley, Allen P. "Zachariah Herndon Gordon: His Life and His Letters on the Battle of King's Mountain." *Georgia Historical Quarterly* 36 (September 1952): 231–249.

Tate, Luke E. *History of Pickens County*. 1935; rpt., Spartanburg, S.C.: Reprint Company, 1978.

Temin, Peter. *Iron and Steel*. Cambridge, Mass.: MIT Press, 1964.

Thomas, William G. *The Iron Way: Railroads, the Civil War, and the Making of Modern America*. New Haven, Conn.: Yale University Press, 2011.

Thompson, C. Mildred. *Reconstruction in Georgia: Economic, Social, Political, 1865–1872*. 1915; rpt., Gloucester, Mass.: Peter Smith, 1964.

Thornton, Russell. "Cherokee Population Losses during the Trail of Tears: A New Perspective and a New Estimate." *Ethnohistory* 31 (1984): 289–300.

Walker, Charles O. *Cherokee Footprints*, vol. 2: *Home and Hearth*. Canton, Ga.: Industrial Printing Service, 1989.

Wallace, Anthony F. C. *The Long, Bitter Trail: Andrew Jackson and the Indians*. New York: Hill and Wang, 1993.

Warren, Mary B., and Eve B. Weeks, comps. *Whites among the Cherokees: Georgia, 1828–1838*. Danielsville, Ga.: Heritage Papers, 1987.

Watson, Samuel J. *Peacekeepers and Conquerors: The Army Officer Corps on the American Frontier, 1821–1846*. Lawrence: University Press of Kansas, 2013.

Wheeler, Kenneth H. "Joseph E. Brown and the Civil War in Cherokee County, Georgia." In *Cherokee County Voices from the Civil War*, 7–29. Canton, Ga.: Cherokee County Civil War Sesquicentennial Committee, 2014.

White, George. *Historical Collections of Georgia*. New York: Pudney & Russell, 1855.

Wigginton, Eliot, ed. *Foxfire 5: Ironmaking, Blacksmithing, Flintlock Rifles, Bear Hunting, and Other Affairs of Plain Living*. New York: Anchor, 1979.

Williams, David. *The Georgia Gold Rush: Twenty-Niners, Cherokees, and Gold Fever.* Columbia: University of South Carolina Press, 1993.

Wills, Gregory A. *Southern Baptist Theological Seminary, 1859–2009.* New York: Oxford University Press, 2009.

Wilms, Douglas C. "Cherokee Land Use in Georgia before Removal." In *Cherokee Removal: Before and After,* edited by William L. Anderson, 1–28. Athens: University of Georgia Press, 1991.

Wilson, John. *Chattanooga's Story.* N.p.: n.p., 1980.

Wolmar, Christian. *The Great Railroad Revolution: The History of Trains in America.* New York: Public Affairs, 2012.

Wood, Richard G. *Stephen Harriman Long, 1784–1864: Army Engineer, Explorer, Inventor.* Glendale, Calif.: Arthur H. Clark, 1966.

Wright, G. Richard, and Kenneth H. Wheeler. "New Men in the Old South: Joseph E. Brown and His Associates in Georgia's Etowah Valley." *Georgia Historical Quarterly* 93 (Winter 2009): 363–387.

Yeates, W. S., S. W. McCallie, and Francis P. King. *A Preliminary Report on a Part of the Gold Deposits of Georgia.* Atlanta, Ga.: Geo. W. Harrison, 1896.

Young, Mary. "The Exercise of Sovereignty in Cherokee Georgia." *Journal of the Early Republic* 10 (Spring 1990): 43–63.

Young, Otis E., Jr. "The Southern Gold Rush, 1828–1836." *Journal of Southern History* 48 (August 1982): 373–392.

Young, Willie Pauline. *A Collection of Upper South Carolina Genealogical and Family Records.* Vol. 1. Easley, S.C.: Southern Historical Press, 1979.

UNPUBLISHED PAPERS, THESES, AND DISSERTATIONS

Ford, Charlotte Adams. "The Public Career of Tomlinson Fort, M.D." MA thesis, Georgia Southern College, 1964.

Gabard, William Montgomery. "Joseph Mackey Brown: A Study in Conservatism." PhD diss., Tulane University, 1963.

Gates, Frederick B. "An Imitative Enterprise: Canal Construction in Georgia, 1820–1850." MA thesis, University of North Carolina, Charlotte, 1995.

Guidry, Jennifer A. "Elizabeth Grisham Brown: 'A Strong and Sunny Soul.'" MA thesis, Georgia College and State University, 2003.

Hornsby, Jane Stroupe, and Michael Stroupe. "History of the Stroup Ironmasters." Unpublished typescript, n.d., in author's possession.

Kearns, Mary Pinckney. "Secession Diplomacy: A Study of Thomas Butler King, Commissioner of Georgia to Europe, 1861." MA thesis, Georgia Southern University, 2006.

Nave, Robert Tipton. "A History of the Iron Industry in Carter County to 1860." MA thesis, East Tennessee State College, 1953.

Nelson, Laura Elizabeth. "A 'Miserable Creature' or 'Remarkable Man': Wilkes Flagg and the Ambiguity of Race in Nineteenth-Century Middle Georgia." MA thesis, University of Georgia, 2018.

Nichols, Annette Davis. "The Political Career of Joseph E. Brown from 1865–1876." MA thesis, Auburn University, 1964.

Rozema, Vicki Bell. "Coveted Lands: Agriculture, Timber, Mining, and Transportation in Cherokee Country before and after Removal." PhD diss., University of Tennessee, 2012.

Taylor, A. Elizabeth. "The Convict Lease System in Georgia, 1866–1908." MA thesis, University of North Carolina, Chapel Hill, 1940.

Wilms, Douglas C. "Cherokee Indian Land Use in Georgia, 1800–1838." PhD diss., University of Georgia, 1973.

INDEX

Atlantic Railroad, 97; death of 105, 115; mentioned, 99
Rowland Springs, 26, 37–43, 88, 90, 92, 105

salt, 97–98
Schofield, Louis, 124
secession, 75, 83, 91, 93–95
Shepard, Charles Upham, 79–81
Sherman, William T., 106–108, 110
Silliman, Benjamin, 68, 79, 81
Simms, William Gilmore, 41
Sixes, Ga., 12, 19, 23
slavery, 73–75, 86–88, 93, 95, 98, 112–113. *See also* slaves
slaves: purchases of, 10–11; owned by Cherokees, 16–17, 25; belonging to Mary Franklin, 19, 77; owned by Tomlinson Fort, 28; who built Rowland Springs, 38; escape from Rowland Springs, 41–42; appraised by Moses Stroup, 51; employed in diverse industries, 58–59, 62; whipped by Joseph E. Brown, 76; harvest wheat with Brown, 81. *See also* slavery
Smith, Gustavus Woodson, 104–107
South Carolina College, 28, 54
Southern Baptist Theological Seminary, 122, 133
Southern Central Agricultural Society, 56–57, 72, 82
Stamp Creek, 52, 59, 72, 114
Stiles, William Henry, 86–87, 92
Stone Mountain, Ga., 56, 62, 118–119
Stroup, Jacob: as iron maker in Carolinas, 44–46; in Habersham County, 46–47; in comparison with Nesbitt Company, 51; on Stamp Creek, 52–53; and Veitch family, 61; economic model of, 51, 61–62; death of, 115; mentioned, 72, 106
Stroup, Moses: as member of iron-producing family, 44–45; builds Habersham furnace, 46; employed by Wilson Nesbitt, 46–52; trip to North, 48–50; in Etowah Valley, 52–60; in Alabama, 60–62, 97; incorporator of Etowah Railroad Company, 73; during Civil War, 97, 111; lasting influence of, 135

Tah-nah-ee, 19–20, 22
Tait, Mr., 19–20, 22
Tannehill, Ala., 61, 97, 111
Tate, Samuel, 75
temperance, 8, 67, 70–71, 75–76, 84–85
Tennessee River, 26–27, 29, 34, 37, 63, 104
Trail of Tears, 8, 24–25
Treaty of New Echota, 22, 24

Unionists, 108–110

Veitch family, 61, 111, 135

Waters, Henry Hawley, 85, 91, 99
Western & Atlantic Railroad: creation and building of, 26–27, 36, 38, 73; land speculation surrounding, 30–38; makes Rowland Springs accessible, 40–41; ambivalence concerning, 43–44; provides transportation for iron products, 44, 52; as purchaser of iron, 54; transports Etowah Mills flour, 54–56; transports coal to Etowah furnaces, 58; connected to ironworks via spur, 72–73, 88; as possible site for convict labor, 74, 85–86, 119–120; promoted by Joseph E. Brown, 74–75; bypasses Cassville, 77; proximity to Canton copper mine, 79; overseen by Joseph E. Brown and John W. Lewis, 83–85; Eugene LeHardy made chief engineer of, 88; Mark A. Cooper as customer of, 92; John S. Rowland replaces John W. Lewis as superintendent of, 97; during Civil War, 101–106, 108; destruction assessed, 110–111; leased, 120–121; controlled by Joseph E. Brown, 124–126, 131; Joseph Mackey Brown works for, 136. *See also* Long, Stephen Harriman
Western Bank of Georgia, 31–33, 35
Wiley, Leroy M., 56, 58, 60, 72–73, 104, 121
Williams, Samuel, 34–35
Wilson, James H., 111–113

Yale College, 67–68, 79, 81, 87